Edexcel
Psychology
for A Level Year 2
Revision Guide

Cara Flanagan
Rob Liddle
Julia Russell
Mandy Wood

Illuminate
Publishing

Acknowledgements

The team who manage and produce this book are simply the best.

Illuminate Publishing, with the psychology list headed by the unique Rick Jackman, and assisted by Clare Jackman, Peter Burton, Saskia Burton and Vikki Mann, represent the best in educational publishing – always looking out for their authors and also for the people who buy the books.

Nic Watson, our editor, puts nothing short of love into ensuring our final product is as perfect as can be. We couldn't do it without her.

The third part of our team is design, fitting the text and pictures on each page. Stephanie White of Kamae Design had the job of implementing the design and has done a fabulous job of it.

A very special thank you to all of you and also to Julia and Mandy who dedicated a huge amount of time and thought to getting this book right, and of course to Rob who provides invaluable support as well as much appreciated humour.

p6 Cover of Edexcel A Level Psychology specification, with the kind permission of Pearson Edexcel; p70 Diagrams of the 1PP and 3PP conditions © Guardia, D., Conversy, L., Jardri, R., Lafargue, G., Thomas, P., Dodin, V. et al. (2012) Imagining One's Own and Someone Else's Body Actions: Dissociation in Anorexia Nervosa. PLoS ONE 7(8): e43241. https://doi.org/10.1371/journal. pone.0043241; p152 Screenshots reproduced with the kind permission of DIMAT INC. (www.dominicinteractive.com).

Picture credits

Cover © Anna Om/Nowik Sylwia/Shutterstock.com

Shutterstock ©: p7 mammoz, oksana2010, Sashkin, marekuliasz; p9 OSTILL is Franck Camhi; p22 Aysezgicmeli; p24 VICHAILAO; p25 aaltair; p26 AndreAnita; p27 alphaspirit; p28 Just dance; p29 LeventeGyori; p30 Evannovostro; p31 Dmitry Guzhanin; p32 Kichigin; p33 Paul Vasarhelyi; p34 hurricanehank; p35 tommaso lizzul; p36 maxuser; p37 VGstockstudio; p38 StudioLaMagica; p39 Elena Elisseeva; p40 Photographee.eu; p41 Monkey Business Images; p44 Sebastian Kaulitzki; p46 blvdone; p47 Jazzmany; p48 Szasz-Fabian Jozsef; p49 Cranach; p50 EvGavrilov; p51 YAKOBCHUK VIACHESLAV; p52 yakub88; p53 xpixel; p54 xpixel; p56 ReflectedLight; p57 Chinnapong; p58 Orkidia; p59 Voyagerix; p60 Gerasymovych Oleksandr; p61 Studio Romantic; p62 TraXXXe; p65 TuiPhotoEngineer; p66 Deb Clark; p67 Africa Studio; p68 Twocoms; p69 Kenishirotie; p72 Andrey_Popov; p73 Andrey_Popov; p75 mrkornflakes; p76 lassedesignen; p77 WAYHOME studio; p79 Marcos Mesa Sam Wordley; p80 Business stock; p81 pathdoc; p82 docstockmedia; p83 Dean Drobot; p85 Bozhko Ekaterina; p86 Africa Studio; p87 Carla Francesca Castagno; p88 Sebastian Kaulitzki; p89 Cartoon Resource; p90 Christian Schulz; p91 Brian A Jackson; p93 Valeriya_Dor; p94 Rawpixel.com; p95 Teguh Mujiono; p97 Javier Brosch; p99 pathdoc; p100 CLIPAREA l Custom media; p101 Teeradej; p102 Monkey Business Images; p103 ra2studio; p104 Kiselev Andrey Valerevich; p105 st-fotograf; p106 Nikolay Gyngazov; p108 Rasulov; p109 Just dance; p110 Leremy; p111 sirtravelalot; p112 Luciano de la Rosa; p113 iofoto; p114 Ammit Jack; p115 wickerwood; p116 sirtravelalot; p117 MicroOne; p119 Alexander_P; p120 Rawpixel.com; p121 AnastasiaNess; p122 A and J King; p123 Look Studio; p124 Tap10; p125 pathdoc; p126 Oksana Kuzmina; p127 Sarah Noda; p128 Rasulov; p130 Rasulov; p132 Radiokafka; p133 Africa Studio; p134 Oksana Kuzmina; p135 Andrey_Kuzmin; p136 Feel Photo Art; p137 WAYHOME studio; p138 Zahraa Saleh; p139 Blackroom; p140 Sebastian Kaulitzki; p141 iodrakon, immfocus studio; p143 ESB Professional; p144 FocusStocker, Artem Kulturen, Alexey Borodin, Dzha33; p145 Dusan Petkovic; p146 Africa Studio; p147 Ocskay Bence; p149 WAYHOME studio; p151 XiXinXing; p153 F. JIMENEZ MECA; p154 CREATISTA; p155 Ebtikar; p156 vchal; p157 Keith Homan; p159 CREATISTA; p160 Monkey Business Images; p161 Cineberg; p162 ra2studio; p163 Andrey_Popov; p164 TanyaJoy; p165 Image Point Fr; p167 mark reinstein; p168 Pan Xunbin Monkey Business Images; p169 Teele Engaste; p170 milias1987; p171 dragon_fang; p172 Vectomart; p173 StanOd; p174 Ksanawo; p175 Mauricio Graiki.

p107 Photo of Colin Stagg, reproduced with the kind permission of Johnny Green/PA Images

p131 Photo of Laura, reproduced with the kind permission of Robertson Films

p166 MEOW MEOW poster (Creative Commons licence)

Other illustrations © Illuminate Publishing

The authors

Cara has written many books for A level Psychology, and she speaks at and organises student conferences. In addition to this, she is senior editor of *Psychology Review*. In a previous life she was a teacher probably for more years than you have been alive and also an examiner for an equally long time. Her spare time (what there is of it) involves travelling with her husband and/or children (all now 25+). She lives in the Highlands of Scotland (despite being American by birth) and loves a long walk in the mountains and night in a bothy.

Julia has been teaching psychology for longer than a life sentence and still loves it. As well as being a Head of Psychology, she has two senior examiner roles in psychology and has authored scores of books and other resources for students and teachers. She lives in a barn on a farm and walks her mad dog whatever the weather.

Mandy has 20 years' experience of teaching psychology. She leads a thriving department, teaching A level and International Baccalaureate and runs popular workshops and training days for teachers. She did take a break for a few years and worked as a psychologist with gorgeous babies and children with Down syndrome. Mandy loves visiting her psychology friends in far-flung places and first got to know Cara on a trip to Auschwitz. When her addled brain is incapable of lucid thought, she likes to cook (Middle Eastern phase at the moment), chain-watch *Grey's Anatomy* and look at the sky. She also drinks tea, a lot of tea.

Rob was an A level Psychology teacher for more than 20 years, before turning to writing. He ventured back into teaching again recently and would like to give a big shout out to his ex-colleagues at Winstanley College. In his spare moments, Rob likes nothing better than to pluck away skill-lessly at his guitar. He is enthusiastically looking forward to *Frozen 2* coming out, even though his granddaughters couldn't care less.

Published in 2019 by Illuminate Publishing Ltd, P.O. Box 1160, Cheltenham, Gloucestershire GL50 9RW

Orders: Please visit www.illuminatepublishing.com or email sales@illuminatepublishing.com

British Library Cataloguing in Publication Data

A catalogue record for this book is available from the British Library

ISBN 978-1-912820-07-8

Printed by Standartu Spaustuvė, Lithuania

03.19

The publisher's policy is to use papers that are natural, renewable and recyclable products made from wood grown in sustainable forests. The logging and manufacturing processes are expected to conform to the environmental regulations of the country of origin.

Every effort has been made to contact copyright holders of material produced in this book. Great care has been taken by the authors and publisher to ensure that either formal permission has been granted for the use of copyright material reproduced, or that copyright material has been used under the provision of fairdealing guidelines in the UK – specifically that it has been used sparingly, solely for the purpose of criticism and review, and has been properly acknowledged. If notified, the publisher will be pleased to rectify any errors or omissions at the earliest opportunity.

Editor: Nic Watson

Design: Kamae Design

Layout: Kamae Design

Contents

A full set of references are available for download from the Illuminate Publishing website. Please visit www.illuminatepublishing.com/edexcelpsychreferences2

In all chapters (except the first chapter on Issues and debates) each spread covers one subtopic in the specification.

The spread **subtopic** is identified here.

On the left-hand page of each spread the **AO1 description** of the subtopic is covered.

Explanations of crime and anti-social behaviour: Personality

AO1
Description

This is the bit in the **specification** that we are covering on this spread.

Spec spotlight

Explanations of crime and anti-social behaviour, with consideration given to gender differences.

6.1.1 Biological explanations, including personality.

Informative picture or dodgy joke.

Crimes against dancing? Looks like it.

Each subtopic is divided into about **four key points** to help your revision. If you can recall something from each point, it will help organise the AO1 content of your answer to an extended response question.

Apply it questions on concepts or methods.

To give you an opportunity to practise applying your knowledge of this subtopic to a scenario.

The *Apply it* questions may be short answer ones (SAQ, worth just a few marks) or essays (extended response questions, ERQs).

The more you practise, the better you will get.

Apply it
Concepts

Luke is a quiet boy who hates being told off for doing something wrong. He is talking with his friends about who is most likely to get arrested. Jake is popular as he is loud and craves excitement – and because he is so reliable. If he says he will do something, he does. Gary has a sharp sense of humour, though his jokes are often hurtful and he can fly into a rage apparently over nothing.

1. (a) Describe **one** example of a boy's neurotic behaviour. (2)
   (b) Describe **one** example of a boy's psychotic behaviour. (2)
2. Explain extraversion and introversion using **two** of the boys as examples. (2)
3. **Context essay:** Discuss why some of the boys' personalities might put them at risk of criminality. (8)

Eysenck's theory of the criminal personality

Two dimensions of personality related to the criminal type.

Extraversion (E)–Introversion

- Extraverts crave excitement and stimulation, so are prone to engage in dangerous, risk-taking behaviour.
- They also tend not to condition easily (they do not learn from their mistakes).
- This means an extravert engaging in criminal behaviour would not be affected as strongly by punishment as an introvert would.

Neuroticism (N)–Stability

- Neurotic individuals are easily agitated and anxious.
- Their general instability means their behaviour is difficult to predict.

According to Eysenck, the typical criminal personality is an extravert–neurotic.

Biological basis

Eysenck's theory is essentially biological in nature.

The personality traits we develop throughout our lives are explained by the type of nervous system we inherit:

- Extraverts have a constant need for excitement. This may be caused by an underactive nervous system which requires unusually high levels of arousal.
- Neurotics are volatile and react strongly to situations others would find less stressful or even neutral.

A third dimension – psychoticism

Eysenck later added another dimension to the criminal type.

Psychoticism (P) is seen in people who are self-centred, cold and lack empathy for others (Eysenck was less clear about the link with the nervous system).

The criminal type scores highly on all three dimensions.

Eysenck developed the *Eysenck Personality Questionnaire* (EPQ), a questionnaire which places respondents along E, N and P dimensions to determine personality type.

The socialisation process

The theory has a biological emphasis but Eysenck acknowledged that the socialisation process in childhood determines whether a person becomes law-abiding or not.

However, the fact that extraverts are natural reward-seekers makes them less receptive to operant conditioning and therefore less affected by punishment for wrongdoing.

Similarly, high neuroticism interferes with efficient learning which may relate to difficulty taking on board social rules.

These factors make extravert–neurotics more likely to behave anti-socially.

To write good exam answers you need to know the facts, but you also must learn to apply your knowledge and evaluation effectively. Study the revision tips throughout this book.

On the right-hand page of each spread the **AO3 evaluation** of the subtopic is covered.

Each evaluative **chain of reasoning** is divided into three segments – **PET**:

P: Making the **Point**.

E: **Elaboration** using an **Example**, **Evidence** and/or **Explanation**.

T: And finally end with '**This** means that …' (if you start a sentence with '**This** shows/suggests/means' or '**Therefore**' – you are writing conclusion and linking the point back to the beginning).

AO3
Evaluation

Explanations of crime and anti-social behaviour: Personality

103

A strength is empirical evidence supporting the existence of a criminal type.

Boduszek et al. (2013) investigated Eysenck's personality traits in repeat offenders (133 violent and 179 non-violent males in a high-security prison).

A criminal thinking 'style' correlated with high psychoticism, neuroticism and extraversion (also linked to criminal friends and criminal identity).

This suggests that Eysenck's theory has validity as the personality types he identified are associated with repeat offending.

CA However, evidence for the criminal personality is not conclusive. Farrington et al. (1982) found little evidence that Eysenck's questionnaire (EPQ) was an adequate measure for predicting offending, in juveniles or adults. This suggests that Eysenck's original ideas about the nature of the criminal personality may lack validity.

A weakness is that there is not just one single criminal personality type.

The five-factor model of personality accepts Eysenck's concepts of extraversion and introversion, but adds openness, conscientiousness and agreeableness (= OCEAN).

Low levels of conscientiousness and agreeableness are related to offending. Also Lipsey and Derzon (1998) claim impulsivity is a better predictor of anti-social behaviour.

This research suggests that the criminal personality may be more complicated than Eysenck suggested.

Another strength is support for the biological basis of criminal personality.

Raine et al. (1990) took physiological measures from participants aged 15 years and related these to later criminal status.

24 years later those who had a criminal record had shown more signs of nervous system under-arousal when aged 15 than non-criminals (e.g. lower resting heart rate).

This suggests a link between biological factors and offending, but the researchers pointed out that there are also social variables that influence criminal behaviour.

Application: Eysenck's theory may help with early crime prevention.

The theory argues that criminal tendencies (e.g. lack of response to conditioning and inability to learn from mistakes) can be identified in early childhood.

Early intervention could modify the socialisation experiences of high-risk people to prevent them becoming offenders (in school or at home with support).

This would suggest that early interventions for vulnerable individuals, based on Eysenck's theory, may be beneficial.

I&D extra: Eysenck's theory integrates different ways of explaining behaviour.

It acknowledges genetic and physiological factors as well as individual differences in personality, and early socialisation.

This is a more integrated and interactionist approach than some of the other explanations discussed in this chapter.

This recognises that crime is a complex social activity that is likely to have different influences.

Unusually for him, Crooked Stan had decided honesty was the best policy.

Revision booster

The details on the specification for 'personality' are not very prescriptive compared with the other biological explanations on the previous spread. You still need to know a range of information thoroughly, but you cannot be asked specific questions about, for example, personality types, although you could be asked about gender differences.

Check it

1. Compare personality with **one** other biological explanation for crime and/or anti-social behaviour. [4]

2. Explain **one** strength of personality as an explanation for crime and/or anti-social behaviour. [2]

3. **Standard essay:** Evaluate personality as an explanation for crime and/or anti-social behaviour. [8] or [16]

4. **Methods essay:** When studying crime, psychologists are interested in the links between personality and anti-social behaviour. Evaluate the validity and reliability of research in this area. [8] or [16]

CA stands for **competing argument**. Use these in an essay to try to provide counterarguments for some of your points ('On the other hand'). This even applies in a 'Discuss' essay with no AO3.

A handy tip to **improve your exam performance**.

A small range of **exam-style questions** to help you understand how the subtopic will be assessed – and so you can practise writing good answers.

Always time yourself when writing exam answers. Aim for about $1\frac{1}{3}$ minutes per mark, which includes planning/thinking time.

You should also aim to write about 20–25 words per minute.

Questions 1 and 2 are **short answer questions** (SAQ).

Question 3 is a **standard essay** (ERQ) on the subtopic. This is the most basic question possible and is a useful platform from which to develop your answers to more complex questions.

Question 4 is a **standard plus essay** – which combines the standard essay with something else. It might focus on methods or have a prompt (see essay types on page 9).

This **I&D evaluation** is an extra – you already have three or even four points which is plenty for an 8-mark essay.

Higher tariff questions (12, 16 and 20 marks) tend to combine subtopics so you will have enough AO3.

I&D essays: These I&D points will also be helpful in the Issues and debates essays on Papers 1 and 3.

We haven't included a **balanced conclusion** at the end, even though it is an important part of a good essay.

You can write your own or read them in our Year 1 and 2 Student books!

Overview of the exam

In this introductory section on understanding the exam we look at key things you should know and give you some exemplar exam answers with comments.

edexcel

A Level
Psychology

Specification
Pearson Edexcel Level 3 Advanced GCE in Psychology (9PS0)
First teaching from September 2015
First certification from 2017
Issue 2

A level (AL)

Paper 1 **Foundations in psychology** 2 hours 90 marks 35% of total qualification	Section A Social psychology	70 marks, mixed question types.
	Section B Cognitive psychology	
	Section C Biological psychology	
	Section D Learning theories	
	Section E Issues and debates	20 marks, two ERQs.

The four topics examined on Paper 1 (social, cognitive, biological and learning) are covered in our Year 1 Revision guide.

Paper 2 **Applications of psychology** 2 hours 90 marks 35% of total qualification	Section A Clinical psychology	54 marks, mixed question types.
	Section B Choose one from three optional topics: • Criminological psychology • Child psychology • Health psychology	36 marks, mixed question types.

On pages 12–15 there are example answers to questions on clinical psychology.

Paper 3 **Psychological skills** 2 hours 80 marks 30% of total qualification	Section A Research methods	24 marks, mixed question types.
	Section B Review of studies	24 marks, mixed question types on psychological studies and one ERQ on classic studies from Paper 1 and from Clinical psychology.
	Section C Issues and debates	32 marks, two ERQs.

On pages 16–17 we explain how to answer questions from Paper 3 Section A.

Research methods are covered in our Year 1 Revision guide.

On pages 18–19 we explain how to answer questions from Paper 3 Section B.

On pages 20–22 we explain how to answer questions from Paper 3 Section C.

Issues and debates are discussed in chapter 1 but also every evaluation page has one criticism related to an issue or debate.

Exam skills

In your answers you are assessed on three skills – called assessment objectives (AOs).

AO1 **Description**	Demonstrate knowledge and understanding of scientific ideas, processes, techniques and procedures.	Good AO1 – aim for one well-detailed and accurate sentence per mark. Command terms, e.g. *state, define, give, describe.*
AO2 **Application**	Apply knowledge and understanding of scientific ideas, processes, techniques and procedures: • In a theoretical context. • In a practical context. • When handling qualitative data. • When handling quantitative data.	Questions have a stem/scenario (the context). Good AO2 – every sentence you write must be linked to the context fully. Command terms, e.g. *using your knowledge* of psychology, *explain* [the context], *discuss* (ERQ with AO1 + AO2).
AO3 **Evaluation** **and analysis**	Analyse, interpret and evaluate scientific information, ideas and evidence, including in relation to issues, to: • Make judgements and reach conclusions. • Develop and refine practical design and procedures.	Good AO3 uses chains of reasoning – PET, make your *point*, *explain* and *elaborate*, *conclude* with a link back to the exam question you are answering with 'This means that …'. Command terms, e.g. *evaluate, assess, to what extent.*

Specialist terms turn your broad-strokes into a detailed answer.

Context is king.

Types of exam question

SAQ	Short answer questions (SAQs).	Marks range from 1 to 7. Marks are awarded for each 'creditworthy' idea. See full-mark examples on pages 10–11.
ERQ	Extended response questions (ERQs), often called 'essays'.	Marks range from 8 to 20 and all have an evaluative component except for 8-markers with the command term *discuss*. ERQs are levels-marked, meaning the examiner will compare your answer to a set of descriptors and choose the set which best describe your essay. See full-mark examples on pages 12–22.

*In answers to ERQs, lists are bad. Do **FEWER** points but explain each carefully.*

To be fair lists are not good in answers to SAQs either. All ideas need to be elaborated really effectively to get marks, so if you try to tackle too many points you leave no time for elaboration = a low mark.

Check it

On every spread in this book you will see two SAQ questions for the subtopic covered on the spread – these are provided to give you a feel for the kind of questions you may be asked. There are more examples for each subtopic in our Year 2 Student book.

There are also example SAQ answers on the next spread.

On every spread you can see examples of application SAQs related to either concepts or research methods.

Edexcel
Psychology
for A Level Year 1 & AS
Revision Guide
Cara Flanagan • Rob Liddle • Julia Russell • Mandy Wood

Illuminate Publishing

In our Year 1 Revision guide we provide further full-mark answers to both SAQs and ERQs.

Straight content	Describe **one** symptom of schizophrenia. (2)	Very predictable description questions with no frills.
	Explain **one** weakness of personality as an explanation for crime and anti-social behaviour. (2)	For each study, know the aims, procedure, findings and conclusions plus the evaluation (strengths and weaknesses).
	Define what is meant by 'privation'. (2)	
Compare	Compare **one** biological and **one** learning explanation for heroin addiction. (4)	Make sure you include at least one similarity and one difference.
Application	There are examples throughout this guide but note that Paper 3 has some lengthier scenarios where you will be expected to apply everything you have learned to slightly more detailed contexts, for example see the question on page 18.	
Prompt	Rosenhan (1973) questioned the validity of diagnosis. Explain **one** issue affecting the validity of diagnosis with reference to research evidence. (3)	These may look like application questions but are not. The question does not require you to address the context.
Methods	Questions related to research methods may be straight content or comparisons but most often they are application questions. For A level there are one or more methods questions on 'unseen' studies (see pages 16 and 17).	
Individual differences and developmental psychology	The specification says 'Individual differences and developmental psychology must be considered' when learning about each subtopic. Therefore, there may be questions such as: With reference to Carlsson et al. (2000), explain why there may be individual differences in schizophrenia. (3)	
Key question	You will have learned about a key question from criminological psychology that is relevant to today's society.	'Describe' questions require an outline of the relevance of your key question to society, including consideration of pros and cons of exploring/ignoring it.
	Explain this key question using concepts, theories and/or research from criminological psychology. (4)	'Explain' questions require you to apply psychological concepts, theories and/or research to your chosen key question.
Practical investigation	As part of your study of biological psychology, you were required to carry out a practical investigation.	
	(a) State a fully operationalised alternate hypothesis for this practical investigation. (2)	
	(b) Describe how you measured the variables in your investigation. (4)	

Standard	Describe and evaluate one subtopic. (Note that these are highly unlikely on Paper 3 where ERQs will be 'review of studies' and 'issues and debates', see below.)	Example answers in our Year 1 Revision guide (pages 12–19).
Context	Context/scenario is given which must be addressed in your answer (i.e. answer applied to context).	
Prompt	Context provided but no application required.	
Methods	Research methods, may just be methods or applied to a subtopic.	
Key question	Describe your key question and apply your psychological evidence. For A level, evaluation is required except for 8-mark discuss questions.	
Practical investigation	Describe aims/procedure/findings/conclusions of your practical investigations. Evaluate strengths and weaknesses.	
Synoptic	Questions include reference to **more than one** topic, i.e. social and cognitive, or psychology in general.	
I&D	Involves **one** issue or debate often (but not always) in relation to a topic (e.g. clinical) or possibly subtopic (e.g. schizophrenia).	
Review of studies	Paper 3, Section B – Questions combine two of the classic studies from topics 1–5 (e.g. Sherif and Rosenhan) with one of the eleven issues and debates.	

Check it

The final two check it questions are ERQs (essays). The first is always labelled **Standard** and the second is one of the other categories described on the left.

Many of the types of exam question on the left can be combined, e.g. I&D/Synoptic or I&D/Methods.

Make up your own

We only have room for two ERQs on each spread in this book but you can adapt the ones throughout each chapter by changing the subtopic in the question.

ERQ command terms

8 marks		16 marks (A level Papers 2 and 3 only)	
Discuss (with context)	AO1 + AO2 (4 + 4)	Evaluate (no context)	AO1 + AO3 (6 + 10)
Evaluate (no context) Assess (no context)	AO1 + AO3 (4 + 4)	Evaluate (with context) Assess (with context) To what extent (with context)	AO1 + AO2 + AO3 (6 + 4 + 6)
12 marks		**20 marks (A level only)**	
Evaluate (no context) To what extent (no context)	AO1 + AO3 (6 + 6)	Evaluate (no context) Assess (no context)	AO1 + AO3 (8 + 12)
Evaluate (with context)	AO1 + AO2 + AO3 (4 + 4 + 4)	To what extent (with context)	AO1 + AO2 + AO3 (8 + 4 + 8)

Practice

No athlete would dream of running a race without doing many practice runs of the right distance and within a set time. Always write exam answers in the allotted time – allow yourself about 12–15 minutes for an 8-mark essay. You should prepare beforehand and maybe even write a few notes, but then write the answer with the clock ticking.

Straight content SAQ

Describe (AO1) then justify or exemplify (AO3).

Explain one strength of the DSM-IV-TR or the DSM-5 as a classification system for mental health. (3)

Full-mark answer *One strength is the DSM-5 is reliable.*

Field trials by Regier found that kappa scores ranged from 0.4 and 0.79 (good to very good) for many disorders including schizophrenia.

This is a strength because it means that if a person is re-assessed (in the future or by another practitioner) 40–79% of them will get the same diagnosis again, which increases the credibility of the diagnosis.

Examiner comments This answer illustrates PET. The point is made at the start, followed by detailed evidence (second paragraph) showing understanding of kappa scores. The final mark is gained by explaining why this is a strength (a conclusion).

Compare SAQ

Maximum mark of 3 out of 4 unless you include at least one similarity and one difference.

Marks are only awarded if both explanations are compared within the point.

Compare two of the following biological explanations for crime and anti-social behaviour: brain injury, the role of the amygdala, XYY syndrome and/or personality. (4)

Full-mark answer *One similarity between brain injury and personality explanations is they can both help screen high-risk individuals. For example, screening first-time offenders for brain injuries could lead to support, thus preventing re-offending. Similarly, the personality explanation suggests children who do not respond to fear conditioning could be targeted for intervention to prevent crime.*

One difference is that the brain injury explanation implies criminality is acquired but the personality account suggests it is innate. This means some people may shows early signs of future criminality due to innate differences, whereas others will show no sign of criminality until after the injury.

Examiner comments The similarity about screening is applied to brain injury and personality explanations clearly, e.g. fear conditioning.

The difference also refers to both explanations and links them with an appropriate connective ('whereas').

There is sufficient depth in both paragraphs for two marks each.

Application SAQ

All sentences must be contextualised in an applications question.

Jaycee has schizophrenia. She works at a local charity shop but sometimes she finds interacting with the other workers stressful. At one time she believed the other workers were trying to poison her. Her therapist wants her to try a non-biological treatment.

Describe one non-biological treatment that could be used to help Jaycee. (3)

Full-mark answer *The therapist might use CBT to help Jaycee identify and manage stressors in her life (e.g. interactions at work) as stress can trigger psychotic episodes in people with an underlying predisposition to schizophrenia.*

Behavioural experiments could be used to differentiate between perceived and actual reality, i.e. comparing Jaycee's delusions to the view shared by others.

For example, Jaycee could record examples of interactions at work and talk through this 'evidence' with the therapist, challenging the idea that the co-workers dislike her.

Examiner comments The answer explains how the treatment would help Jaycee, i.e. by minimising stress, thus combining knowledge of CBT for schizophrenia and elements from the context.

Good understanding of behavioural experiments is linked to the context, e.g. 'co-workers dislike her'.

Prompt SAQ

The prompt may help you think of ways to answer the question, but you don't have to refer to it.

Recovering from addiction is not easy and treatments can present a variety of problems.

Explain one practical issue relating to a treatment for drug addiction. (3)

Full-mark answer *One practical issue is non-adherence, meaning that people drop out because the treatment programme is unpleasant in some way.*

For example, aversion therapy might use electric shocks or emetics which make people feel sick, while drug treatments can lead to stomach cramps, depression and dizziness.

These punishing consequences mean some people, especially those with little social support, may fail to complete the programme, meaning their addiction continues.

Examiner comments The issue is described in the first sentence. Next, detailed knowledge of aversion therapy and drug treatments is clearly articulated. The final sentence addresses the command term (explain) by noting how and why the issue impacts recovery.

Methods SAQ

Explain one way that researchers in child psychology are affected by the UNCRC (1989) which aims to protect children's rights. (2)

Full-mark answer *Article 12 of the UNCRC states that children have the right to express their views, feelings and wishes in matters affecting them.*

This means researchers should seek informed consent from the children themselves and provide age-appropriate information, i.e. modified so it is meaningful to their level of development.

Examiner comments The point shows good knowledge of the UNCRC. Furthermore, there is an explanation for *how* this can be achieved, e.g. by providing age-appropriate information.

As this question asks for **one** way it is important not to bring in more than one idea, meaning that your second mark must come from explaining the initial point made. Describe (AO1) your point and then justify or exemplify it (AO3) carefully.

Individual differences and developmental psychology SAQ

With reference to the contemporary study by Carlsson *et al.* (2000), explain why there may be individual differences in schizophrenia. (3)

Full-mark answer *Some people with schizophrenia exhibit more positive symptoms (e.g. hallucinations and delusions) while others exhibit more negative symptoms (e.g. flat affect and alogia).*

Carlsson explains this in terms of hypoglutamatergia in different brain regions leading to differing symptoms.

For example, hypoglutamatergia in the cerebral cortex is related to negative symptoms whereas hypoglutamatergia in the basal ganglia results in positive symptoms.

Examiner comments The answer starts well by stating how individuals with schizophrenia differ and then succinctly links this to Carlsson *et al.*'s review to explain why these differences arise (hypoglutamatergia in differing brain regions).

Questions related to individual differences or developmental psychology can be linked to any subtopic.

Key question SAQ

State your key question and explain it using psychological concepts, theories and research from clinical psychology. (4)

Full-mark answer *My key question is: 'How do different societies define mental health disorders?'*

Although it was developed in the US, the DSM is used around the world to define mental health disorders. However, comparing a person's behaviour to the social norms of a society with whom they do not identify can be misleading because, what appears abnormal in one culture, may not be so in another.

This means a person's behaviour may be wrongly defined as 'deviant', leading to stigmatisation and attempts to treat or even detain the person. The DSM-5 Section 3 tries to avoid this problem by detailing ways in which cultural differences affect the presentation of clinical symptoms. This should help clinicians avoid being influenced by their own ethnocentric biases which can lead to invalid diagnoses.

Examiner comments The candidate is careful to provide a match between the key question and the material that follows, e.g. the words 'define' and 'society' are used. Therefore, both paragraphs are focused on applying clinical psychology to the stem.

As this is a 4-marker, the answer is organised into two detailed paragraphs, the first stating the problem and the second outlining the implications and ways that the problem may be resolved.

This is an application (AO2) question, which means you are required to focus on applying clinical knowledge to your key question as opposed to *describing* the key question.

Be aware that when answering the key question you can draw on knowledge from across the specification not just the named topic area.

Practical investigation SAQ

Explain one problem that you faced when conducting your practical investigation for health psychology. (2)

Full-mark answer *One problem was that it was hard to establish inter-rater reliability in our content analysis of drug references in pop songs from 1967 and 2017.*

This was because we were using qualitative data and found that this led to subjectivity in the way that we interpreted the lyrics. Our interpretations were dependent on our own knowledge of the words associated with drug-taking.

Examiner comments A problem (inter-rater reliability) is identified. The next paragraph explains why this problem arose (individual differences in interpretation).

Requires a description of the problem (AO1) and a well-reasoned explanation (AO3), both referencing specific details of *your* practical.

Evaluate Carlsson *et al.*'s (2000) contemporary study on schizophrenia. (8)

Examiner comments

The answer on the right begins with a short paragraph on Carlsson *et al.*'s study – just the aim and one example is covered. This is a sensible approach to dealing with such a complex study. When revising select a few key details that you can use effectively.

The second paragraph is AO3. Compare this with page 55 in this book and you will see how a chain of reasoning has been produced to fit the demands of this short essay.

Paragraph 3 supplies more AO3. It starts with a link to the previous paragraph, showing a logical development of ideas throughout the essay and delivers a competing argument.

Next we have a further AO1 paragraph which is followed up in the final AO3 paragraph (i.e. 'a wider range of neurotransmitters') which gives an application of Carlsson *et al.*'s work.

Thus, in total there is a fairly even distribution of AO1 and AO3 paragraphs.

The essay ends with a balanced conclusion which is required for an 'evaluate' essay.

Full-mark answer

Carlsson et al. (2000) looked at research that went beyond the dopamine explanation for schizophrenia. For example, they looked at the role of glutamate. Low levels of glutamate (hypoglutamatergia) can act as an accelerator on dopamine or a brake on GABA, both of which produce schizophrenia symptoms.

This is supported by Carlsson and Carlsson (1989) who found that continued use of MK-801, which reduces glutamate and thus increases serotonin and dopamine, resulted in psychotic-like behaviour. This suggests that schizophrenia may be caused by glutamate irregularity.

However, this research was conducted on mice and one consequence of basing conclusions on animal research is that the role of culture is ignored. For example, Luhrmann (2015) showed that US participants with schizophrenia were more likely to hear violent and frightening voices whereas Ghanaian people had more positive experiences. This suggests that animal models would fail to capture the holistic lived experience of people with schizophrenia – including the role of other people's reactions to the symptoms of a person with schizophrenia.

Carlsson et al. (2000) note that hypoglutamatergia in the cerebral cortex can lead to negative symptoms whereas positive symptoms result from hypoglutamatergia in the basal ganglia (which includes the striatum). In this brain region, glutamate signals to GABA to inhibit dopamine release. Therefore, when there is insufficient glutamate, the GABA system fails to regulate dopamine.

Carlsson et al.'s focus on a wider range of neurotransmitters is a strength because it leads to improved drug treatments. For example, glutamate agonists could be used to reduce both positive and negative symptoms. This is important as typical antipsychotics often fail to treat negative symptoms and result in side effects such as tardive dyskinesia, which may lead to non-compliance.

In conclusion, Carlsson et al.'s research is valuable in providing a comprehensive review and highlighting new areas for research and treatment such as glutamate agonists. However, the reliance on animal models ignores the role of social and cognitive factors which could also be exploited in treatment.

328 words

Mark scheme for 8-mark *evaluate* questions

> The grid summarises the levels-based mark scheme used for such questions.

AO1 (4 marks)   AO3 (4 marks)   Candidates must demonstrate an equal emphasis on knowledge and understanding vs evaluation/conclusion in their answer.

Level	Mark	Description (AO1) Knowledge and understanding	Evaluation (AO3)	Chains of reasoning (AO3)	Competing arguments (AO3)	Conclusion (AO3)
0	0	No rewardable material.				
1	1–2	Isolated elements.	Limited attempt to address the question.	Limited supporting evidence.		Generic.
2	3–4	Mostly accurate.	Statements with some development.	Mostly accurate and relevant factual material.		Superficial.
3	5–6	Accurate.	Arguments developed but may be imbalanced.	Mostly coherent.	Grasp of competing arguments.	Arguments lead to a conclusion.
4	7–8	Accurate and thorough.	Well-developed and logical.	Logical throughout.	Demonstrates an awareness of competing arguments.	Balanced conclusion. (Nuanced)

The mark schemes used in this book are <u>illustrative</u> of the levels-based mark schemes (LBMS) used by Edexcel. Always ask your teacher for up-to-date advice about the Edexcel mark schemes, as these may have been amended.

Paul discovered that his aunt was diagnosed with schizophrenia. He is a clinical psychologist and finds this quite interesting but his son Matthew is a bit worried as he has heard that schizophrenia is biological and can be inherited.

Discuss **one** non-biological explanation for schizophrenia that Paul might mention to reassure his son. [8]

Full-mark answer

Matthew believes that schizophrenia may be a heritable condition and is worried about developing it himself. His father, Paul should explain that a possible biological vulnerability for schizophrenia only develops if social factors create stress (a social causation explanation).

One example of this is social adversity. It may be that Matthew's aunt grew up in an unfavourable environment and this creates stress which acts a trigger. An example of this might be unemployment or poverty. So, if Matthew grew up in a fairly well-off family and enjoyed a good relationship with his father, this would reduce his risk.

Urbanicity is another factor linked to schizophrenia. Perhaps Paul's aunt lived in a city where there are many stressors such as noise, light pollution, criminality, faster pace and anonymity. High population density makes life more competitive, which may increase the experience of chronic social defeat (a stressor). If Matthew lives in a rural area and is happy, with good friends and a loving family, his risk will be much reduced.

A further factor is being an immigrant. Research shows greater risk of schizophrenia for first- and second-generation immigrants. Therefore, if Paul's aunt immigrated to the UK, this might even influence Paul's risk as a second-generation immigrant. However, Veling et al. (2008) found that only people with weak ethnic identity had an increased risk of schizophrenia. So, if Paul's family maintained a strong sense of ethnic identity this would reduce their risk, which is an important message to pass on to Matthew.

The risk of schizophrenia increases as the number of people from the same ethnic background decreases. This can be linked to social isolation. People who have developed schizophrenia can be cut off from feedback about what behaviours are inappropriate and this can increase the development of strange behaviour and thoughts. So Matthew should be aware that, given his possible risk, his friends are an important defence.

Knowledge of these factors should help reassure Matthew that being related to someone diagnosed with schizophrenia may only marginally increase his risk but he can do a lot to avoid those social factors which in turn would reduce his risk.

355 words

Examiner comments

Discuss questions require AO1 plus AO2. There is no credit for evaluation (AO3).

As AO3 is unnecessary the answer can just focus on one side of the argument (environmental triggers) and, for example, does not need to look at biological evidence that supports Matthew's view. Competing arguments can simply come from looking at multiple aspects of the selected non-biological explanation.

The answer starts by showing understanding that Matthew is concerned about heritability before delivering four concise paragraphs each linking theoretical knowledge to the extract (context). The paragraphs are organised by theme, e.g. social adversity, urbanicity, immigration/ ethnic identity and social isolation. Research by Veling *et al.* is introduced as a competing argument.

All ideas are developed fully and links to Matthew, Paul and their relative are sustained.

Mark scheme for 8-mark *discuss* questions

'Discuss' questions have a scenario. The grid summarises the levels-based mark scheme used for such questions.

AO1 (4 marks)   AO2 (4 marks)   Candidates must demonstrate an equal emphasis on knowledge and understanding vs application in their answer.

Level	Mark	Description (AO1) Knowledge and understanding	Argument (AO2)	Chains of reasoning (AO2)	Competing arguments (AO2)	Application (scientific ideas, processes, techniques or procedures) (AO2)
0	0	No rewardable material.				
1	1–2	Isolated elements.	Little or no reference to relevant evidence from the context.			
2	3–4	Mostly accurate.	Partially developed.	Superficial.	Imbalanced.	Occasionally supported through the application of relevant evidence.
3	5–6	Accurate.	Arguments developed.	Mostly coherent.	Grasp of competing arguments but discussion may be imbalanced or contain superficial material.	Supported by applying relevant evidence from the context.
4	7–8	Accurate and thorough.	Well-developed and logical.	Logical.	Demonstrates a thorough awareness of competing arguments.	Supported by sustained application of relevant evidence from the context.

ERQs – example questions and answers

Papers 1 and 2 Prompt essay

Examiner comments

Research methods are explained and evaluated in our Year 1 Revision guide but they are examined in relation to *all* topics – Year 1 and Year 2 ones as well (clinical, criminological, child and health).

For the Year 2 topics, the specification lists the specific research methods you need to know for that topic. For clinical psychology, one of the requirements is detailed knowledge of two additional studies as examples of case studies and interviews (see pages 56 and 57). However, the question on this page does not require detailed knowledge of specific studies, as the focus is on the methods themselves.

This is a prompt question which means you do not have to address the stem, however the key feature of the question itself is that it requires you to apply your answer to clinical psychology.

In fact each point you make should be linked to examples from clinical psychology, as has been done here. Notice that, in this essay, the examples are insightful rather than just the odd mention of the words 'clinical psychology' or 'mental illness'.

Another important feature of the question is that it requires *two or more* research methods. In reality it is difficult to distinguish between a research method (such as a case study) and something that is more a research technique (such as collecting qualitative data). The key point is that 'two or more' may make you feel you have to write about lots of methods to get high marks – but you don't. It is better to focus on fewer methods and ensure a thorough description and evaluation of each, as has been done here.

Evidence-based practice matters in clinical psychology because it is important that people are offered treatments that are supported by research evidence. Assess the use of **two** or more methods for researching mental health. (20)

Full-mark answer

Two methods used in clinical psychology are case studies and interviews.

Clinical psychologists use in-depth case studies to examine single events, groups or individuals, e.g. a specific person with schizophrenia or a group receiving cognitive-behavioural treatment. Case studies are usually longitudinal, involving years of work between a clinical psychologist and their client. A case study often includes a case history of a client to provide useful background information, often constructed from secondary data (existing records made for some other purpose). Hospital notes, school reports or even old diaries may be useful sources of contextual information.

Case studies may also include qualitative data, e.g. group therapy sessions may be observed and field notes recorded. Interviews may be conducted with the client. Family members may provide information about how the person/family feels about their experiences. Interview transcripts and field notes provide rich qualitative data which can be analysed in terms of themes, e.g. frustration with a therapist. However, clinical case studies usually also include quantitative data, e.g. the Beck Depression Inventory may be used to represent the severity of a disorder and also to track progress.

One strength of case studies is the use of multiple research methods and types of data. For example, a depressed client may appear to have made unexpectedly rapid improvement, as measured by a questionnaire. More probing questions in an interview could reveal that increased family support aided the person's recovery. This is important as it shows how triangulation of methods can improve the validity of the findings. This is especially important when researching clinical treatments, which can be costly.

However, a weakness is that case studies lack generalisability, due to the unique features of the 'case'. For example, a treatment may only be effective due to the talents of a specific therapist, including their ability to form a good rapport with their clients. This means readers must be cautious about expecting similar findings with their own clients, i.e. they must think about ways in which their clinical setting may differ as these factors may mean that therapy is more or less effective.

On the other hand, case data may still be relevant to other settings and should not be written off simply because only one set of experiences are represented. In fact, the focus on only one person or therapist means that information is generally richer in detail and in greater depth. This is important as this level of detail should mean readers are able to decide whether the outcomes would generalise well to their own clinical setting or not and this therefore is a strength of the case study in clinical psychology.

The second method that is often used by clinical psychologists is interviews. These can take three forms. Structured interviews have predetermined questions and interviewers cannot deviate from the set order. Structured interviews are basically a questionnaire which is read out to the interviewee. Structured interviews may be used to determine the number, duration and severity of symptoms based on the DSM or ICD criteria.

The other two kinds of interview, semi-structured and unstructured interviews, permit interviewers to develop questions in response to the answers given. In a semi-structured interview, the interviewer might start with a few predetermined questions such as, 'Tell me about your childhood' or 'How do you feel about your diagnosis?', but then develop further questions depending on the answers given. This approach allows the interviewer to probe into unexpected answers. In an unstructured interview no questions are decided in advance.

The interviewer will have some general aims, e.g. finding out about a therapist's experiences in treating certain clients. The interviewer will ask very open-ended questions such as, 'How do you feel about that?' just to keep the conversation going.

Answer continues on facing page.

Full-mark answer (continued)

One weakness with all types of interviews is interviewer bias. For example, an interviewer may have preconceptions of how a person with depression is likely to answer and might nod when the person gives the expected answer, showing their agreement. This is important as when interviewers consciously or unconsciously communicate expectations or approval/disapproval this can affect the interviewee's subsequent responses. This means the interviewer essentially ends up with data that reinforces their own preconceptions, thus reducing internal validity.

This said, a specific advantage of semi-structured interviews is that validity can be improved by asking further questions, based on the interviewee's answers. For example, when unsure of an interviewee's meaning, the interviewer can ask for clarification. This may be particularly important in diagnostic interviews, as errors can be avoided by further probing questions, e.g. the interviewer can pick up on things the person has said about their past, helping reveal whether symptoms have actually been present for longer than initially assumed.

This contrasts with structured interviews where the questions cannot be changed. Although this makes structured interviews with clinical clients replicable (to check validity), it can also be a weakness because it does not permit an interviewer to shape questions to client needs. For example, when a client fails to understand a question or gives an incomplete answer then there is no opportunity to offer assistance. The end result is that the data about mental health problems will lack validity.

Overall, whilst case studies (which usually include interviews) provide a large amount of in-depth information, they require considerable time and may lack generalisability. Interviews alone can also collect large amounts of in-depth qualitative information and take less time than a comprehensive case study, so greater numbers of participants can be involved.

910 words

Examiner comments (continued)

A further consideration is balance. First of all balance in the amounts of AO1 and AO3. In a 20-mark assess essay this is a 40/60 split (2:3). This is not easy to keep track of – one approach is to have a sense of what 80 words (one paragraph) in your handwriting looks like and then you can keep a rough count of what you have done. For every two AO1 paragraphs you should write three AO3 paragraphs.

One advantage of focusing on this 80-word chunk is that, if you know you need to write a bit more on an AO1 or AO2 point then it may encourage you to squeeze out a little bit more explanation. You might omit this demonstration of your understanding in your hurry to get everything down. It is the *quality* of your explanations that is important.

Balance is also related to the AO3 points you write. You need strengths and weaknesses in equal proportion. Here we have two strengths and a weakness for case studies and two weaknesses and one strength for interviews.

The final conclusion succinctly balances the benefits of each research method reviewed.

Mark scheme for 20-mark *assess* questions

AO1 (8 marks)   AO3 (12 marks)   Candidates must demonstrate a greater emphasis on evaluation/conclusion vs knowledge and understanding in their answer. Knowledge and understanding is capped at maximum 8 marks.

The grid summarises the levels-based mark scheme used for such questions.

Level	Mark	Description (AO1) Knowledge and understanding	Evaluation (AO3)	Chains of reasoning (AO3)	Competing arguments (AO3)	Conclusion (AO3)
0	0	No rewardable material.				
1	1–4	Isolated elements.	Limited attempt to address the question.	Limited supporting evidence.		Generic.
2	5–8	Mostly accurate.	Statements with some development.	Mostly accurate and relevant factual material.		Superficial.
3	9–12	Accurate.	Arguments developed but may be imbalanced.	Mostly coherent.	Grasp of competing arguments.	Arguments lead to a conclusion/judgement.
4	13–16	Accurate and thorough.	Developed and logical.	Logical throughout.	Demonstrates an understanding of competing arguments.	Conclusion/judgement may be imbalanced.
5	17–20	Accurate and thorough.	Well-developed and logical.	Logical throughout.	Demonstrates a full awareness of competing arguments.	Balanced conclusion.

The mark schemes used in this book are <u>illustrative</u> of the levels-based mark schemes (LBMS) used by Edexcel. Always ask your teacher for up-to-date advice about the Edexcel mark schemes, as these may have been amended.

Examiner comments

Paper 3 Section A examines your knowledge of Research methods. There are 24 marks available in total distributed between one or more short extracts from 'unseen' studies (we have included two here).

You must use the extract carefully to contextualise every point – if you don't contextualise, marks can be lost very easily despite evidence of detailed knowledge.

1. Arachnophobia is an extreme fear of spiders. This phobia can be treated using virtual reality (VR). In one study people with arachnophobia were asked to estimate the size of a real 7.5 cm wide tarantula. These estimates were compared with estimates made by a non-phobic control group. All participants also rated their fear on a scale of 1–10 as the spider was brought closer to them.

Later all participants were confronted with four 'digital spiders' for five minutes using a virtual reality (VR) headset. This was repeated four times. Two weeks later, participants were shown the real tarantula again and asked to estimate its size and rate their fear level. Not all of the original participants came back for the second stage of the study.

Table 1: Tarantula size estimates before and after VR exposure treatment for participants with and without arachnophobia.

	Estimate of tarantula's size	
	Participants with arachnophobia	Participants without arachnophobia (control group)
Time 1: Before VR treatment	13.5 cm	8.3 cm
Time 2: After VR treatment	8.5 cm	8.1 cm

(Source: Adapted from Shiban *et al.* 2016)

(a) Describe one conclusion that can be determined from the figures in Table 1. (2)

You must state the conclusion and include actual figures from the extract. You must also state what can be inferred from the figures.

Full-mark answer *One possible conclusion is that arachnophobia is linked to an exaggerated perception of spider size. Before therapy, participants estimated the spider as considerably bigger than its real size (estimate of 13.5 cm compared with real size of 7.5 cm). After therapy, estimates were far more accurate, they were just one centimetre wrong (8.5 cm compared with 7.5 cm).*

(b) Explain why the researcher used a control group in this study. (3)

An accurate reason is given and then thoroughly explained. Sound understanding of the study is displayed through reference to the independent and dependent variables.

Full-mark answer *Using a control group allowed the researcher to see whether the estimated spider size and the fear ratings (dependent variables) were different in the participants with arachnophobia and those without arachnophobia (the independent variable). The comparison would be useful because it could explain the higher fear ratings of those with arachnophobia, i.e. they were more scared because of their misperception of the spiders as bigger.*

(c) The researcher wishes to know whether the reduction in the estimate of the spider's size before and after VR treatment is statistically significant for the participants with arachnophobia. State which statistical test should be used and why. (3)

The candidate identifies the test and concisely gives the three necessary conditions for choosing the appropriate test, systematically linking each of these conditions to the extract context.

Full-mark answer *The researcher would use a Wilcoxon test because: (1) they are testing for a difference between two conditions (before and after VR treatment), (2) the experimental design is repeated measures as they are looking at the same groups of participants (people with arachnophobia) before and after VR treatment, (3) the level of measurement for estimated spider size is interval (centimetres are standardised units) and this can be collapsed to ordinal data.*

(d) Explain two possible problems with this study which mean that VR treatment is not as effective as it may seem. (4)

The secret to a good answer is to state the problem and then explain it with specific reference to details of the study.

It is important to use the correct terminology wherever possible to demonstrate your detailed knowledge.

Full-mark answer *First, internal validity may be low if participants gave smaller spider size estimates the second time due to demand characteristics. They knew they were expected to feel better after treatment and may have said what they thought the researcher expected to hear, maybe to avoid further VR sessions.*

Second, the study arguably lacks generalisability because some participants did not attend stage two. The non-attenders may have found the VR terrifying, so their fear ratings and size estimates would have been much higher. Their lack of attendance means the treatments may have appeared to be more effective than they were.

2. Sabrina has come across an interesting study showing that the more countries a person has visited, the more likely they were to cheat on a computerised quiz, if given the opportunity to do so.

She decided to investigate this for herself. She asked nine of her friends how many countries they had visited and then presented them with a questionnaire including ten moral dilemmas. Her friends were asked to select one of four possible answers to describe what they would do in each dilemma. Sabrina calculated a self-reported morality score out of 40 for each friend. The higher the score the higher their level of morality.

(Source: Adapted from Lu *et al.* 2017)

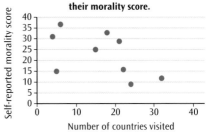

A scatter diagram to show the relationship between the number of countries a person has visited and their morality score.

(a) State a fully operationalised directional hypothesis for Sabrina's study. (2)

Full-mark answer *There is a negative correlation between the number of countries visited and morality scores based on moral dilemmas (maximum score of 40, where a high score equals greater morality).*

Both co-variables are operationalised using information from the extract.

(b) Analyse the data from the scatter diagram, with reference to the original study on which Sabrina based her investigation. (3)

Full-mark answer *The scatter diagram shows a moderate, negative correlation. This supports the original study as the more countries a person had visited, the lower they scored on the morality questionnaire (i.e. less moral).*

There is one outlier – the person who visited the fewest countries (5) scored 15 on the questionnaire. Removing this score would increase the correlation coefficient providing solid support for Lu et al.

The answer is analytical as it considers not only the trend shown by the majority of data but also the possible impact of the outlier. Both points are contextualised well and the data used effectively in support.

(c) Measuring morality using self-report may not be valid. Suggest one way that Sabrina could measure morality that has greater validity. (3)

Full-mark answer *Sabrina could leave some money on the bar in a pub, making it look like someone had forgotten their change and then observe people's reactions.*

A scoring system could be used to rate the morality of different actions, e.g. 1 = take the money, 2 = give it to the bartender, 3 = put it in a charity donation box.

Validity would be higher because people do not know they are being watched whereas they might give socially desirable answers in a questionnaire.

A sensible proposal is made showing understanding of validity – testing what you mean to test (moral behaviour). This is elaborated successfully for the second and third mark.

(d) Sabrina calculated the correlation coefficient using Spearman's test and got a value of –.583. Using the appropriate critical values table, explain whether she can accept her directional hypothesis or not. (2)

Full-mark answer *The critical value for nine participants (5% level of significance and a one-tailed test) is 0.600.*

The observed (calculated) value of rho (.583, ignoring the sign) is less than the critical value (0.600). Therefore, Sabrina must accept the null hypothesis and conclude that there is not a significant negative correlation between the number of countries visited and morality scores based on moral dilemmas (maximum score of 40, where a high score equals greater morality) (p > 0.05).

The correct decision has been made based on a comparison of the observed and critical values, both of which are quoted. A full explanation for why 0.600 was chosen has been given. The final sentence states the conclusion.

(e) Explain one weakness of the use of quantitative data in Sabrina's study. (2)

Full-mark answer *A weakness is that the data for morality may not represent a person's actual feelings because there are only four possible answers for each moral dilemma. This means that participants may be forced to choose an answer which does not really match what they would do in that situation meaning their answer is not valid.*

The weakness has been given in a two-step process – first the issue is stated and second it is explained. Each sentence is clearly related to the extract.

Examiner comments

Section B may also include 'unseen' studies as is the case with question 3 on our Paper 3 – a synopsis of an unknown study, followed by two or more SAQs which add up to 8 marks. The first SAQ is usually methods/statistics-oriented while the second usually involves commenting on the usefulness of a named psychological theory to explain the unseen study's findings.

Section B finishes with a 16-mark essay (see facing page) requiring you to evaluate two classic studies in terms of an issue/debate.

3. 'Footie fathers'

A small study conducted in New Mexico USA, examined variations in hormone levels in eighteen fathers (mean age 47), before and after watching their children play in a number of football matches at a local tournament.

Testosterone levels were measured using saliva swabs. The fathers also completed questionnaires about their perception of the various games, e.g. the fairness of the referee, whether the team played to their full potential and how much their own child contributed to the end result. Post-match testosterone levels increased by 81%.

It was also noted that fathers who perceived unfairness tended to have higher post-match testosterone levels, and increases in testosterone post-match were greater for fathers watching their sons compared with fathers watching their daughters.

Also fathers who perceived that sport was less important to their children experienced greater testosterone levels post-match than those fathers who perceived sport to be more important to their children.

(Source: Adapted from Alvarado *et al.* 2018)

(a) Explain **one** weakness of the 'footie fathers' study. (2)

In this answer, the first sentence identifies a problem in the study, i.e. lack of control.

The second sentence presents a well-developed relevant example (implications of crowd size) and notes the impact of this, i.e. reduced validity.

Full-mark answer

One weakness of this study is that hormone levels may be affected by a variety of factors which could not have been controlled in this naturalistic study. For example, crowd size was not controlled and this lack of control would reduce the validity of the findings because hormone levels may only fluctuate in this manner under certain circumstances.

(b) Explain how useful evolutionary theory can be in accounting for the findings of the 'footie fathers' study. (6)

The focus of this question is the application (AO2) of an area of your knowledge, in this case evolutionary theory. So the first step is to think about relevant content that could be used to explain the extract, e.g. natural selection, sexual selection.

Next you need to think about what the question actually says: 'Explain how useful…'. So you need to explain the study's findings in terms of evolutionary theory and then also consider strengths and weaknesses (AO3) of your explanations, i.e. the usefulness of the theory.

This answer is split into two paragraphs, each starting with relevant knowledge of evolutionary theory which is explicitly linked to the study's findings (AO2). The final sentence of each paragraph gives a justification/ judgement relating to the ideas presented in the first section (AO3). These sentences cover supporting evidence (e.g. Dabbs and Hargrove) and methodological criticism (limitations of correlational studies).

Full-mark answer

From an evolutionary perspective, parents who were prepared to fight to protect their young would have been more likely to be represented in future generations. This explains the fathers' increased testosterone in response to what they perceived as unfair refereeing as a threat to their child. This is supported by Dabbs and Hargrove who found that testosterone levels in saliva were associated with aggressive dominance. This suggests that evolutionary processes might be a useful approach to understanding the fathers' response to the referee.

Evolutionary psychologists suggest aggression is more common in males than females as males needed to fight off rivals to be successful reproductively. This offers an explanation for why the boys may have fouled more than the girls. Although chimpanzee studies support the idea that the boys might have played rougher than the girls, studies such as these are correlational. This means cause and effect cannot be established, reducing the usefulness of evolutionary explanations for the fathers' behaviour.

> **Mark scheme**
>
> **AO2** Up to 3 marks for application of the theory to the findings of the study.
>
> **AO3** Up to 3 marks for judgement/justification of the theory to the findings of the study.

4. Evaluate the classic studies by Sherif *et al.* (1954/61) and Watson and Rayner (1920) with reference to the use of psychological knowledge in society. (16)

Full-mark answer

Sherif et al. *ran a camp at Robbers Cave State Park with 22 middle-class boys, splitting them into two teams, the Rattlers and Eagles. Competition was created by manipulating aspects of camp life and seeing how this affected interactions both within and between the two groups. Sherif* et al. *created hostility between the groups through a competition with knives and medals as prizes. This created prejudice towards the outgroup and increased ingroup solidarity. He restored harmony by creating situations with superordinate goals where all the boys had to work to fix a broken water supply and get a truck out of the mud.*

A strength of this study is it can be applied to the reduction of prejudice. For example, Aronson and Bridgeman's (1979) jigsaw classroom tackled racial prejudice in American schools using cooperative group learning tasks. Students reported increased liking and empathy for each other and black students improved in academic performance. This shows that Sherif et al.'s *study has helped students to reach their potential, regardless of ethnicity.*

One weakness of using cooperation to reduce prejudice is both Sherif's and Aronson's studies were conducted in America, which is high on individualism and low on power distance index. Differing strategies may be required in collectivist societies or cultures stratified by social status or rank.

This is supported by Orpen (1971) who examined prejudices held by white South African 16-year-olds, who experienced cultural pressure to accept prejudice towards black people. This highlights the importance of tackling cultural norms in wider society.

Watson and Rayner aimed to classically condition nine-month-old Little Albert to fear a white rat. Initially he was unafraid of various stimuli, including a white rat, cotton wool and wooden blocks but had an unconditioned fear of loud noise (steel bar hit with a hammer). When Albert was 11 months, learning trials started, showing Albert a rat and then making the loud noise. Albert returned to the lab several times for further pairings and his reactions were tested. Albert developed a conditioned fear response, crying and crawling away on seeing the rat. His fear generalised to some of the other furry stimuli but to a lesser extent.

One strength of this study is that it led to behavioural treatments, e.g. systematic desensitisation (SD), based on classical conditioning. Gilroy et al. (2003) treated arachnophobia using SD and clients were still much improved 33 months later. This shows that knowledge gained from Watson and Rayner's study could help people with phobias.

This said, Gilroy et al. only looked at arachnophobia (a fear of one specific thing). Multiple phobias or those linked to trauma/abuse may be much harder to treat. In Little Albert's case, his artificially created fear appeared to diminish rapidly on its own, yet in real life, 'unlearning' may be much more complex.

A further problem is that behavioural treatment does not target thought patterns, which would not have been an issue with Little Albert, who was just a baby. However, it may be an issue with older clients whose irrational thoughts could be discussed. This is especially true for social phobias where a cognitive therapy may be more successful. This suggests that the classical conditioning approach derived from Watson and Rayner's study may be over-simplistic. Nevertheless, the study has been hugely influential and inspired a range of therapies, from simple exposure therapy to the use of virtual reality.

In conclusion, both studies have made useful contributions to society, but may offer an over-simplistic view of human behaviour, for example prejudice interventions may be superficial and therefore not long-lasting and, in the case of SD, the underlying cognitive issues may be ignored. This challenges the usefulness of these studies.

610 words

Examiner comments

This section of the exam is about the classic studies so you will need your Year 1 book/ class notes. But don't forget, this review of studies essay can also refer to Rosenhan's classic study from clinical psychology.

These 16-mark essays need to be about 600–700 words in length with an AO1:AO3 ratio of roughly 1:2, i.e. roughly 100 words of description and 200 words of evaluation for each study, where the AO3 is specific to the named issue/debate.

Here, both studies are summarised in about 100 words. This is a great skill to practise for all classic studies.

Each description is followed by a strength relating to one specific application of the study to society. These strengths follow the PET structure – point, relevant evidence (e.g. Gilroy) before linking back to the classic study. (Why not colour in the three parts for P-E-T?)

Well-developed competing arguments are presented, including appropriate terminology and further accurate AO1 knowledge.

The strengths are balanced with well-supported weaknesses.

The essay closes by identifying a problem which is shared by each application, a thoughtful way of drawing the two studies together.

Mark scheme for 16-mark *evaluate* questions

See mark scheme on page 12 for 8-mark *evaluate* questions. For 16-mark essays the marks at each level are altered, for example Level 1 is 1–4 marks instead of 1–2 marks and Level 4 is 13–16 marks instead of 7–8 marks.

In addition there is a greater requirement for AO3 as 16 marks = 6 AO1 and 10 AO3.

LRQs - example questions and answers

Paper 3
Section C
Issues and debates essay

5. Luna has played the flute for many years but experiences severe 'performance anxiety'. This is a type of phobia where a person experiences an extreme fear of performing in front of others.

Evaluate the extent to which Luna could be helped to overcome her performance anxiety using concepts, theories and/or research from biological psychology and learning theories. [12]

Examiner comments

Section C will comprise one 12-mark essay, which is likely to include a context and require one or more topics to be used to explain the context. Section C also includes a 20-mark essay (see facing page).

You need to be flexible in questions such as this one about Luna, where you will be faced with behaviours which are not part of your specification. You are expected to put together arguments based on the material that you have learned, using those theories/studies in new and creative ways.

This answer uses the 'sandwich' approach, alternating paragraphs of AO1 and AO3, with AO2 embedded throughout.

AO1 paragraphs link relevant knowledge to Luna (AO2). The section on creating a fear hierarchy for Luna is a good example of applied knowledge.

AO3 paragraphs combine supporting evidence (e.g. Maletzky et al.) with counterarguments and sustained links to Luna's situation (AO2), e.g. the evaluation of SD with links to trauma.

This answer specifically addresses the extent to which Luna's anxiety could be overcome. Engaging fully with what you have been asked is a critical skill so take your time to thoughtfully pick the question apart before putting pen to paper!

Full-mark answer

Biological psychologists might think Luna is genetically predisposed to high stress levels, e.g. a gene mutation may have caused an abnormality in the way that her brain produces those neurotransmitters linked to anxiety, such as GABA or serotonin.

This is supported by Egan et al. (2001) who found that inheriting two copies of the Val allele (a specific form of the COMT gene, which regulates dopamine) made people 50% more likely to develop schizophrenia. Luna's anxiety may also be caused by genes involved in regulating stress, arguably making her anxiety hard to overcome. This said, the diathesis stress model suggests that although genetic factors increase vulnerability, other biological or environmental triggers are also necessary. Therefore, Luna's anxiety may subside if the triggers can be identified and removed.

A biological psychologist might also suggest that medication could be used to overcome Luna's anxiety. As she perceives the audience as a stressor, her hypothalamus signals her adrenal glands to produce adrenaline, making her heart race. Blocking the effects of increased hormone levels could therefore be helpful.

This is supported by Maletzky et al. (2006) who lowered testosterone levels using Depo-Provera. This drug successfully reduced sexual aggression in offenders suggesting that drugs to block adrenaline could help reduce Luna's anxiety. However, medication can have unpleasant side effects and she may prefer cognitive therapy to help her to see the audience as less of a threat.

Learning theorists believe that learned behaviours can be unlearned, providing hope for Luna. She could undergo systematic desensitisation (SD) involving the creation of a fear hierarchy, starting with the least scary thing, e.g. playing at home to her mum. She would gradually move up to the scariest thing, e.g. playing a complex piece in front of experienced musicians.

SD is well supported by research, for example, Capafóns et al. (1998) significantly reduced fear of flying in 90% of their sample using SD, suggesting this could work for Luna. However, not everyone benefits from SD. If Luna's anxiety stems from some form of trauma, a therapy that focuses on changing beliefs might work better for her.

Another learning theory therapy is flooding where there is no anxiety hierarchy. Luna would be plunged into the highest level of her anxiety whilst practising relaxation until her anxiety subsides. The problem is that, when playing the flute, it would be difficult to simultaneously focus on relaxing as one might with, for example, a spider phobia.

In conclusion, Luna should be hopeful that she can overcome her anxiety about performing. Drug therapy offers a temporary solution but therapies based on learning theories are more long-lasting and less invasive, however it will require more effort and can take time.

445 words

The grid summarises the levels-based mark scheme used for such questions.

We only have room to show the criteria for level 4.

Mark scheme for 12-mark *evaluate* questions with a scenario

AO1 (4 marks)   AO2 (4 marks)   AO3 (4 marks)   Candidates must demonstrate an equal emphasis between knowledge and understanding vs application vs evaluation/conclusion in their answer.

Level	Mark	Description (AO1) Knowledge and understanding	Line(s) of argument based on relevant evidence from the context (AO2)	Ability to integrate and synthesise relevant knowledge (AO2)	Chains of reasoning (AO3)	Competing arguments (AO3)	Conclusion (AO3)
4	10–12	Accurate and thorough.	Argument sustained.	Demonstrates.	Well-developed and logical throughout.	Demonstrates an awareness of competing arguments.	Balanced conclusion.

6. Assess the issue of socially sensitive research in psychology. (20)

Full-mark answer

Sieber and Stanley define socially sensitive research as studies that have potential consequences or implications for the participants or social group that they represent. This essay will look at two such areas of research: the authoritarian personality from social psychology and research by Adrian Raine, from biological psychology.

In the 1950s, Allport developed the idea of the authoritarian personality, pointing out that such people tend to think in rigid 'black and white' ways and require 'cognitive closure'. They have an inflexible thinking style and a preference for clear answers as opposed to being willing to debate with others. Altemeyer further developed this idea and he renamed it right wing authoritarianism (RWA). He suggested RWA was more common in people who were closed to new experiences and overly conscientious, as well as those who perceived the world to be dangerous and threatening. RWA can make people suspicious and behave in a hostile manner towards anyone who defies the norm or seems different. This has been linked to things such as nationalism, ethnocentrism and also prejudice towards a range of minority groups in society including women and those who identify as LGBT.

This research is socially sensitive as it is arguably offensive and divisive. Altemeyer's research could offend people with right wing attitudes due to the link to prejudice, which is generally seen as undesirable. Also, the link with cognitive closure might be used to support the view that right wingers are less capable of critical thinking. This is important because psychological research should not be used to denigrate people who hold certain views, particularly as 'scientific' research is often seen as adding credence to a particular viewpoint.

This said, research in this area should not be prevented because anything which helps us to understand the origins of prejudice could be important in reducing it and protecting people from minority groups. For example, if RWA results from seeing the world as a dangerous place, strategies to challenge this view could be implemented such as promoting a global sense of self in schools and encouraging connections between people from different walks of life.

It should be remembered however, that lack of balance continues to be a problem for research in this area. Democrats outnumber Republicans 12:1 in US psychology departments (Duarte et al.). This is socially sensitive because a lack of political diversity means certain types of research may be favoured over others, leading to a one-sided evidence base that exaggerates some issues and minimises others.

A second area of socially sensitive research is that of Adrian Raine, who studied the biological basis of criminality. His classic study (Raine et al. 1997) was of murderers who pleaded not guilty by reason of insanity (NGRI). He compared glucose metabolism in various brain regions for 41 murderers in comparison with a matched control group. Participants had to identify targets on a screen by pressing a button, following an injection of a radioactive tracer. Ten images (slices) were then taken at 10 mm intervals through their brains. The scans showed differing glucose metabolism in various cortical and subcortical regions compared with non-murderers and several brain regions were identified that had not previously been linked to violence, e.g. occipital lobe, right amygdala, right medial temporal lobe and right thalamus. The overarching implication of this work is that some murderers may be unable to control their behaviour due to biologically-based brain abnormalities.

This research is socially sensitive as it could be used to support changes in public policy, which may not always have the individual or society's best interests at heart. For example, Raine et al.'s research raises questions – if crimes are due to pre-existing brain abnormalities (nature not nurture), then the criminal is not responsible for their behaviour and rehabilitation may not be possible. This is important as rehabilitation is expensive and therefore evidence to support the view that it may be ineffective could affect government spending.

Answer continues on next page.

Examiner comments

The final question on Paper 3 tests your understanding of issues and debates topics and your ability to apply this understanding to all you have learned.

However, this doesn't mean slinging in examples willy-nilly! If you try to stuff everything in you will fail to demonstrate the depth of your understanding.

The brief introduction in this answer shows a clear understanding of socially sensitive research (SSR). This is AO1 material, as are paragraphs 2 and 6. These two main AO1 paragraphs focus on theory/research which can be discussed in terms of SSR.

In paragraph 6 the study by Raine et al. is summarised including all the important details (aim, procedure, findings and importantly the implications), demonstrating how a study can be condensed to just 150 words – a skill that needs to be practised so that important detail is not sacrificed.

Each AO1 block is about 150 words followed by three shorter AO3 paragraphs (about 75 words each). This ensures the required 2:3 split between AO1 and AO3 (8 marks AO1 and 12 marks AO3). It helps to develop a rule like this to ensure you get the balance between assessment objectives right.

You also need to ensure balanced AO3 – arguments both for and against. This is achieved by first presenting an argument against the research in terms of its social sensitivity and then arguing in favour of the research continuing. The third AO3 paragraph adds a further competing argument ensuring that the AO3 has both breadth and depth.

Examiner comments (continued)

To gain high marks, it's important to show that you genuinely grasp the significance of what you are saying. A good example in this essay is the discussion of lack of political diversity in US psychology departments which may lead to a lack of scientific evidence for certain views not because they are wrong but because research does not exist in this area.

The essay finishes with a conclusion. In longer essays, this can be an important differentiator between levels 4 and 5. The conclusion to this essay shows a sensitive awareness of the implications of SSR, with reference to some of the research reviewed.

Full-mark answer (continued)

However, one should take care with socially sensitive research if there are issues of validity. Raine et al. argue that there were some important uncontrolled variables in this study which could reduce internal validity. For example, 23 of the murderers had a history of head injury. This is important as it suggests that differences between the brains of murderers and non-murderers may be due to something else. Raine et al. draw attention to the importance of understanding what can and cannot be logically deduced from the findings.

One further issue with Raine et al.'s research in terms of social sensitivity is the possibility of predicting future criminality on the basis of brain scanning. Although this could be an important step in protecting people from potential violent offenders, it removes free will, which opens society up to human rights abuses. Brain scans may indicate potential for future criminality, however, knowledge of the findings of such scans could lead to self-fulfilling prophecy.

In conclusion it is apparent that topics such as prejudice and dealing with criminals produce socially sensitive findings. Once the findings are in the public domain, politically-motivated reporting can lead the research to be used to legitimise certain views, such as locking criminals up for life. However, psychologists should not solve this problem by avoiding such research but must ensure that the research they produce is valid and they should monitor the way it is interpreted and used.

888 words

Mark scheme for 20-mark *assess* questions
See page 15.

"IT'S NOT ABOUT BEING THE BEST IT'S ABOUT BEING BETTER THAN YOU WERE YESTERDAY"

How to impress in a 20-mark answer – five top tips

1. Choose your AO1 content wisely.
   Do not try to impress the examiner with everything you know. Focus on a few areas of knowledge and provide succinct detail.

2. AO3 must be logical.
   Give yourself time to develop all points fully using PET chains of reasoning. Less is more.

3. Balance.
   The whole response (not just the conclusion) needs to be balanced, meaning an equal proportion of arguments for and against. A short 'tick list' before you start is all you need to help you keep on track.

4. Avoid being generic.
   When writing each paragraph make sure you have addressed the key elements of the question set.

5. Leave yourself time to write a 'cracking conclusion'.
   You should consider both sides of the argument and demonstrate your understanding of issues that make it difficult to come down firmly on either side.

Ethics in human research (BPS code)

Respect Respect for others can be shown in many ways.	Privacy – confidentiality of data safeguards identity and so protects privacy (e.g. the study of HM). Informed consent – respect the right to choose to take part. • HM could not fully understand he was a participant. • Children may have a limited understanding. • Not possible in covert observations nor with deception. Deception – avoid if possible or seek approval from an ethical committee or by consulting with colleagues (e.g. Milgram).
Competence	Researchers must be skilled and up-to-date in research area. e.g. mental health therapies as part of research are conducted only by qualified researchers.
Responsibility	Researchers must consider participants and psychology in general (people could lose faith in psychology). e.g. in Hofling et al. (1966) the nurses were distressed about their errors, people could be less willing to trust health services.
Integrity	Researchers should be honest and fair. e.g. avoid deception, give experimental and control groups in therapy studies equal access to most effective therapy.

Ethics in animal research

Animals (Scientific Procedures) Act 1986	Consider causes of psychological distress and physical pain in animals (e.g. housing, feeding, social companions). Social isolation and food deprivation (e.g. Skinner box) cause animals distress.
Home Office regulations	Compliance with the Act is monitored (Home Office inspectors). e.g. researchers must show animals were killed humanely.
The three Rs	Replacement with non-animal alternatives. Reduction of the number used to the minimum needed. Refinement of procedures to minimise suffering.
Justifying animal research	For • More procedures and controls can be used with animals. • There are parallels (e.g. in brain structure and function). Against • We are so different from animals (e.g. language). • We don't have the right to harm other species.

An *ethical issue* is a dilemma about right and wrong. The dilemma arises because researchers wish to investigate behaviour to benefit our understanding of people and improve our world, but there are costs to participants.

✓ Check it

In this chapter all of the Check it questions are I&D essays and some are also synoptic (i.e. include more than one topic). See pages 9 and 20–22 for more on such essays.

1. Assess whether research in biological psychology is ethical. [8]

2. Many contemporary psychologists believe that psychological research has become more ethical.

   Evaluate whether your chosen contemporary studies from social psychology and learning theories can be considered to be ethical. [12]

3. Assess the extent to which psychological research could be considered to be ethical. [20]

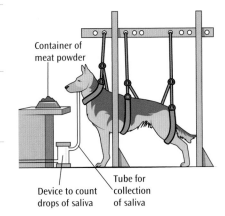

Container of meat powder

Tube for collection of saliva

Device to count drops of saliva

Pavlov's studies on dogs may have caused physical pain in the procedure to insert the salivary drain tube.

Does it do what it says on the tin? If the answer's yes, then it's got validity.

Validity refers to trueness or legitimacy.

Reliability is consistency.

 Check it

1. Discuss the practical issues faced by psychologists when designing and implementing research in social and biological psychology. [8]

2. Evaluate the practical issues in the design and implementation of Watson and Rayner's (1920) study. [12]

3. Applications in psychology include clinical psychology, criminological psychology, child psychology and health psychology.

   Assess the practical issues faced by psychologists when designing and implementing research, with reference to any **two** of these applications. [20]

Validity

Validity versus ethics	High validity – deception reduces demand characteristics.
	But ethical issues arise if concealing aims.
Social desirability	Questionnaires/interviews – design so that participants' wish to 'look good' is limited, e.g. don't make people with mental health issues feel bad about revealing their symptoms.
Measurement Measuring variables in valid ways.	Psychodynamic approach – measures of the unconscious have poor credibility ('id' cannot be observed).
	Brain functions/clinical psychology – measures themselves are valid but it is hard to interpret what brain activity means.
Controls Confounding variables.	Controlling confounding variables enhances validity.
	e.g. Skinner box controls what a rat sees, hears and feels. Also the rats' weight is controlled so they are hungry and will press a bar for food.
Ecological validity	Setting/task may mean findings can't apply to other situations.
	e.g. memory studies use nonsense syllables (control), but real-world memory rarely involves such material.
	Applies to both lab and field experiments.

Reliability

Standardisation	Increases reliability – procedures identical for participants.
	Easy in lab studies but harder to achieve in field experiments.
Reliability over time Test-retest reliability.	Detects whether measurement in studies is consistent from one time to the next.
	Only reliable measures can ensure that observed changes in the dependent variable are due to the independent variable.
Reliability between researchers	Interviewers compare data from same person (inter-interviewer).
	Observers compare observations of same behaviour (inter-observer).
	Qualitative data is interpreted, and therefore there are differences between researchers (quantitative is more objective, so more reliable).

Generalisability

The sample	Wider samples are more generalisable but sometimes narrow samples needed (e.g. to focus on special groups).
Generalising from animals	Complexity of human brains, cognition, etc. may mean animal research lacks relevance to people.

The debate: reductionism versus holism

Examples of reductionism	Biological psychology explains emotion/behaviour in terms of: • Brain regions (e.g. *limbic system* for aggression). • Cells (neurons) or chemicals (neurotransmitters). • Genes controlling production and/or function of cells or chemicals (genetic reductionism). Cognitive psychology explains emotion/behaviour in terms of: • Information processors (e.g. multi-store model), machine reductionism.
Examples of holism	Social learning theory considers the influence of models in the environment and the cognitive features of the individual. Multi-store model (three 'levels' of memory) is more holistic than the working memory model (just short-term memory).
Arguments for reductionism	Simplicity • Individual units are simpler so more readily understood and explained than the 'whole'. • By studying each 'unit' (e.g. memory store), psychologists isolate functions that work independently (e.g. STM and LTM) and the biological structures involved (e.g. *hippocampus*). Easy to study • When units are isolated (e.g. in lab studies) the whole can be better understood (many factors do not act at once). e.g. to explain working memory, control visuo-spatial information to identify influential factors.

Arguments against reductionism	Ignores interactions
	• A 'whole' explained in terms of its units will be perceived as a simple arrangement of those components, ignoring interactions between components.
	  e.g. biological explanation of aggression ignores interactions with social factors which moderate responses.
	  e.g. the visuo-spatial sketchpad and phonological loop are independent, but less is known about how they interact.
	
	Overlooks complexities
	• Isolating variables (as in controlled lab experiments) is hard because human systems are complex.
	• Controlled research produces theories that cannot explain complex interactions.
	  e.g. simpler behavioural systems in animals than humans, but simplicity means not representative of humans (no interaction between cognitive and social factors).

'The whole is greater than the sum of its parts'. Where cake is concerned, she's inclined to agree.

Reductionism is the view that human behaviour is best explained by breaking it down into smaller constituent parts. The 'whole' is explained in terms of the separate units.

Holism is the view that it only makes sense to study an indivisible system rather than its constituent parts.

On each spread in the other chapters in this book there are more 'Check it' questions where we have included further practice questions on issues and debates.

✓ Check it

1. Assess whether social psychology is reductionist. (8)

2. Evaluate how reductionism has benefited our understanding of either memory or prejudice. (12)

3. Some people say biological and cognitive explanations for human behaviour are reductionist.
   To what extent would you consider this statement to be true? (20)

Comparison between ways of explaining behaviour using different themes

As the only Accrington Stanley supporter, Brian (fifth row, third from the left) felt very much in the minority. Maybe it wasn't about football.

Revision booster

It helps to draw a table listing all four themes across the top and down the side. In each box consider similarities and differences. Try to vary your examples, e.g. don't always mention Milgram or Pavlov – dig deep for your examples.

Exam questions may not ask you to make comparisons between themes but it is one way to structure your answers.

The term 'themes' is used to refer to the topics you studied in Year 1, i.e. social, cognitive, learning and biological.

✓ Check it

1. Discuss ways of explaining behaviour using biological and learning themes. [8]

2. Assess the explanation of behaviour using social and cognitive themes. [16]

3. People are all very different from each other, some are shy, others are overfriendly, some are aggressive whereas others are peace-loving.

   To what extent can biological and learning themes explain these individual differences in behaviour? [20]

Making comparisons between Year 1 topics

Social psychology

Social – aims to understand people in social context.

Similar to learning theories, e.g. role models in social learning.

Social – explains aggression.

Similar to biological psychology, using evolution, hormones, brain structures.

Social – focuses on roles other people play in behaviour (e.g. authority figures).

Differs from cognitive psychology which does not use other people as part of the explanation, e.g. others contribute to *schemas* but do not explain them.

Cognitive psychology

Cognitive – aims to find out how mental processes affect behaviour (e.g. process of rehearsal in multi-store model).

Similar to the idea of repetition in learning theories and build-up of associations/synapses in biological psychology.

Cognitive – studies unseen behaviours (thoughts) and needs different research methods (e.g. tests of recognition or recall).

Differs from social and learning theories (observable behaviour studied).

Biological psychology

Biological – underpins all explanations, e.g. evolution, genes, brain structure, neurotransmitters, etc.

Similar to learning theories which explain response to rewards (reinforcement), e.g. through *dopamine* reward system.

Biological – a reductionist approach, e.g. explanations for gender differences.

Differs from social which is more holistic, looks at influences of people/culture.

Biological approach focuses on physical therapies (drugs).

Differs from cognitive (cognitive-behavioural treatment) and learning (behaviourist approach in aversion therapy).

Learning theories

Learning theory – classical and operant conditioning.

Similar to biological, e.g. reinforcement and the dopamine reward system.

Learning theory – behaviour acquired through social learning.

Similar to cognitive and social approaches.

Learning theory – studies observable behaviour, which affects methods used, e.g. observation.

Differs from cognitive focus on thoughts and biological investigation of hidden biological factors.

Science is a means of acquiring knowledge through systematic and objective investigation. The aim is to discover general laws.

Psychology *is* a science

The scientific method	Psychology uses the scientific method and controlled experiments, e.g. controls confounding variables.
	Standardised procedures allow replication to check validity.
	Human behaviour can be objectively measured, tested and ideas falsified.
Some psychology is 'hard' science	Biological, genetic and behavioural psychology (learning theories) are based on subject matter derived from 'hard' sciences (clearly scientific).
'Hard' science is imperfect too	Problems exist in hard sciences, e.g. demand characteristics.
	Heisenberg (1927) argued we cannot even measure a subatomic particle without altering its 'behaviour' (uncertainty principle is an experimenter effect).
'Soft' science can be scientific	Data from interviews, observations etc. can be triangulated.
	Objectivity and validity of qualitative data can be established.

Psychology *is not* a science

Falsifiability	Some ideas in psychology are not falsifiable, e.g. Freudian theories of the unconscious cannot be shown to be untrue.
Objectivity	Studies looking at feelings and conscious experience use subjective measurements – not objective scientific evidence.
Pseudoscience	Using the scientific method doesn't make psychology a science.
	Miller (1983) argues psychologists use scientific tools (e.g. statistics, experiments) but they are just 'dressing up'.
Describing not explaining	Koch (1992) reviewed psychological studies and concluded that the research produced verifiable *descriptions* of behaviour, but the explanations were opinion not fact.
Lack of a single paradigm	Kuhn (1962) claims psychology is not a science as it has no single paradigm (shared set of assumptions and methods).
	Psychology has seen paradigm shifts (e.g. from behaviourism to cognitive psychology), has yet to find its scientific basis.
	'Mini' paradigms co-exist (evolutionary, behaviourist, cognitive), each with its own explanations and methods (psychology is a 'pre-science').
Low validity	Experiments may lack internal validity due to demand characteristics.
	May lack external validity if procedures unlike everyday life.
	e.g. Baddeley (1966) tested memory with word lists.

Falsification is about never having to say you're right.

Check it

1. Assess Milgram's study as an example of psychology as a science. [8]

2. To what extent were the procedures of your practical investigations for social psychology and learning theories scientific? [12]

3. Evaluate whether the classic studies by Bandura *et al.* (1961) and Rosenhan (1973) demonstrate the 'scientific status of psychology'. [16]

Culture and gender

Culture refers to the ideas, customs and social behaviour of a particular group of people or society.

Picture below shows an alpha male, alpha = exaggerates importance. Same for alpha bias.

Gender refers to the psychological and cultural differences between males and females including attitudes, behaviour and social role.

✓ Check it

1. Evaluate culture and gender issues that arise in research within cognitive and biological psychology. [8]

2. Different areas of psychology present different problems for research, such as taking gender and culture into account.

   Evaluate the extent to which research from social and cognitive psychology takes culture and gender into account. [12]

3. Many studies in psychology have only used American males as participants.

   Assess culture and gender issues in psychological research. [20]

Culture

Cultural differences	Plan research to avoid bias. e.g. diagnostic errors because people from different cultures describe symptoms differently.
The assumption of universality	Findings generalised to all people because it is assumed all people are the same. Research often uses WEIRD samples (Western, Educated, Industrialised, Rich, Democratic).
Cultural biases Etics and emics.	Etic approach – an 'outsider' studies people from a culture other than their own to find cultural universals. e.g. memory study (Steyvers and Hemmer 2012) used 'natural scenes' but only 'natural' for some cultures. Emic approach – studies cultural uniqueness, ideally from an internal view (e.g. indigenous researcher). e.g. Sebastián and Hernández-Gil (2012) explored the digit spans of Spanish children.

Gender

Assumptions about gender differences	Differences may be due to biology or learning. Implications: • People expect men to be 'naturally' aggressive which suggests they are less able to control their aggression. • Women may be guided away from certain careers.
The assumption of universality	If gender differences exist then samples of just one gender should not lead to conclusions about 'people in general'.
Findings about gender differences	Some gender differences have been explored and explained: • Bandura *et al.* (1961) showed that male models were more powerful for both genders in modelling physical aggression. • Clinical psychology has found many gender differences in rates and onset of schizophrenia (e.g. more common and earlier onset in men than women).
Gender biases Alpha and beta.	Alpha bias – arises when research emphasises gender differences. e.g. males are more aggressive because of testosterone – but this difference is exaggerated as females do also produce testosterone and higher levels increase their aggression. Beta bias – ignores or underestimates gender differences. e.g. research based on male samples sets standards and then females appear deficient or abnormal.

Nature

Inherited predispositions	Present at birth or develop as we mature, both genetic. e.g. cognitive problems linked with dyslexia (and Alzheimer's disease) are partly governed by nature.
Genes and evolution	Behaviours that evolved via natural selection are genetic. e.g. ancestral males who aggressively guarded partners were reproductively more successful (so this characteristic was selected).
Innate behaviours	Naturally selected behaviours are the same in all people. e.g. babies born with innate ability to suck when roof of their mouth is touched (so feed without learning). Innate reflexes are simple reactions. e.g. salivating is an unconditioned response to the smell of food.

Nurture

Many ways to learn Environment influences behaviour.	Classical conditioning – neutral stimulus associated with unconditioned stimulus, becomes conditioned stimulus. Operant conditioning – consequences are from environment (reinforcement and punishment). Social learning – models are sources of vicarious reinforcement.
Experience Environment provides more than just opportunities to learn.	Chemical environment affects foetus pre-birth. e.g. hormones affect brain development. Cultural and family environments are part of 'experience'.

Testing the nature–nurture debate

Evidence for nature Twin studies.	If MZ twin has schizophrenia, co-twin is 42 times more likely to have it than someone in the general population (risk in DZ twins only 9 times, Gottesman and Shields 1966).
Evidence for nurture Cultural differences.	The !Kung San of Southern Africa discourage aggression, Yanomami of Brazil accept aggression to gain social status (Wolfgang and Ferracuti 1967). If aggression was genetic (i.e. nature), cultural differences would be far smaller.
Evidence for interactionist approach	Most behaviours affected by genes and environments. e.g. Brendgen et al. (2005) showed physical aggression mostly due to nature, but social aggression largely due to nurture.

'It says in here that genetic similarity may cause people to behave, think and dress in the same way,' said Len. 'Sounds like baloney to me,' replied Ken.

The question of whether behaviour is determined more by 'nature' (inherited and genetic factors) or 'nurture' (all influences after conception, e.g. experience) is not a debate about one or the other but about the contributions of each, as well as their interaction with each other.

Revision booster

Questions on Paper 3 may begin with a scenario. We have tended not to include examples of such scenario questions in this chapter because of space (you can see an example on page 20). The example in question 3 below is a prompt and not a scenario – you are therefore not required to address it in your answer but it may provide a useful stimulus.

Check it

1. To what extent do theories from social psychology and learning theories favour nurture more than nature? (12)

2. Evaluate the classic studies by Watson and Rayner (1920) and Raine et al. (1997) in terms of how nurture influences our behaviour. (16)

3. Some psychologists believe that a disorder such as schizophrenia can mainly be explained in terms of biology.

   Assess the role of nature and nurture in the development of schizophrenia. (20)

An understanding of how psychological understanding has developed over time

This is Norm. People don't mess with Norm. Over the years, the norms of psychology may have created cultural bias.

✓ Check it

1. Assess whether psychological understanding in social psychology and learning theories has developed over time. [8]

2. To what extent have cognitive and biological psychology developed over time? [12]

3. Applications in psychology include clinical psychology, criminological psychology, child psychology and health psychology.

   Assess how psychological understanding has developed over time, with reference to any **two** of these applications. [20]

Using the past to inform the present

Past theories are a platform from which we develop new theories.

Scientific process begins with observations of the world or research evidence – leads to a theory which is tested by research studies.

If the hypothesis is not supported the theory is modified, e.g.

- Studies in the 1950s/60s led to a view of memory as a set of stores and processes – the multi-store model.
- Further research (e.g. KF case study) challenged the model (STM is more than one store).
- New model developed – working memory (acoustic and visual short-term store).
- This model continues to be developed by research.

Change depends on 'how' as well as 'what'

Theoretical approaches change, but so do methods.

Research techniques develop, producing more detailed information.

- Early research used post-mortem studies of dead brain (e.g. Broca, speech production).
- In the 1960s CAT scans showed structural abnormalities in a live brain.
- Later PET scans showed the brain in action (e.g. Raine *et al.* 1997).

Change is both reductionist and holistic

Each step forward focuses on smaller (reductionist) elements – but individual parts may also be drawn together, so contribute to a bigger picture (holistic).

e.g. Carlsson *et al.*'s (2000) review relies on reductionist studies but holistic overview.

The influence of non-psychological factors

Historical events

- The Holocaust led social psychologists to study obedience – world events drew attention to behaviour.

Social needs

- Work on dementia is driven by a need to understand its causes and identify ways to slow cognitive decline.

Social norms, affected by academic views

- Darwin's theory of evolution led to explanations based on 'nature' (e.g. innate gender differences).
- Influence of behaviourists led to a focus on nurture and the environment for new ways to improve lives.

Technological change

- Rise of information processing led to use of computer concepts (multi-store model).
- Information technology paved the way for sophisticated theories and techniques (e.g. virtual reality).

Uses of social control

Obedience	An authority figure giving an order leads to behaviour change.
	Acceptable, even if order is unpleasant (e.g. cold cross-country run).
	Milgram felt that being able to enter the agentic state was essential for a stable society.
Prejudice	Reducing prejudice involves social control, imposing beliefs and behaviours of one group (non-prejudiced) on another.
	e.g. This is achieved using strategies such as arranging for ingroup and outgroup members to work cooperatively (Sherif *et al.* 1954/1961).
Improving mental health	In systematic desensitisation (SD) and flooding the therapist controls the behaviour (or thoughts) of the client.
	Mental health policies advocate using drugs to control symptoms of mental illnesses.
	e.g. Clinicians administer drugs, almost always with the client's consent but client may still feel their behaviour is controlled.

Misuses of social control

Obedience	An individual may distort society by creating situational factors. Social control is so powerful that even when the recipient of the order does not want to follow it they may still obey.
	e.g. Milgram showed that wearing a uniform (experimenter's coat) makes disobedience difficult.
	Psychologists in the military design strategies to maintain obedience so soldiers follow orders even when harm involved.
	e.g. using binding factors to reduce moral strain (reduce perceived suffering by using dehumanising language).
Treating mental illness	Behaviour modification in mental health or prison settings rewards desirable behaviour – but may be unethical.
	e.g. when the choice of 'desirable' lies with staff who just want cooperative behaviour for an easy life.
	Drugs can be misused.
	e.g. pseudopatients in Rosenhan's (1973) study given drugs to keep them quiet.
Operant conditioning	In his book *Walden Two*, Skinner (1948) described his ideal world where behaviour was controlled by reinforcement, but the social control imposed by such a system would infringe personal freedoms (unacceptable if you value liberty).
	This may be happening around us.
	e.g. store cards reinforce our 'shopping behaviour' with points so we return to the shop.

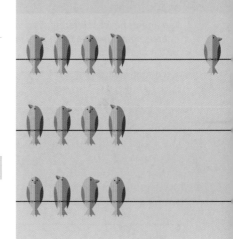

Not everyone succumbs to social pressure.

Check it

1. To what extent can social psychology and learning theories explain social control? [12]

2. Social control is often seen as a negative influence but in some situations it is beneficial to both individuals and society.

   Assess ways in which learning theories and biological psychology have been used for social control. [12]

3. Evaluate the classic studies by Sherif *et al.* (1954/1961) and Rosenhan (1973) in terms of how they could be used as a means of social control. [16]

The use of psychological knowledge in society

Teri knew she was different. Very few people would have paired a grey jacket with a blue scarf.

Revision booster

12-mark questions on issues and debates may appear on Paper 1 (Section E) and Paper 3 (Section C). On Paper 1 these are very straightforward but on Paper 3 they are likely to have a lengthy scenario which must be addressed in your answer. There are examples of both types of question below.

✓ Check it

1. Assess ways in which psychological knowledge about recreational drugs could be useful to society. [8]

2. Evaluate the usefulness to society of the psychological knowledge of social and cognitive psychology. [12]

3. Kirsty was an only child, raised by her father on a farm quite far from the nearest village. She was happy playing with all the animals and enjoyed walks in the fields. But she never really learned how to get on with other people and tended to be quite a loner at school. Her father also preferred not to seek the company of others despite having grown up in a large family.

    Evaluate the extent to which the biological approach can explain human behaviour such as preferring to be alone. You must make reference to the context in your answer. [12]

Cognitive psychology Memory.	Multi-store model shows that chunking material should help us hold more in STM.
	Research can help improve episodic/working memory in people with specific impairments (e.g. dementia).
	Children with dyslexia may have central executive problems – a systematic teaching programme can help them avoid distractions (detectable changes in brain activity, Shaywitz and Shaywitz 2004).
Biological psychology Recreational drugs.	Recreational drugs bring problems for society (e.g. health risks reducing quality of life, increased pressure on health services).
	Psychology helps these problems with strategies (e.g. *naloxone* for heroin addiction).
	This is based on understanding the mode of action of drugs – heroin is an agonist so euphoric effects can be prevented by an antagonist drug (i.e. naloxone blocks action of heroin).
Learning theories Systematic desensitisation.	People with severe phobias may not contribute to society (afraid to go outside to work and diminished quality of life).
	Systematic desensitisation (SD) is based on learning theory.
	Anxiety hierarchy is created and worked through during deep relaxation – cannot feel tense and relaxed at the same time (reciprocal inhibition) so new response (calmness) is associated with feared object or situation (classical conditioning).
	Gilroy *et al.* (2003) showed that SD improved the quality of life of people with spider phobia, even 33 months later.
Clinical psychology Therapies.	People with mental disorders can be helped using psychological techniques, improves well-being, reduces burden on society.
	Treatment helps them contribute more fully to society (e.g. to work, contribute to economy, provide for selves and family).
	CBT is not an 'off-the-peg' treatment (like drugs), but tailor-made for each individual.
	Therapist helps the client identify their irrational thoughts and work on how to recognise and cope with personal triggers.
	Using CBT to target delusions and hallucinations produced improvement in people with schizophrenia for whom drugs were ineffective (Kuipers *et al.* 1997).
Criminological, child and health psychology	Criminological psychology – identifying and rehabilitating criminals, improving eye-witness testimony.
	Child psychology – advice about effective childcare, better institutional care, looking after hospitalised children.
	Health psychology – aversion therapy for addictions, developing effective anti-drug campaigns.

Socially-sensitive psychological research

Implications of research	Research may present issues which offend or divide people. e.g. research supporting existing prejudices. Realistic conflict theory might 'justify' discrimination as a legitimate response.
Public policy and other uses	Impact of publishing findings should be considered, could the knowledge be dangerous in the wrong hands? e.g. Raine *et al.*'s (1997) findings might lead to the conclusion that murder is 'not the murderer's fault'. Then criminal courts could not punish such murderers because they are not responsible.
Validity	Psychologists should not avoid carrying out certain research, but should pay attention to biases and interpretations. e.g. in thematic analysis biases are more likely to affect validity, so extra steps ensure findings reflect reality.

No one could accuse Janet of being 'socially sensitive'.

Sieber and Stanley (1988) define socially-sensitive research as 'studies in which there are potential consequences or implications, either directly for the participants in the research or for the class of individuals represented by the research'.

The need for socially-sensitive research

Research on TV viewing	Bandura *et al.* (1961, 1963) showed that when children watch aggression it increases the risk of them displaying aggression. Socially-sensitive issue because parents may feel irresponsible for letting their children see aggressive behaviour on television or computer games. But such research is important because it identifies dangers and enables people to reduce children's exposure.
Researching Alzheimer's disease	Research identifies cognitive deficits linked to losses in brain areas (e.g. *hippocampus*) – explains why people with Alzheimer's first lose episodic memories (e.g. experiences) and later semantic memories (e.g. naming objects). Research is socially sensitive because it may create a negative image of people with Alzheimer's which threatens their dignity. But the research is valuable as it helps improve quality of life (e.g. targeting different kinds of help at different stages).
Investigating authoritarianism	Allport (1954) argued that people with right wing (authoritarian) views are less capable of critical thinking. Research is socially-sensitive because it has implications for how right wing opinions are regarded in society. But the research is valuable because, as authoritarian personalities also tend to be prejudiced, the findings could help to protect the rights of minority groups.

Revision booster

Socially-sensitive research is an issue that is hard to grasp. It isn't just about ethics, it is about the tension between doing important research but being aware of the impact of certain kinds of research on marginal groups. The answer is not to avoid such research. It must be done but special focus is required so it does not harm the groups of people concerned.

 Check it

1. Evaluate the issues related to conducting socially-sensitive research in cognitive and social psychology. [8]

2. To what extent is research in biological psychology and learning theories socially sensitive? [12]

3. Research in certain areas of psychology may have consequences for certain individuals or for groups of people in society.

   Assess psychological research in terms of social sensitivity. [20]

When Shelley asked for a blue rinse, she got more than she bargained for.

The 4Ds of diagnosis = deviance, dysfunction, distress, danger.

Apply it Concepts

Steve sometimes finds himself wandering at the side of the motorway and doesn't know why. He is frightened by feelings he says make him do it. When he is really scared he spends whole days in his wardrobe to stop the feelings. Steve may be diagnosed by a clinician using four criteria: deviance, dysfunction, distress and danger.

1. Explain how 'distress' and 'danger' is used in diagnosing Steve. (4)

2. Explain **one** strength and **two** weaknesses of using the four features to diagnose Steve. (6)

3. **Context essay:** Discuss the use of deviance, dysfunction, distress and danger to decide if Steve has a mental disorder. (8)

The term 'clinician' refers to a health care professional who works directly with people/clients/patients. This may include psychiatrists, clinical psychologists, nurse practitioners, doctors. Note that a psychiatrist is medically trained whereas a psychologist is not.

When a diagnosis is helpful	With physical illness, a clinician might take your temperature or do a blood test/scan to see if outcomes are 'abnormal'.
	Diagnosing mental disorders is harder – but the 4Ds can help determine when a mental health 'issue' could be considered a mental health 'disorder'.
	This is a crucial decision, with implications for treatment and the potential for being stigmatised as 'mentally ill'.
Deviance Deviant behaviours are unusual, undesirable and even bizarre.	• Statistical norms – these are used to measure the unusualness of any behaviour. • Social norms – desirability of the behaviour depends on historical context, and the culture, age and/or gender of the individual. Failure to conform to statistical and/or social norms may lead to negative attention from others and social exclusion (so norm-breaking is a useful indicator of psychological abnormality).
Dysfunction Symptoms that distract, confuse or interfere with ability to carry out roles and responsibilities.	Psychologists use a variety of objective measures to assess everyday functioning. e.g. the WHODAS II – questionnaire assessing a person's understanding of what is going on around them, communication and deterioration in self-care, etc. Dysfunction can also include trouble getting up in the morning, failure to complete tasks at work or college and problems participating in routine activities (e.g. socialising).
Distress When symptoms cause emotional pain or anxiety.	Sometimes psychological distress shows as physical symptoms (e.g. aches and pains, palpitations, feeling tired all the time), so these are important for diagnosis. Distress could be seen as normal depending on the situation (e.g. it would be normal in relation to a job loss or bereavement). A clinician considers the intensity or duration of the distress, as well as a person's level of functioning, when making a diagnosis. Quantitative data can be collected using scales such as the *Kessler Psychological Distress Scale* (K10), a 10-item self-report scale focusing on experiences in the past four weeks.
Danger Careless, hostile or hazardous behaviour jeopardises safety of the person and/or others.	Predicting violent behaviour is difficult but a history of aggression makes another incident more likely. In the UK, a person may be detained under the Mental Health Act ('sectioned') if three professionals agree they are a danger to themselves or others. The person can be taken (without consent) to hospital for treatment.

A strength of the 4Ds is that using all four helps avoid erroneous diagnosis.

For example, more factors than just deviance from statistical or social norms are considered when making a diagnosis.

This avoids situations in which eccentric but harmless people are seen as abnormal, and those with common but debilitating symptoms of depression are missed.

The importance of this is that a valid system should be neither over- nor under-inclusive (like this one).

CA However, there are no hard and fast rules about how to combine the Ds, e.g. someone struggling to cope (signs of distress and dysfunction), but with no signs of danger or deviance, may not require a diagnosis. It could be the situation causing the problem (so could not be resolved by treatment, which is the purpose of a diagnosis).

A weakness is that the 4Ds lack objectivity.

Various methods try to increase objectivity, but this is unlikely (for example because ratings are being made of feelings).

4Ds compare individual with others, so decisions would be better if made in comparison to a reference group (more objective), not using the clinician's view (more subjective).

This shows that if the 4Ds are to be applied meaningfully, a clinician needs information not only about the person, but also their community.

Another weakness is that the 4Ds create labels.

For example, 'danger' as a criterion for mental disorder leads people to equate mental illness with being dangerous.

This becomes distorted in the media, but most people with schizophrenia are no more dangerous than people without it (Fazel et al. 2009).

This matters because such attitudes may become 'self-fulfilling prophecies' – stereotypes lead people to act as predicted by the stereotype.

Application: 4Ds are effectively applied to diagnosis of mental disorders.

The 4Ds are used by clinicians in conjunction with classification manuals (e.g. DSM-5 and ICD-10, see following spreads). There are different mixes of Ds in different disorders.

For example, deviance from statistical norms helps define intellectual disability, while deviance from social norms, dysfunction and danger help define anti-social personality disorder.

This shows that each of the 4Ds is used in diagnosis.

I&D extra: There is potential for social control and abuse of power.

Those who breach social norms or challenge government policies can be quieted by being labelled as mentally disturbed.

For example, Russian psychiatrist Koryagin (1981) described how the KGB pressured psychiatrists in the 1960s to diagnose and imprison dissidents.

This shows how misusing psychiatric diagnosis can 'legitimise' punitive treatments and social exclusion (Moncrieff 2010).

Unexpected item in the bagging area...

'CA' stands for 'competing argument'.

Revision booster

If you can't think of an evaluation point, remember the fifth D, 'duration', which you can use as a strength or a weakness. It is a strength because in many disorders the symptoms have to be present for a certain time. It is a weakness because the symptoms of some disorders may make it difficult for the patient to decide how long they have been experiencing the symptoms.

✓ Check it

1. Explain how the concept of 'dysfunction' could be used to make a diagnosis. [2]

2. Explain **one** weakness of using the concept of 'deviance' when diagnosing mental disorders. [2]

3. **Standard essay:** Evaluate the concepts of 'deviance' and 'distress' as ways of deciding whether or not to make a diagnosis. [8] or [20]

4. **I&D/Synoptic essay:** Assess the issue of social control. Refer to the diagnosis of mental disorders and examples from **one** other application of psychology (e.g. criminological, child or health). [20]

Spec spotlight

5.1.2 Classification systems (DSM-IV-TR or DSM-V and ICD) for mental health, including reliability and validity of diagnoses.

What is the DSM?

Diagnostic and Statistical Manual.

Describes and classifies symptoms, features and associated risk factors of over 300 mental and behavioural disorders (22 categories), used throughout the US and in many nations across the world.

Arguably this is an important first step on the journey to appropriate support and treatment.

The DSM-V (or DSM-5)

Most recent edition (2013) with three sections.

Section One
- Guidance about using the new system.

Section Two
- Details of disorders, categorised according to current understanding of underlying causes and similarities between symptoms.
- Examines symptoms of some disorders differently from previous editions, e.g. the five subtypes of schizophrenia have been removed and a dimensional assessment added.

Section Three
- Suggestions for new disorders (e.g. internet gaming disorder) that should have further investigation.
- Includes information about impact of culture on presentation of symptoms and how symptoms are communicated (especially when the clinician is from a different cultural background).

Dave's dream of building a robot that could fix his car whilst making a brew remained unrealised, but at least it could put the shape in the right hole.

Making a diagnosis using the DSM

Generally based on unstructured (clinical) interviews but many structured interview schedules are also available, based on symptom lists (e.g. *Beck Depression Inventory*, BDI).

Diagnosis often involves ruling out disorders which do not match the person's symptoms sufficiently.

Uncomplicated problems may take a GP ten minutes to diagnose. Difficult cases may take weeks or months in order to understand the consistency of symptoms over time.

Apply it Concepts

Dr Lu trained in the UK but works in Africa. He diagnosed two patients using the DSM but is unfamiliar with this system. He gave one person a diagnosis of schizophrenia, but the other person had a disorder he could not identify.

1. (a) Explain how Dr Lu would make a diagnosis using the DSM, such as for schizophrenia. (4)
   (b) Explain **two** possible ways that the DSM could be helpful for Dr Lu's other patient. (4)

2. Explain the validity of the DSM, using Dr Lu as an example. (4)

3. **Context essay:** To what extent is the DSM the best classification system for Dr Lu to use on his patients? (20)

How reliability and validity are assessed

Reliability = consistency of diagnosis.

Validity = whether a real disorder has been diagnosed.

Reliability of the DSM-III checked using *Cohen's kappa* = proportion of people who get the same diagnosis when assessed and then re-assessed, either at a later time (test-retest reliability) or by an alternative practitioner (inter-rater reliability). 0.7 is 'good agreement' (Spitzer *et al.* 2012).

Several types of validity are relevant to diagnosis:
- *Descriptive validity* – two people with the same diagnosis exhibit similar symptoms.
- *Aetiological validity* – two people with the same diagnosis share similar causal factors.
- *Concurrent validity* – a clinician uses more than one method or technique to reach the same diagnosis.
- *Predictive validity* – accurately predicting outcomes for an individual from their diagnosis (e.g. prognosis).

Reliability of the DSM

A strength of the DSM-5 is a good level of agreement for some disorders.

Field trials demonstrated impressive agreement between clinicians for a variety of disorders.	Three disorders (e.g. PTSD) had kappa values of 0.60–0.79 (very good). Seven more disorders (e.g. schizophrenia) had values of 0.40–0.59 (good, Regier *et al.* 2013).	This is important because the criteria for PTSD have changed (e.g. specific symptoms for a diagnosis) and clinicians have clearly adapted well.

A weakness of the DSM-5 is the issue of falling standards.

The 'acceptable' level of agreement has fallen over the last 35 years.	0.2–0.4 was classified as 'acceptable' (Cooper 2014). Major depressive disorder was one of the least reliable diagnoses (0.28, Regier *et al.* 2013).	This suggests the DSM-5 may be less reliable than previous versions (e.g. diagnoses of MDD may have been mistaken, with other cases missed.

CA However, clinicians in the DSM-5 field trials were asked to 'work as they usually would' (e.g. take clients as they come), to mirror normal practice. In contrast, the DSM-III used carefully screened 'test' clients, and clinicians had detailed training. So it is no surprise that DSM-5 trials had lower reliability (Kupfer and Kraemer 2012).

Validity of the DSM

A strength of the DSM is support for the validity of conduct disorder (CD).

Kim-Cohen *et al.* (2005) showed validity for CD. Concurrent – interviews of children and mothers, observation of anti-social behaviour, questionnaires with teachers.	Aetiological – risk factors common (e.g. male, low income). Predictive – 5-year-olds with CD more likely to have behavioural problems at 7.	This is a strength as accurate diagnosis helps reduce adult mental health problems preceded by symptoms of CD.

A weakness of the DSM is that labels tell us nothing about causes.

Merely naming or classifying a disorder does not actually tell us anything about its causes.	Circular logic – Why does someone hear voices? They have schizophrenia. How do we know they have schizophrenia? They hear voices.	The result of a diagnosis is simply a label that lacks validity and tells us nothing useful.

I&D extra: One issue is making comparisons between different explanations.

The *trauma-informed approach* has been gaining interest amongst clinicians (Johnstone and Miners 2018).	'Symptoms' are 'survival strategies', e.g. hostile voices can often be identified as a person who abused or hurt them.	Therefore, it makes sense to treat the 'symptom' in terms of its meaning rather than trying to diagnose a disorder.

So, Jeff, you can boss the midfield whilst our wing backs get down the channels putting pressure on their back line...

Revision booster

You can be asked questions about validity and reliability in the context of diagnosis. When writing answers about this, be sure to consider the validity and reliability of *diagnosis*, not simply examples of validity and reliability in research. Remember to tailor your answer to include evidence of different types of validity: descriptive, aetiological, concurrent and predictive.

Check it

1. Explain **one** reason why it might be difficult to make a diagnosis using either the DSM-IV-TR or the DSM-5. (2)

2. Explain **two** strengths of either the DSM-IV-TR or the DSM-5. (4)

3. **Standard essay:** Evaluate the validity of the DSM-IV-TR or the DSM-5. (8) or (20)

4. **Methods essay:** Assess the use of interviews as a way of making a diagnosis in clinical psychology using classification systems such as the DSM. (8) or (20)

Mary was the kind of person who always did everything by the book.

Apply it Concepts

Dr James prefers to use the DSM when diagnosing a mental disorder but has changed jobs and must use the ICD. His new employers say this is because he will be working in a multicultural area. He is worried the ICD is less valid and reliable than the DSM.

1. Describe why Dr James' employers think the ICD is better for a multicultural area. (3)

2. (a) Explain **two** reasons why Dr James' employers may say the ICD is more reliable. (4)

   (b) Explain **two** reasons why Dr James' employers may say the ICD is more valid. (4)

3. **Context essay:** To what extent are his employers justified in believing that the ICD is a better classification system for Dr James? (20)

What is the ICD?

International Statistical Classification of Diseases and Related Health Problems.

Developed since 1893 to monitor global mortality and morbidity statistics (data on death and disease).

Revised often, current version (ICD-10) published in 1992 (ICD-11 due soon).

A multilingual freely available resource used around the world, provides a 'common language' so that data collected in different countries can be usefully compared.

Mental disorders and ICD codes

Chapter 5 of the ICD-10 is 'Mental and Behavioural Disorders'.

Each disorder has a code (starting with F), disorders are listed consecutively and there are 11 sections. For example:

- F20–F29 is 'Schizophrenia, schizotypal and delusional disorders'.
- F20 is the subcategory of 'Schizophrenia'.
- F20.0 is 'Paranoid schizophrenia', F20.1 is 'Hebephrenic schizophrenia', etc.

Each section has 'leftover' codes, so new disorders can be added without having to recode the others (e.g. F48 is 'Other nonpsychotic mental disorders').

Codes are used to index medical records (easy to find people with specific conditions for research).

The system tries to be comprehensive enough to include all known conditions but also avoid repetition or overlap.

Making a diagnosis using the ICD-10

ICD contains both physical and psychological disorders.

The clinician making the diagnosis:

- Selects key words from the client interview relating to symptoms (e.g. hallucinations, delusions).
- Looks up the symptoms in an alphabetic index or may go straight to an obvious section (e.g. schizophrenia).
- Uses other symptoms to locate a subcategory (e.g. select F20 and then F20.1 based on presenting symptoms).

Improvements to the ICD-10

Presentation, communication and interpretation of symptoms are shaped by language and culture, leads to culture bias.

'Culture bias' means clients from one culture could be given a different diagnosis when diagnosed by clinicians from another culture because of different cultural norms or language use.

Poses problems for the international community served by the ICD. So a research programme was set up to review differences in diagnostic practice and terminology across the world. Now the ICD-10 is available in different languages and cultural forms.

This review process also revealed inconsistencies, ambiguities and overlaps between disorders. These were removed from the ICD, so it is now clear, simple and logically organised.

Reliability of the ICD

A strength is improved reliability between the ICD-9 and ICD-10.

Ponizovsky et al. (2006) compared the reliability of the ICD-9 and ICD-10 using PPV (positive predictive value), the proportion of people who get the same diagnosis when reassessed.

PPV scores for schizophrenia increased from 68% in 1989 (ICD-9) to 94.2% in 2003 (ICD-10), an increase of 26.2%.

This clearly shows improved reliability and suggests that the increased number of disorders from the ICD-9 to ICD-10 has not detracted from the reliability of those diagnoses.

Helen prided herself on her reliability. Unfortunately the meeting had started at 5.

CA On the other hand high reliability is meaningless without a high level of validity. A demonstration of high stability of diagnoses, i.e. reliability of a given diagnostic system, does not mean that the system is valid. Reliability on its own tells us nothing about the true meaning of the diagnosis.

Another strength of the ICD-10 is it has good inter-rater reliability.

Two researchers carried out a joint interview with 100 clients (Galeazzi et al. 2004).

Looking at psychosomatic symptoms, kappa values ranged from 0.69 to 0.97 (very high agreement).

This encourages confidence in using the ICD-10 at least for some disorders.

Validity of the ICD

Another strength is good predictive validity for schizophrenia.

Mason et al. (1997) compared different ways of making a diagnosis.

The ICD-9 and ICD-10 were reasonably good at predicting disability in 99 people with schizophrenia 13 years later.

This shows that the initial diagnosis was useful and meaningful in terms of its ability to accurately predict future outcomes.

Application: The ICD-10 continues to be effectively applied to diagnosis.

The WHO (World Health Organization) aims to improve the 'clinical utility' of the system in the ICD-11 by conducting research.

An international survey of clinicians found a preference for simplicity and flexibility, so the ICD-11 task force is now cautious about adding new disorders.

The system should become more 'user-friendly', which means validity of diagnosis should also improve.

I&D extra: Illustrates how psychology has developed over time.

Both the DSM and ICD have been revised a number of times.

This is in response to criticisms about reliability and validity.

Therefore, both systems should provide a more accurate diagnosis and one that is useful (i.e. leads to an appropriate treatment).

Revision booster

Some strengths and weaknesses of the DSM and the ICD can be turned on their heads to become weaknesses or strengths of the alternative classification system. Watch out for these when you are revising and make a note so you can make economies on how much you have to learn.

✓ Check it

1. Compare the DSM and the ICD. (4)

2. Explain **one** weakness of the ICD. (2)

3. **Standard essay:** Evaluate the reliability of diagnosis using the ICD. (8) or (20)

4. **Context essay:** While classification systems such as the DSM and the ICD can help people get treatment, many argue that psychiatric labels are at best meaningless and at worst dangerous.

   Assess the validity of classifications systems such as the DSM and the ICD. You must refer to the issues raised in the context. (8)

Schizophrenia: Symptoms and features

Spec spotlight

5.1.3 For schizophrenia: description of symptoms and features, including thought insertion, hallucinations, delusions, disordered thinking.

Schizophrenia can be shattering for the individual and their family.

Schizophrenia is a compulsory topic to study but the remaining three mental disorders (anorexia nervosa (AN), obsessive compulsive disorder (OCD) and unipolar depression) are options – you must study one of these three.

- AN starts on page 58.
- OCD starts on page 72.
- Unipolar depression starts on page 86.

Apply it Concepts

Brian thinks his neighbour is sending thoughts through the wall and into Brian's head. Brian is sure he smells and feels things his neighbour is experiencing and is convinced this is because he is an extra-terrestrial interpreter sent from outer space. He finds that if he tries to describe this to other people it is hard to explain himself clearly.

1. Explain how Brian's symptoms illustrate thought insertion and disorganised thought. (4)

2. Distinguish between delusions and hallucinations using Brian's symptoms as examples. (4)

3. Context essay: Discuss how Brian's experiences could lead to a diagnosis of schizophrenia. (8)

Schizophrenia

DSM-5 – diagnosis requires at least two of the four key symptoms listed below (one must be delusions, hallucinations or disorganised speech/thought).

The person must have at least one month of active symptoms and six months of disturbance to everyday functioning.

ICD-10 – less focus on dysfunction and six months of disturbance is not necessary. Six subtypes are listed.

Four key symptoms

Schizophrenia is divided into positive symptoms such as delusions, hallucinations and disorganised speech/thought and movement.

Negative symptoms may also be present, e.g. lack of emotion or speech, flat affect and mutism.

Thought insertion

- Person believes their thoughts do not belong to them and have been implanted by an external source.
- Experience 'blurring' between self and others.

Hallucinations

- Involuntary and vivid perceptual experiences that occur in the absence of external stimuli.
- Visual, olfactory (smell), somatosensory (bodily feelings).
- Auditory are most common in schizophrenia (experienced as hearing voices, distinct from own inner voice/thoughts).

Delusions

- 'Fixed beliefs that are not amenable to change in the light of conflicting evidence' (DSM-5).
- May relate to everyday life, or may be 'bizarre'.
- Many forms, e.g. persecutory (someone is trying to harm you), referential (environmental cues have personal meanings) and/or grandiose (you are exceptional).

Disorganised thought

- Inferred from speech – derailment (unrelated ideas) or tangentiality (going off on a different topic).
- Difficult to follow the person's train of thought.
- 'Word salad' (random stringing together of words), 'neologism' (blending words to create new words).
- Mixing up words is common so this is only classed as symptomatic if it leads to dysfunctional communication.

Features

Lifetime prevalence is 0.3–0.7% (varies with ethnicity, nationality and geographic origin in immigrants).

Onset is slightly earlier in males (early- to mid-20s) than females (late-20s) and males have a poorer prognosis.

Prognosis is variable and hard to predict – a minority recover, most experience chronic, episodic impairment and some show progressive deterioration. Positive symptoms reduce over time but negative symptoms often remain.

A strength is that schizophrenia can be reliably diagnosed.

Schizophrenia diagnosis is highly consistent (this is true of diagnosis made with both the DSM-5 and ICD-10).

Kappa value was 0.46 ('good') in field trials of the DSM-5 (Regier *et al*. 2013) while Sartorius *et al*. (1995) found a very high kappa value of 0.86. Only 3.8% of clinicians 'lacked confidence' in their diagnoses using the ICD-10.

This is important because it suggests that the descriptors for schizophrenia are sufficiently detailed to allow clinicians to distinguish this condition from others with shared symptoms and features.

People with schizophrenia may require plenty of support.

CA This said, diagnosing schizophrenia is not easy as it shares symptoms with various other disorders. For example, hallucinations can be experienced by people with depression and post-traumatic stress disorder. Hallucinations can also be caused by drug withdrawal, metabolic disorders, stress and sleep deprivation. Catatonic behaviour can be symptomatic of major depression or bipolar disorder.

A weakness is that cultural differences can make diagnosis difficult.

Identifying disorganised thinking can be hard if the client is from a different cultural background from the clinician.

For example, Rastafarians use neologisms (new words) which are a play on English words (e.g. 'downpress' for 'oppress'). Could be seen as a sign of disorganised thought when interviewing someone showing signs of mental distress.

This demonstrates that an accurate diagnosis of schizophrenia requires an awareness of and sensitivity to cultural and linguistic differences.

A case study of schizophrenia

Melissa started university late, having had a few years off after school. She made friends in her first year but in her second year people noticed that she was getting stranger and stranger. She told her friends she could hear someone talking to her inside her head and she was convinced that one of her flatmates was stealing money from her room when she was out. One week she disappeared for a few days and when she came back she was quite dirty as if she had been sleeping in the street. She had always loved to sing in the university choir and also to play the piano but she had given all that up. She just spent most of the day in her room listening to the radio.

One of her friends got quite worried and contacted Melissa's family who came to visit her. They were shocked by Melissa's appearance. She looked pale and sad. Melissa told her parents that she wanted to quit university as she really had lost interest in the music course she was doing. She also told them about things that were bothering her, for example she said that her flatmates had drilled holes in the ceiling of her room so they could spy on her. When her father said he couldn't see the holes Melissa said they were very tiny and really only she could see them. She had put up a tent in her room so her flatmates couldn't spy on her.

Her parents arranged for Melissa to talk to their family doctor. They told the doctor that Melissa's grandmother had had a serious illness and been in a mental hospital for many many years but didn't know specifically what she had been diagnosed with.

Adapted from several different case studies.

Check it

1. Define the term 'thought insertion' with reference to **one** example. [2]

2. Describe **two** features of schizophrenia. [4]

3. **Standard essay:** Evaluate **two** of the key symptoms of schizophrenia. [8]

4. **I&D essay:** Assess the issues of culture and gender in relation to the diagnosis of schizophrenia. [20]

Excess dopamine in the mesolimbic pathway has been linked to positive symptoms of schizophrenia while low levels of dopamine in the mesocortical pathway have been linked to negative symptoms of schizophrenia.

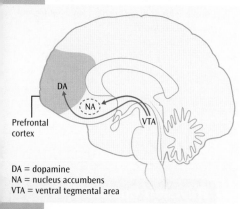

DA = dopamine
NA = nucleus accumbens
VTA = ventral tegmental area

The term 'psychosis' tends now to be used instead of schizophrenia because it is broader. It refers to severe mental disorder where a person's thought processes and emotions are so impaired that they have lost contact with external reality. The whole person is affected, behaviour is qualitatively different from before and the person lacks insight into their condition (as distinct from a neurosis).

 **Methods**

Pansy is altering neurotransmitter levels in rats to simulate symptoms of schizophrenia. She measures disorganised thinking by counting the mistakes they make on a familiar task and negative symptoms by scoring social withdrawal and lack of movement.

1. Suggest how social withdrawal and lack of movement in rats could be operationalised. (4)

2. Explain why Pansy's measure of disorganised thinking may be more objective than her other measures. (2)

3. **Context/Methods essay:** To what extent are animal studies more useful than human case studies in understanding schizophrenia? Refer to the context in your answer. (20)

Excess dopamine
Hyperdopaminergia.

Antipsychotic drugs *chlorpromazine* and *reserpine* help symptoms of schizophrenia – but also induce side effects of tremors and muscle rigidity.

These are symptoms of *Parkinson's disease* (low *dopamine*) – so schizophrenia was linked to high dopamine (hyperdopaminergia).

But the causes of excess levels were unclear. Two theories gained favour:

- Low levels of *beta hydroxylase* (enzyme breaks down dopamine) may build up excess dopamine in synapses.

- Proliferation of *D2 dopamine receptors* on postsynaptic cells may be responsible for hyperdopaminergic activity.

Dopamine deficiency
Hypodopaminergia.

Davis *et al.* (1991) suggest that:

- Positive symptoms of schizophrenia (e.g. delusions and hallucinations) may result from *excess* dopaminergic activity in the *mesolimbic pathway*.

- Negative symptoms (e.g. flat affect and mutism) may result from *hypodopaminergia*, a lack of dopaminergic activity in the *mesocortical pathway*.

Serotonin and negative symptoms

Later research focused on the roles of other neurotransmitters (*GABA*, *glutamate* and *serotonin*).

Newer antipsychotic drug (*clozapine*) binds to *D1* and *D4 dopamine receptors*, but only weakly to D2 receptors.

The effectiveness of this drug called into question the original dopamine hypothesis (with its focus on D2 receptors).

Clozapine also binds to serotonin receptors and reduces positive and negative symptoms of schizophrenia – so negative symptoms may be caused by irregular serotonergic activity.

Research then focused on the interactions between different neurotransmitters (e.g. serotonin regulates dopamine levels in the mesolimbic pathway).

Dopamine dysregulation

Howes and Kapur's (2009) version of the hypothesis:

- Dopamine dysregulation in the *striatum* is the common pathway to psychosis (schizophrenia).

- Attention should turn to high presynaptic dopamine levels as opposed to irregularities of D2 receptors.

- Focus on interactions between genetic, environmental and sociocultural factors.

- Dopamine hypothesis should be softened and viewed as an explanation for 'psychosis proneness', not as an explanation specifically for schizophrenia.

A strength is support from amphetamine-induced psychosis in rats.

Tenn et al. (2003) found that rats given nine amphetamine injections over three weeks showed various schizophrenia-like symptoms.

Dopamine antagonists (drugs that block D1 receptors) successfully reversed these effects.

This experimental evidence suggests that increased dopamine levels may be a cause of schizophrenia in humans.

CA However, Dépatie and Lal (2001) showed that apomorphine (dopamine agonist which stimulates D2 receptors) does not induce psychotic symptoms in non-psychotic clients and does not worsen symptoms in those already diagnosed. This challenges the suggestion that hyperdopaminergia is responsible for positive symptoms.

A weakness is evidence of schizophrenia in second-generation immigrants.

Neurochemical theories cannot explain why certain groups, (e.g. second-generation immigrants) are more likely to be diagnosed with schizophrenia.

Veling et al. (2008) showed that Moroccan immigrants were more likely to be diagnosed than Turkish immigrants (likelihood correlated with the discrimination faced by each group).

This suggests that environmental factors (social stress) may interact with internal neurochemistry making some people more prone to psychosis because of both factors.

Another strength is support for the role of D2 receptors.

Snyder (1985) found that chlorpromazine is an antagonist at many dopamine receptors (D1 and D2) and has an antipsychotic effect.

He also found that the dopamine antagonist haloperidol is more effective even though it has a narrower range of biochemical effects.

This finding suggests that excess activity at specific (but not all) dopamine receptors is implicated in development of symptoms.

Application: Research into neurotransmitters has led to drug treatments.

Research shows that dopamine antagonists binding to D2 receptors (e.g. haloperidol and spiroperidol) can successfully reduce positive symptoms.

Also, atypical drugs (e.g. clozapine) which also block serotonin receptors have been successful in treating both positive and negative symptoms.

This means that people with schizophrenia can live in the community without need of residential care because their symptoms are controlled.

I&D extra: Biological explanations may be reductionist.

A complex disorder involving multiple symptoms is explained in terms of the action of one neurotransmitter.

But the 'lived-in' experience of someone with schizophrenia is not represented at this lower, biological level.

Therefore, explanations that focus solely on dopamine are unlikely to represent the full nature of schizophrenia.

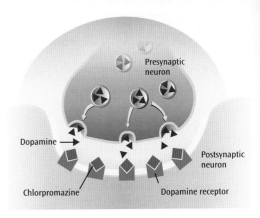

The original dopamine hypothesis proposed that schizophrenia is associated with high levels of dopamine.

Chlorpromazine works by binding to postsynaptic D2 dopamine receptors and so reduces the effects of dopamine on postsynaptic neurons.

✓ Check it

1. Describe how symptoms of schizophrenia can be explained by the function of neurotransmitters. [3]

2. Explain **one** strength of the function of neurotransmitters as an explanation for schizophrenia. [4]

3. **Standard essay:** Assess **one** explanation for schizophrenia. [8] or [20]

4. **Standard plus essay:** Evaluate the role of **two** or more neurotransmitters as explanations for schizophrenia. [8] or [20]

Schizophrenia: One other biological explanation

AO1
Description

Spec spotlight

5.1.3 For schizophrenia: One other biological theory/explanation.

Methods

Clyde is a mental health nurse. He has ethical permission to use clients' records and has searched for adults who have previously participated in genetic research and are known to have genetic variations that increase vulnerability to schizophrenia. He has identified 12 clients and has found quantitative data about sources of stress in their lives. 10 lived in a city, 4 had harsh parents and 6 took drugs.

1. Calculate the percentage of the clients Clyde identified who lived in a city. (1)

2. Calculate the ratio of all **three** sources of stress. (2)

3. Clyde also collected qualitative data by listening to his 12 clients in conversation in group sessions. Clyde was an overt non-participant observer.

   Explain **one** advantage of this strategy for Clyde. (2)

4. **Context/Methods essay:** Evaluate Clyde's use of different types of data. (8)

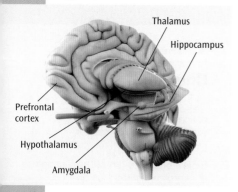

Abnormality in the DISC1 gene has been related to changes in the limbic system (consists of, for example, the hypothalamus, amygdala, hippocampus and thalamus).

Abnormality in the COMT gene has been related to changes in the prefrontal cortex.

Genetic explanation for schizophrenia	The human genome comprises some 23,000 genes, each with specific instructions about how to build a unique person.
	Genes consist of DNA strands and DNA holds 'instructions' for specific features linked to psychological functioning.
	Genetic variation may explain some of the neurochemical irregularities described on the previous spread.
Schizophrenia as a heritable condition	Heritability of schizophrenia may be 79% (Hilker *et al.* 2018), suggesting a large role for genetic factors in causation.
	One approach is to identify responsible genes present in family members diagnosed with schizophrenia – up to 700 genes identified (Wright 2014) and probably a lot more.
Gene mutations Schizophrenia can appear without a family history.	DNA in one or more genes may change (mutate).
	Mutations can result from an environmental factor or an error in cell division (e.g. deletion or duplication of a DNA strand).
	e.g. *DiGeorge Syndrome* is caused by the deletion of 30–40 neighbouring genes in a specific region of chromosome 22 (up to 25% of people with this condition develop schizophrenia).

Candidate genes

Specific genes have been identified that are linked to schizophrenia.

COMT gene

- The link between DiGeorge Syndrome and schizophrenia may be due to deletion of the COMT gene.
- COMT gene creates *catechol-O-methyltransferase* (enzyme breaks down neurotransmitters such as *dopamine* in the *prefrontal cortex*).
- Deletion would mean poor regulation of dopamine levels resulting in schizophrenic symptoms.

DISC1 gene

- People with an abnormality to the gene *Disrupted-in-Schizophrenia 1* (DISC1) are 1.4 times more likely to develop schizophrenia than people without (Kim *et al.* 2012).
- Codes for creation of *GABA*, which regulates *glutamate* and dopamine in the *limbic system* (see diagram left).

Diathesis-stress model Genes are more likely to create a vulnerability for schizophrenia than to cause it.	A person may possess 'schizophrenia' genes (diathesis) but it is only triggered by other biological or environmental effects – genetic explanation because genes are the required element.
	Original diathesis-stress model saw 'stress' as psychological (e.g. harsh parenting, the 'refrigerator mother').
	The definition of 'stress' is now broader and includes anything that might trigger schizophrenia (Houston *et al.* 2008). For example, recent research into factors triggering a schizophrenic episode shows that cannabis use increases risk by up to seven times (cannabis interferes with the dopamine system).

A strength is research support showing schizophrenia runs in families.

Gottesman (see right) found a relationship between genetic similarity and the probability of two people both having schizophrenia.

Gottesman and Shields (1966) identified a concordance rate of 42% for MZ twins and 9% for DZ twins.

The greater rate for MZs shows that while schizophrenia is not entirely a genetic disorder, biology certainly plays a significant role.

CA We should be cautious in interpreting the findings of twin studies. MZs not only share more DNA than DZs, they are also treated more similarly (similar appearance and always the same sex – see equal environments assumption on page 61). Also, similarity between genetic relatives may be as much due to shared environment as shared genes. This reduces the validity of the conclusion that the greater shared DNA is responsible for the similar pathology.

A weakness is research that identifies protective environmental factors.

Concordance rates in twin studies are far from 100% even for MZ twins, suggesting a significant role for the environment.

Pedersen and Mortensen (2006) show the risk of developing schizophrenia increases with greater exposure to city life and higher population density.

This suggests that rural dwelling may help protect a person from developing a disorder to which they are genetically predisposed.

Another strength is the considerable research evidence on DISC1 and COMT.

Dahoun et al. (2017) concluded that DISC1 is associated with presynaptic dopamine dysregulation, a key factor in schizophrenia.

Egan et al. (2001) found a link between decreased dopamine activity in the prefrontal cortex and one form of the COMT gene – the 'Val' allele (inheriting two copies increases risk of schizophrenia by 50%).

This shows how genetic variations underpin neurochemical differences which can predispose a person towards schizophrenia.

Application: Knowledge of genetics has been used in genetic counselling.

When a family member receives a diagnosis of schizophrenia, the family may want more information about heritability.

'Recurrence risk' can be calculated and the counsellor will then help the family to interpret this information.

This can provide support, help allay fears about developing schizophrenia and inform choices about family planning.

I&D extra: A relevant debate is the interaction between nature and nurture.

Tienari et al.'s (1994) 21-year longitudinal adoption study supports the diathesis-stress model.

Adopted children whose biological mothers were diagnosed with schizophrenia were more affected by dysfunction in the adoptive home than those from low-risk backgrounds.

This supports an interactionist approach to explaining schizophrenia.

Graph showing that as genetic similarity increases so does the probability of sharing schizophrenia (Gottesman 1991).

Relationship to person with schizophrenia

General population	1%
First cousins	2%
Uncles/aunts	2%
Nephews/nieces	4%
Grandchildren	5%
Half-siblings	6%
Parents	6%
Siblings	9%
Children	13%
DZ twins	17%
MZ twins	48%

Risk of developing schizophrenia

Genes shared
	☐ Unrelated
12.5%	▨ 3rd degree relatives
25%	▩ 2nd degree relatives
50%	▦ 1st degree relatives
100%	■ MZ twins

'MZ' stands for monozygotic. These are identical twins who formed from one egg (zygote) and have the same genome. DZ twins are formed from two eggs so they are genetically as similar as any siblings.

Revision booster

You learned about twin studies as part of the Year 1 course. The twin studies on this spread could be used when answering questions in general on twin studies.

✓ Check it

1. Explain **one** strength of **one** biological explanation for schizophrenia other than the function of neurotransmitters. (2)

2. Compare **two** biological explanations for schizophrenia. (4)

3. **Standard essay:** Assess **one** biological explanation for schizophrenia other than the function of neurotransmitters. (8) or (20)

4. **Prompt essay:** Many people think schizophrenia has more to do with nature than nurture.

   Assess biological explanations for schizophrenia. You must include a comparison with at least **one** non-biological explanation in your answer. (8) or (20)

Life in the big city – but could it also contribute to a rise in stress levels?

Josh is conducting a meta-analysis about past factors in the lives of adults with schizophrenia. The factors he is considering include parental unemployment, moving house often, whether they moved into or out of a city and the number of neighbours they can recall well.

1. (a) Explain how Josh will conduct his meta-analysis. (4)

   (b) Explain the importance of **two** of Josh's variables. (2)

2. Explain **one** way Josh can make sure his study is high in validity. (2)

3. Explain **one** reliability problem in Josh's study. (2)

4. **Context/Methods essay:** Discuss how structured interviews could have been used to collect the data used in Josh's study. (8)

Social causation hypothesis	The human world (people around you) is a major cause of schizophrenia (or at least of relapse).
	Many environmental risk factors contribute (e.g. family dysfunction, childhood trauma), the four main ones are covered below.
Social adversity Failure to meet needs can be stressful.	All humans have the same basic needs, e.g. physical but also intellectual, emotional and social.
	Some children grow up in unfavourable environments – this makes them vulnerable to mental health disorders in the future (e.g. unemployment and poverty expose some families to stress).
	People from lower socioeconomic groups may not be able to access treatment. This makes their problems worse.
Urbanicity Link between urban living and schizophrenia.	City life is more stressful than rural life – noise, light pollution, criminality, faster pace, anonymity.
	Long-term exposure may make a person more vulnerable to having an episode of schizophrenia.
	High population density makes life more competitive, which may increase experience of *chronic social defeat* (a stressor that occurs when a person is exposed to hostile confrontations from another individual, such as bullying).
Social isolation People with schizophrenia withdraw.	People with schizophrenia find contact with others stressful (Faris 1934).
	Self-imposed isolation cuts them off from feedback about what behaviours or thoughts are inappropriate – they begin to behave 'strangely' without this corrective feedback.
Immigration and minority status Immigrants are at greater risk of schizophrenia than the general population.	Research shows greater risk for first- and second-generation immigrants in many countries.
	Risk decreases as the number of people from the same ethnic background increases – minority or *outgroup* status is key, not belonging to a particular ethnic group.
	This implies marginalisation of outgroups may leave people vulnerable to schizophrenia.
	Veling (2008) suggests schizophrenia may be a reaction against chronic experience of prejudice and discrimination. Second-generation immigrants are at greater risk than first-generation because:

- They have a weaker cultural identity.
- They have learned to fit in with the norms of the indigenous society.
- Their beliefs and expectations may be at odds with those of their parents and extended family.

This creates stress which worsens vulnerability to schizophrenia.

A strength is meta-analyses supporting the role of urban dwelling.

Vassos *et al.* (2012) analysed data from four studies to correlate location (urban to rural) with schizophrenia risk.

The risk was 2.37 times higher for people living in the most urban environments compared with the most rural.

This shows that relative risk of schizophrenia increases in line with population density.

CA However, the data is correlational, so we cannot say that schizophrenia is caused by urbanicity or adversity. The *social drift hypothesis* suggests the reverse is true – people with schizophrenia find it hard to hold down a job, so they 'drift' into a lower social class than their parents and siblings, migrating into deprived inner-city areas. So schizophrenia leads to urbanicity rather than vice versa.

A weakness of the social causation hypothesis is twin study evidence.

Social causation is not a complete explanation for schizophrenia.

We know there is a genetic contribution to the development of schizophrenia (see previous spread).

Therefore, environmental factors may trigger schizophrenia in people genetically predisposed (diathesis-stress).

A strength of Veling's explanation is research into ethnic identity.

Veling *et al.* (2010) studied people classed as *marginalised* (weak national and ethnic identity) and *assimilated* (strong national identity but weak ethnic identity).

They were at greater risk of schizophrenia than people classed as *integrated* (strong national and ethnic identity) or *separated* (weak national but strong ethnic identity).

This suggests that a strong ethnic identity (identifying with and embracing ethnic 'differentness') may be a protective factor against schizophrenia.

Application: The hypothesis has been applied to treating schizophrenia.

The social causation hypothesis can help treat schizophrenia by drawing attention to factors affecting mental health at community level.

Housing projects which reduce overcrowding and celebrate cultural diversity foster resilience and help communities arm themselves against mental breakdown.

This is a critical step in developing a sense of collective social responsibility for not only our own mental well-being, but also that of other people.

I&D extra: The nature–nurture debate is again relevant here.

Tienari *et al.* (1994) looked at adopted children whose biological mothers had been diagnosed with schizophrenia – the environment was critical.

None of the children adopted into healthy (or even mildly disturbed families) developed schizophrenia – it only appeared where the environment was significantly disturbed.

This demonstrates the importance of nurture in people with a genetic predisposition for mental disturbance.

A strong ethnic identity may be a protective factor in schizophrenia.

Revision booster

In total you will have learned three different explanations for schizophrenia. Remember that you often need a 'competing' argument in an essay – you may be able to 'borrow' a competing argument from one of the other explanations.

You can also often use one of the explanations as evidence against another – but take care because this might not always be the case! Two different explanations for a phenomenon might not be mutually exclusive. That is, it might be possible for both explanations to exist side-by-side, so neither one is 'wrong'.

✓ Check it

1. Describe **two** features of **one** non-biological explanation for schizophrenia. [4]

2. Explain **one** weakness of **one** non-biological explanation for schizophrenia. [2]

3. **Standard essay:** Assess **one** non-biological explanation for schizophrenia. [8] or [20]

4. **Methods essay:** Assess the scientific status of research into **one** non-biological explanation for schizophrenia. [8] or [20]

Schizophrenia: One biological treatment

Spec spotlight

5.1.4 For schizophrenia: One biological treatment.

Dodgy habits like these can disrupt the effects of antipsychotics.

Drug treatments for schizophrenia	If schizophrenia is caused by an excess or a deficiency of a certain neurochemical (discussed on page 42), then medication can be used to correct this imbalance.
Typical or first-generation antipsychotics (FGAs) *Chlorpromazine* was the first antipsychotic medication in 1950s.	*Dopamine* antagonist – reduces positive symptoms by blocking postsynaptic dopamine receptors without activating them. Most effective FGAs bind to D2 receptors (one of the main receptors implicated in schizophrenia). FGAs reduce positive symptoms for many but up to 40% gain no relief at all and many still experience negative symptoms (Barlow and Durand 1995). Side effects, e.g. *tardive dyskinesia* – uncontrollable stiff or slow, writhing movements of the face and body).
Atypical or second-generation antipsychotics (SGAs) *Clozapine* and *risperidone*.	Clozapine Developed in the 1960s, blocks dopamine in the same way as FGAs. But also acts on *serotonin* and *glutamate* receptors, e.g. blocking serotonin receptors (antagonist). Reduces both positive and negative symptoms. Side effect – *agranulocytosis* (potentially fatal blood condition). So the drug has fallen out of favour, but still used with treatment-resistant clients, providing relief for up 60% (Lally and MacCabe 2015). Regular blood tests help avoid agranulocytosis.
	Risperidone More recently developed SGA, believed to bind to serotonin as well as dopamine. Binds more strongly to dopamine receptors than clozapine so effective in smaller doses than most antipsychotics.
Protocol	Medication is started quickly for greatest effectiveness. In the first week after a psychotic episode, the aim is to decrease hostility and return client to normal functioning (e.g. sleeping). Careful monitoring for changes in symptoms and side effects. When symptoms subside, a maintenance dose is prescribed: • Encourages socialisation, self-care and improves mood. • Combats relapse – relapse occurs in 18–32% who take medication, but in 60–80% who don't. • Continued for at least 12 months after remission (absence of symptoms).
Additional considerations	Amphetamines, alcohol, caffeine and nicotine can all disrupt the effectiveness of antipsychotic medications. Drug treatments often fail to bring relief to people who have experienced symptoms for many years – the first five years following an acute episode can lead to the most significant changes in the brain (Patel *et al.* 2014).

Apply it Concepts

Dr Fry has many clients with schizophrenia who have had treatment problems. Some do not take their medication, others still experience symptoms even when they are taking their medication and there is one who will not take tablets. A very small number have experienced side effects from the medication, both minor and severe ones.

1. (a) Explain **two** of Dr Fry's clients' problems with their medication. (4)

   (b) Describe **one** serious side effect which Dr Fry's clients may have experienced. (3)

2. Suggest **one** way to overcome **one** of Dr Fry's clients' problems. (4)

3. Context essay: Discuss why it may be difficult for Dr Fry to check her clients' adherence to biological treatment. (8)

A strength is good empirical evidence for drugs from a large meta-analysis.

Zhao et al. (2016) compared 18 antipsychotics using data from 56 randomised controlled trials (RCTs) with over 10,000 people.	They found that 17 of the antipsychotics tested had significantly lower relapse rates than placebo treatment.	This means that drug treatments for people with schizophrenia can help avoid the emotional and financial costs of hospital treatments.

CA 20% of people with schizophrenia show little improvement after multiple FGA trials and 45% experience partial or inadequate improvement and unacceptable side effects (Patel et al. 2014). Many people with schizophrenia who are taking drugs fail to function well in everyday life (e.g. most are unemployed).

Does animal research tell us anything about the human brain?

Side effects can lead to poor compliance and subsequent relapse.

A weakness is that much of the data comes from research with animals.

Kapur et al. (2000) point out that high doses of medication can be given to animals to block D2 receptors effectively (but these doses produce severe side effects in humans).	Animal models cannot show how such side effects would interfere with everyday life or whether this would lead to lack of compliance.	Therefore, lab research can't always replicate the lived experience of taking daily medication and coping with incapacitating side effects (which lead clients to stop taking medication).

Another weakness is that there is bias in some of the supporting evidence.

There is a publication bias towards studies showing a positive outcome of antipsychotic drugs (Turner et al. 2012).	Much research is funded by drug companies who promote continuing success of drugs.	Therefore, drug effectiveness is exaggerated, and doctors may make inappropriate treatment decisions.

Application: Drug treatment has led to de-institutionalisation.

The advent of antipsychotics (1950s) meant an enormous change in the way people with schizophrenia could live their lives.	People with a diagnosis of schizophrenia had the chance to remain in the community (avoiding institutionalisation and inability to cope).	This is important because segregation of people with mental health problems into hospitals increases stigmatisation through lack of contact with the rest of the community.

I&D extra: One relevant issue is that of social control.

Supporters of the anti-psychiatry movement call drug treatments 'chemical straitjackets' and suggest they lead to disempowerment.	They believe it is wrong that some people in society have the power to control others using drugs to change their behaviour.	This is an important alternative view, especially as people from nonindustrialised societies have better prognoses (i.e. sociocultural factors play a central role in shaping the outcome of the disorder).

Revision booster

The points you have learned as strengths and weaknesses can also be used to answer a 'compare' question. For example, consider that a strength of FGAs is being good at treating positive symptoms, this can be compared to a strength of SGAs which, in contrast, are good at additionally treating negative symptoms. Similarly, you could compare the effective doses of FGAs and SGAs and relative risks of side effects.

✓ Check it

1. Describe **one** biological treatment for schizophrenia. [4]

2. With reference to research evidence, explain **one** weakness of biological treatments for schizophrenia. [3]

3. **Standard essay:** Assess **one** biological treatment for schizophrenia. [8] or [20]

4. **Context essay:** Jordan has been prescribed daily medication for schizophrenia. Things have improved but his mother worries that he is still very socially withdrawn.

   To what extent is a full recovery likely if Jordan takes his medication as prescribed? [20]

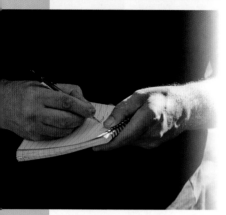

Note to self: remember to write note to self.

Fenn is attending CBT sessions for schizophrenia. He has delusions that he is from another planet and experiences hallucinations of a voice speaking to him from miles away. He believes nobody likes him and he rarely speaks to anyone as he is always waiting to hear the faraway voices.

1. **(a)** Suggest **one** way that CBT could help to combat Fenn's delusions. (3)

   (b) Suggest **one** way that CBT could help to combat Fenn's hallucinations. (3)

2. Explain how behavioural activation could help Fenn. (3)

3. **Context essay:** To what extent would **one** non-biological treatment help to relieve Fenn's symptoms? (20)

Cognitive-behavioural treatment (CBT) for schizophrenia	Key elements of CBT: • Cognitive approach (how a person thinks). • Learning approach to change behaviour (e.g. reinforcement). Commonly used to treat clients with schizophrenia usually in five to 20 sessions (group or individual).
Irrational thoughts	CBT helps client identify irrational thoughts and change them. Managing symptoms – people with schizophrenia lack coping skills, so are vulnerable to stress which then triggers relapse. Altering how the person thinks can help prevent *decompensation* (decline from normal functioning into a psychotic episode). Self-awareness is enhanced by the therapist by helping the client understand more about their condition – to recognise specific situations preceding decompensation and to learn to use coping strategies (e.g. meditation).
Delusions	People with schizophrenia typically experience delusions and hallucinations (related to irrational thinking). CBT helps make sense of how delusions and hallucinations affect feelings and behaviour. e.g. it is very scary to hear voices and believe they are demons – giving a non-biological explanation can help reduce anxiety.
Behavioural experiments	'Reality testing' is a kind of personal experiment: • Combats delusions and hallucinations by verbally challenging clients' perceived reality. • Client 'tests' whether delusions are real – often better than trying to talk client out of their false belief. e.g. a client who believes someone is trying to harm them could keep a record of evidence to support this. • Evidence is discussed to debunk false beliefs – helps client differentiate between 'confirmed reality' and 'perceived reality'.

Behavioural activation	Schizophrenia is linked with motivational deficits, e.g. social withdrawal and *anhedonia* (lack of enjoyment or pleasure).
	
	Can be reduced by rewarding positive behaviours.
	
	  e.g. becoming more socially active and expanding the activities the client is involved in.
	
	The client's sense of 'self' may also be addressed.
	
	  e.g. helping them recognise there are more ways to define themselves than 'I am schizophrenic'.

A strength is that CBT is supported by evidence from NICE.

NICE (2014) conducted a meta-analysis of high quality studies of CBT (e.g. randomised controlled trials) and found support for CBT.	Rehospitalisation rates were reduced (for up to 18 months), time spent in hospital reduced (average 8.26 days), symptom severity reduced (at the end of treatment and 12 months later).	This is good evidence to support the value of CBT as a treatment for schizophrenia.

A weakness is that CBT may not reduce symptoms or prevent relapse.

McKenna and Kingdon (2014) compared CBT with routine treatment or a control non-biological intervention.	CBT was only superior in two out of nine trials. In one of the studies with a positive result the blinding procedure lapsed (therefore the findings may not have been valid).	This suggests that CBT may not be as effective as the NICE (2014) report suggests.

Therapy session (aerial view).

CA However, meta-analyses using only quantitative data overlook the unique experiences of people in therapy. Whereas case studies which take an idiographic approach such as Bradshaw (1998), demonstrate that a strong relationship between CBT therapist and client, developed over many months, can support the process of personal recovery. This suggests that CBT can have value.

Another strength is support from studies of drug-resistant clients.

Kuipers *et al.* (1997) conducted a randomised controlled trial (RCT) of CBT for schizophrenia.	Drug-resistant clients improved when given CBT targeting their delusions and hallucinations.	This is important because many people with schizophrenia do not respond to antipsychotics (useful to have a second line of therapy to offer).

Application: CBT used to develop independent living skills.

CBT can target ways to improve a person's quality of life by discussing and developing personal and social skills.	This can be achieved through challenges to irrational thoughts, so the person relates better to others (plus specific use of social skills training).	This kind of approach offers a more long-lasting solution than drug therapy.

I&D extra: One issue relevant to CBT for people with schizophrenia is ethics.

CBT relies on collaboration between therapist and client.	But challenging a client's delusions can be distressing, so must be managed with sensitivity (also true of behavioural experiments).	This means that such aspects of the treatment must be approached with care (avoiding psychological harm).

Check it

1. Explain how **one** non-biological treatment could be used to target **one** specific symptom of schizophrenia. [3]

2. Explain **two** strengths of a non-biological treatment for schizophrenia. [4]

3. **Standard essay:** Assess **one** non-biological treatment for schizophrenia. [8] or [20]

4. **I&D essay/Synoptic:** Assess the scientific status of non-biological treatments of human behaviour. Your answer must refer to schizophrenia **and** phobias (from the learning theories topic). [20]

Spec spotlight

5.3.1 Classic study: Rosenhan (1973)
On being sane in insane places.

Tim Burton (director of films such as Edward Scissorhands), said, 'One person's craziness is another person's reality'.

Apply it Methods

Dr Kohl plans to find out whether GPs diagnose depression using just one symptom. He will ask his students to book appointments at their local surgery, saying they cry all the time, e.g. in lectures, at TV adverts and at night. The students had recently studied Rosenhan (1973) and identified three ethical points of concern:

Concern 1: The GPs' diagnoses will not be confidential.

Concern 2: Deception of the doctors.

Concern 3: A risk to future real patients once the doctors were aware of their previous errors.

1. Explain each of the **three** concerns identified by the students. (6)

2. **Context/Methods essay:** Discuss the ethical issues raised by Dr Kohl's study. (8)

Aims

To show that psychiatrists are unable to distinguish 'the sane from the insane'.

To provide evidence that 'mental disorders' lie not within the individual but in the diagnostic process.

Procedure

Initial study

- Pseudopatients visited 12 psychiatric hospitals (in five US states), hearing a voice saying 'empty', 'hollow' and 'thud'.
- All information pseudopatients gave was true (except to protect identity). If the pseudopatients were asked they said they were no longer hearing voices.
- Once admitted, pseudopatients behaved normally and kept records of observations.

Follow-up study

- Hospitals were told to expect pseudopatients (none sent).
- Staff rated every patient 1–10 (1 = patient was a fake).

Mini-experiment

- Pseudopatients approached a staff member in hospital grounds and asked a polite question about their release.
- Responses were compared with a similar encounter between people on the Stanford University campus.

Findings

Initial study

- All pseudopatients were admitted (seven with schizophrenia), most released with 'schizophrenia in remission'.
- Length of stay was 7 to 52 days (average 19 days).
- About 30% of real patients were suspicious of pseudopatients.

Follow-up study

- 41/193 patients wrongly reported as fake by at least one member of staff, 23 by at least one psychiatrist, and a further 19 by at least one psychiatrist and one other staff member.

Mini-experiment

- 4% of pseudopatients received an answer from a psychiatrist and 0.5% from a nurse.
- 100% people on campus stopped to talk.

Conclusions

'We cannot distinguish the sane from the insane in psychiatric hospitals' (Rosenhan).

Hospital environment created situational factors leading to depersonalisation and segregation.

Overdiagnosis occurred because clinicians avoided calling a sick person healthy (potentially dangerous).

But in the follow-up study, staff erred in the opposite direction to avoid labelling a healthy person as sick.

A strength of Rosenhan's study is that it was well-designed.

Rosenhan used covert participant observation and collected both qualitative and quantitative data.	Staff were unaware the pseudopatients were researchers, so their behaviour would have been more natural.	Therefore, the data had high ecological validity, enhanced by the wealth of data collected by naturalistic observation.

CA However, it could be argued that the validity of the study is poor. Pseudopatients may have only recorded instances of negative interactions between staff and patients as they were all supporters of Rosenhan. Also, there was only one pseudopatient per hospital so no way to check the reliability of the data each person collected.

A weakness is that demand characteristics may explain the diagnosis.

Psychiatrists admitted pseudopatients on flimsy evidence because they did not suspect someone would fake symptoms.	They would assume that anyone seeking admission must have a good reason to do so.	This may challenge the validity of some of the study's conclusions.

A strength of the study is it provided support for the anti-psychiatry movement.

Psychiatrist Szasz (1960) argued that mental illnesses are problems in living, not diseases, and therefore it is inappropriate to use a medical model for diagnosis of mental illness.	Rosenhan's study supported this because it showed that diagnosis of mental states was invalid. He also argued that labels for mental illness, once given, were 'sticky' so patients would forever be labelled 'schizophrenic'.	Thus the study shows a need for psychiatry reform, to avoid misuse of diagnostic labels. Rosenhan wanted to replace the system with a more behavioural approach to avoid labels.

Application: This study led to changes being made to the DSM-III.

Spitzer saw the DSM-III revision as an opportunity to address the issues raised by Rosenhan.	'…the issue of defining boundaries of mental and medical disorder cannot be ignored… there is pressure… [on] psychiatry…to define its area of prime responsibility' (Healy 1997).	Therefore, the study arguably paved the way for critical reforms to the diagnostic process, though this was not Rosenhan's intention.

I&D extra: One issue relevant to this study is ethics.

The study led to long-term benefits to society but there were risks to the pseudopatients, clinicians and real patients.	For example, clinicians were made to feel incompetent and real patients may have been discriminated against if clinicians believed they were fake (psychological harm).	These are important considerations as the benefits of scientific research should always be weighed carefully against potential harm to participants and society.

I told my psychiatrist that everyone hates me. He said I was being ridiculous – everyone hasn't met me yet.

 Check it

1. Describe Rosenhan's (1973) classic study. [5]

2. Explain **one** practical application of Rosenhan's (1973) classic study. [2]

3. **Standard essay:** Assess the classic study by Rosenhan (1973). [8] or [20]

4. **Review of studies essay:** Evaluate the psychological knowledge gained in the classic studies of Rosenhan (1973) and Watson and Rayner (1920) with regard to its use in society. [16]

Contemporary study on schizophrenia: Carlsson *et al.* (2000)

Spec spotlight

5.3.2 One contemporary study on schizophrenia: Carlsson et al. (2000) Network interactions in schizophrenia – therapeutic implications.

Hyperactive child – 'hypo' is the opposite.

Psychotic is another term used to describe schizophrenia – see explanation on page 42.

Apply it Concepts

Emma is using animals to study the role of neurotransmitters in schizophrenia, researching the idea that GABA and glutamate can have opposing effects on the release of dopamine. She is using M100907 and a new drug *Volinanserin*, which is a powerful serotonin receptor antagonist.

1. Explain why the new drug Volinanserin is of interest to Emma. (2)

2. **(a)** Emma tests the new drug on male and female animals. Explain why she does this. (2)

   (b) Emma tests the effectiveness of the different drugs in different countries. Explain why she does this. (3)

3. **Context/Methods essay:** Evaluate the use of animals in studies such as Emma's in clinical psychology. (8)

Aims	Review evidence for and against the *dopamine* hypothesis.
	Consider other neurotransmitters (e.g. *glutamate, serotonin*).
	Explore new antipsychotics (help with treatment resistance).
1. Dopamine hypothesis revisited	Evidence still supports this hypothesis, e.g. studies using PET scans show *amphetamine* (dopamine agonist) enhances psychotic symptoms. But this doesn't apply to all people with schizophrenia.
2. Beyond dopamine	Glutamate – *PCP* ('angel dust') induces schizophrenia-like symptoms, antagonist of *NDMA* (glutamate) *receptors*.
	Leads to increased dopamine activity (acts as 'accelerator').
3. Glutamatergic control of dopamine release	Glutamate also affects release of *GABA*, with opposite effect (a 'brake', reducing dopamine activity).
	Therefore, low glutamate (*hypoglutamatergia*) may cause an increase or decrease in dopamine.
	Normally there is a balance between 'accelerator' and 'brake' but disruption of either can produce schizophrenia symptoms.
4. Glutamate– dopamine interaction	Hypoglutamatergia in cerebral cortex → negative symptoms.
	Hypoglutamatergia in basal ganglia → positive symptoms.
	Dopamine + glutamate pathways interact and affect striatum.
5. Thalamic filter	In suggested *psychotogenic pathway* the *thalamus* may be 'turned' on or off depending on which pathway is activated.
	Normally the inhibitory glutamate pathway dominates.
6. Comparing two experimental schizophrenia models	1. Hyperdopaminergic model – traditional view of dopamine (increase produces psychotic symptoms) is not challenged by the second model, merely extended.
	2. Hypoglutamatergic model – glutamate can produce an increase or a decrease in dopamine activity, depending on whether the accelerator or the brake is applied.
	Haloperidol tackles hyperdopaminergia, M100907 tackles hypoglutamatergia (affecting GABA via serotonin).
	People with different symptoms could be treated with different drugs. Or use combined drugs to tackle both problems.
7. Is the therapeutic potential exhausted?	Understanding mechanisms that moderate dopamine activity may show new ways to stabilise dopamine system.
	May avoid some negative effects of current antipsychotics.
8. Concluding remarks	More attention could be focused on other neurotransmitters (e.g. *acetylcholine*) and other pathways in the brain.

AO3
Evaluation

Contemporary study on schizophrenia:
Carlsson et al. (2000)

55

A strength of the study is support from research on glutamate antagonists.

Carlsson and Carlsson (1989) gave mice a drug to reduce motor activity followed by MK-801 (reduces glutamate and increases serotonin and dopamine in the *nucleus accumbens*).

MK-801 restarted motor activity but continued use resulted in highly abnormal, psychotic-like behaviour.

This suggests that schizophrenia may be caused by glutamate irregularity and also implies that glutamate agonists may be effective treatments.

CA However, this is not the full story. Since the study, two further neurotransmitters (*anandamide* and *nitric oxide*) have been identified as important in psychosis and may lead to new treatments (Crippa et al. 2015). It has also been suggested that neurotransmitter imbalances may arise from autoimmune problems (Severance et al. 2018) – this means even glutamate is not the end of the story.

Striatum — Caudate nucleus / Putamen
Cerebral cortex
Globus pallidus
Subthalamic nucleus
Substantia nigra
Thalamus

A vertical (coronal) slice through the brain showing the key areas mentioned in this article. The basal ganglia consists of the five areas identified in red.

A weakness is that the research ignores the role of culture.

Luhrmann (2015) showed that US participants were more likely to hear violent and frightening voices whereas Ghanaian and Indian people had more positive experiences.

It may be that the review ignored cultural factors because the conclusions of the research studies in the review are based on animal models.

Thus animal models may fail to capture the holistic lived experience of schizophrenia, which includes other people's reactions to the symptoms (truer reflection).

Another weakness is that the evidence overlooks the wider experience.

Some evidence for the dopamine hypothesis was based on people with schizophrenia during acute episodes.

But people with chronic schizophrenia may respond differently to drugs when they are between episodes (e.g. more side effects).

Therefore, research should consider all the phases of the disorder so better conclusions can be made about efficacy and adherence.

Application: The research has led to the development of new drug treatments.

Serotonin antagonists and glutamate agonists are effective in reducing both positive and negative symptoms.

By tackling more precisely the disturbances of neurotransmitter systems, their action is less likely to have detrimental effects.

These advances have helped people who were treatment-resistant or who experienced side effects (e.g. *tardive dyskinesia*).

I&D extra: An issue relevant to this study is gender.

On average, age of onset for schizophrenia is later in women and prognosis is generally more positive.

The main female sex hormone *oestrogen* has a neuroprotective role which helps regulate glutamate, serotonin and dopamine (Gogos et al. 2015).

This suggests that gender-related oestrogen-based medications may provide yet another pathway for treating schizophrenia.

Revision booster

The links between neurotransmitters and their effects that are described in Carlsson et al.'s study are quite complex and the terms make them easy to confuse. Simplify the task of understanding the links by creating a flowchart of the neurotransmitters and changes they produce. You will need to interlink parts of the flowchart. Use different colours for the neurotransmitters, effects and drugs used to test them.

✓ Check it

1. Describe **one** aim and **one** conclusion of Carlsson et al.'s (2000) research study. (2)

2. Compare the classic and contemporary studies of Rosenhan (1973) and Carlsson et al. (2000). (4)

3. **Standard essay:** Assess Carlsson et al.'s (2000) study on schizophrenia. (8) or (20)

4. **Methods essay:** Assess the use of primary and secondary data in clinical psychology, with reference to the contemporary study of schizophrenia by Carlsson et al. (2000). (8) or (20)

Clinical psychology

Spec spotlight

5.2.3 The use of case studies, to include an example study: e.g. Lavarenne et al. *(2013) Containing psychotic patients with fragile boundaries: a single group case study.*

The purpose of this case study (and the interview study on the facing page) is to enable you to apply your understanding of case studies/interviews to an example study.

We discussed case studies in the Research methods chapter of the Year 1 Student book. A case study explores one event, group of people or person in depth. Qualitative data is usually collected (e.g. what people say or feel) and can be summarised by using examples. This can be turned into quantitative data by counting instances of themes.

Case studies allow us to study the complex interactions of many factors. However, it can be hard to generalise from individuals/groups because of their unique characteristics. Recall of past events can be unreliable and researchers may lack objectivity because of their involvement.

A famous case.

✓ Check it

1. Describe **two** features of case studies as a research method in clinical psychology. [4]

2. Explain **one** strength and **one** weakness of the case study as a research method in clinical psychology. [2]

3. **Methods essay:** Assess the use of case studies in clinical psychology. [8] or [20]

An example case study: Lavarenne *et al.* (2013)

Aims	To describe how a therapy group can provide a firm boundary (a container) within which individuals can explore their own fragile ego boundaries (i.e. their sense of self).
	The group aimed to develop a feeling of connectedness among individuals who are fairly isolated.

Procedure	Therapy group met regularly, usually with ten members (all with vulnerability to psychosis and receiving drug treatments).
	Four members were absent from this session, three had difficulty attending regularly.
	Sessions were not taped or video-recorded. Coding system recorded the emotions expressed (e.g. joy, sadness) as well as thoughts/behaviours (psychotic, manic or depressed).
	Verbal content was also coded (e.g. expressions of humour, loneliness, whether a person was engaged with the group).

Findings	**Earl**
	Reacted to Brett who gave everyone a Christmas card.
	His rejection of the gifts might represent his fear of being annihilated (self-disintegration).
	He responded by discussing a grandiose oil project running a pipeline around the world – interpreted as an attempt to hold the pieces of his self together, symbolising a way to identify a boundary between Earl's self and the selves of others.
	Running a pipeline round the world is analogous to a boundary around himself – choice of oil production may relate to a wish to merge his identity with that of his father (an oil engineer).

	Dan
	Had been silent for the first six months of attending the group but now didn't stop talking.
	Described an out-of-body experience where he was scared he wouldn't be able to get his spirit back into his body.
	May relate to him coping with demands from his girlfriend to clearly define the boundaries in their relationship.

Conclusions	Notes show that all group members were working hard to hold themselves together.
	Interactions with others threaten fragile boundaries – they cut off from human relations in the outer world, driving them more and more into an inner world of isolation (Earl).
	This session report showed an impressive tolerance, acceptance and containment from group members.
	This enabled group members to wrestle with their fragile egos and hopefully foster psychological growth.

An example interview: Vallentine et al. (2010)

Aims	Investigated usefulness of psychoeducational material as part of groupwork for patients in a high-security psychiatric hospital.
Procedure	42 male patients were referred to the *Understanding Mental Illness'* (UMI) psycho-educational group.
	Judged as either able to gain from further information and/or currently lacked insight about their condition.
	80% of the sample were diagnosed with schizophrenia, schizotypal and delusional disorders (ICD-10).
	Four 20-session UMI groups run over a period of three years.
	Patients were assessed pre- and post-group:
	• *Clinical outcomes in routine evaluation – Outcome measure* (CORE-OM) assesses subjective well-being, problems/symptoms, social/life functioning, risk to others.
	• *Self-concept questionnaire* (SCQ) assesses self-esteem.
	Also interviewed (semi-structured) to assess experience of the group (e.g. what patients felt they had gained).
	Interviews analysed by identifying themes, content analysis.
	Another rater repeated the analysis (60% average agreement).
Findings	Inferential statistics compared groups – those who completed the UMI (31 'completers') and non-completers – no significant differences found between groups on any of the tests.
	CORE-OM – clinically significant changes occurred across all four scales (only one participant showed a reliable change).
	SCQ – more cases of reliable change and over 50% reported improved self-esteem (some showed a negative shift).
	Data from interviews was analysed into four main categories:
	1. What participants valued and why (e.g. 'Knowing basic stuff gives peace of mind that you can get out, gives you hope').
	2. What was helpful about the group (e.g. 'It helped me understand symptoms and how different treatments help').
	3. Clinical implications identified by patients (e.g. 'If you know what's happening it helps you understand and calm down').
	4. What was difficult/unhelpful (e.g. 'It was difficult talking in front of the group').
Conclusions	Should further consider absence of reliable changes and the negative changes in some patients.
	Qualitative analysis of the interviews showed that patients did value the sense of hope and empowerment provided.

Spec spotlight

5.2.4 The use of interviews in clinical psychology, to include an example study: e.g. Vallentine et al. (2010) Psycho-educational group for detained offender patients: understanding mental illness.

When did you first notice you'd glued your fingers together, Mr Stevenson?

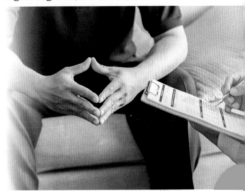

We discussed interviews in the Research methods chapter of the Year 1 Student book. Interviews may be structured (all questions determined in advance), unstructured (no questions determined in advance) or semi-structured (some questions determined in advance but most are follow-up questions related to the previous answers given).

Interviews are a useful way to find out what people think and feel. Such cognitive insights are important for diagnosis in clinical psychology. Interview data may lack validity because of a *social desirability bias* – people may wish to present themselves in a 'good light' and underplay their problems (or some people may exaggerate their symptoms to get attention).

Check it

1. Describe the use of interviews as a research method in clinical psychology. [4]

2. Compare the use of case studies and interviews in clinical psychology. [4]

3. **I&D/Synoptic essay:** Assess practical issues relating to the design and implementation of interviews as a research method. You must refer to clinical and social psychology in your answer. [20]

Anorexia nervosa: symptoms and features

Spec spotlight

Students study schizophrenia and one other disorder from anorexia nervosa, obsessive compulsive disorder and unipolar depression.

5.1.3 For anorexia nervosa: Description of symptoms and features.

Schizophrenia is a compulsory topic to study but the remaining three mental disorders (anorexia nervosa (AN), obsessive compulsive disorder (OCD) and unipolar depression) are options – you must study one of these three.

Anorexia can involve distorted perception of one's body shape and size.

Apply it
Concepts

Vince is researching young people's ability to judge their body image. He has a full-length distorting mirror that makes the reflection thinner or fatter. Participants control the mirror until they think their own image looks correct. He also asks participants to guess the calories in a snack they are offered for participating.

1. (a) Explain how a person with anorexia nervosa (AN) would be likely to adjust the mirror. (2)

   (b) Explain how a person with AN would judge the snack. (2)

2. Suggest **one** test Vince could use to explore his aim. (2)

3. **Context essay:** To what extent is a study such as Vince's adequate to explore symptoms of anorexia? (20)

Anorexia nervosa (AN)	Diagnosis under the DSM-5 requires all three symptoms below. ICD-10 overlaps with DSM-5, but there are also differences (e.g. unlike ICD-10, the DSM-5 includes measure of severity of disorder).
Three key symptoms	Symptom 1 – restriction of energy intake: • Significantly low body weight (for age, sex, etc.), though the DSM-5 does not specify how low. • ICD-10 defines it as 'maintained at least 15% below expected…or BMI (body mass index) is 17.5 or less'. Symptom 2 – fear of weight gain/interfering behaviours: • 'Intense fear of gaining weight or becoming fat' (DSM-5). • May behave in ways to prevent gaining weight (not just avoiding fattening foods). • ICD-10 includes self-induced vomiting and/or purging, excessive exercise, using appetite suppressants, etc. Symptom 3 – disturbed experience of body weight/shape: • Cognitive element, ICD-10 calls it 'body-image distortion'. • Weight and/or shape has a disproportionate influence on self-evaluation (how they perceive/feel about themselves). • May fail to recognise how serious their low body weight is.
Subtypes	*Restricting* subtype – no bingeing or purging (e.g. vomiting, laxative use) in the three months before diagnosis (DSM-5). Weight loss is achieved through dieting (e.g. one meal a day, one type/colour of food) and/or excessive exercise. *Binge-eating/purging* subtype – bingeing and/or purging in the previous three months (usually with restricting energy intake).
Severity	The DSM-5 also allows for assessment of severity in terms of BMI. Categories ('specifiers') of AN are mild (BMI >17), moderate (16–16.99), severe (15–15.99), extreme (<15).
Features of AN	Lifetime prevalence rate for females, 1.7–3.6% (0.1% in males). Incidence (rate of new cases) in 16–20-year age group, 6.05 new cases per 10,000-person years (i.e. total number of years people followed). Female incidence much higher than male. Prognosis – six times as many deaths as expected for females with AN (highest mortality of all mental disorders). Being younger and staying longer in hospital during first hospitalisation predicts better outcomes (survival and recovery).

A strength is evidence that diagnosis of AN using the DSM-5 is reliable.

Sysko et al. (2012) assessed participants by telephone interview using the DSM-5 criteria for AN, and repeated this with a different assessor a few days later.

The extent of agreement across the two occasions (test-retest reliability) was described by the researchers as 'excellent'.

This suggests that trained assessors can reliably diagnose AN using the DSM-5 criteria.

CA However, this finding does not necessarily support the view that the DSM-5 criteria for AN are reliable. Thomas et al. (2015) point out that many studies go beyond the DSM-5 criteria in operationally defining AN.

For instance, many use a researcher-defined cut-off point for 'significantly low weight' because none is specified in the DSM-5. This means reliability estimates in research studies are higher than they would be in real-life clinical practice (because it is easier to achieve agreement between raters when criteria are defined in detail).

A weakness is that the DMS-5's severity ratings may lack validity.

Smith et al. (2017) looked at the validity of the four severity specifiers (see facing page).

In 109 adults diagnosed with AN, higher BMI (low severity) was linked to *greater* eating disorder psychopathology – the opposite of the expected outcome.

This is an issue for the DSM-5 severity specifiers, as they fail to distinguish accurately between people and therefore lack validity.

People with anorexia monitor every mouthful.

Revision booster

You will have studied schizophrenia in addition to anorexia nervosa. In order to avoid confusing the symptoms and features of each, draw a two-column table listing the key symptoms/features of each disorder, one in each column. It is possible to make comparisons between some of the symptoms/features, such as looking at cognitive symptoms and at gender issues. Making a note of these comparisons in a third column will be invaluable for answering 'comparison' questions.

Case studies of anorexia nervosa

Carol is a typical 16-year-old in most ways but she has anorexia nervosa. She almost always makes some reference to her body size and shape when she talks about herself. She pays a lot of attention to details, and this includes her weight which she is always 'keeping an eye on'. She avoids 'fatty foods'. But this includes foods she knows are good for her but 'make her feel fat'. She frequently skips meals, eating rice cakes to fill up and continuing to lose weight.

She doesn't see it, but Carol is actually really very thin. Her friends tell her she is too skinny but she takes no notice and thinks they are just 'jealous'. Her hair is falling out, she bruises easily and she has no energy.

Joan developed anorexia when she was 29 years old. She lived with her parents after her marriage broke up, and they looked after her and her son Charlie. This made Joan feel more like Charlie's sister than his mum. After a disastrous relationship with an alcoholic Joan started a strict diet to lose some weight. She had a cup of coffee and a muffin during the day and then very little for dinner with her parents. She regularly used laxatives after eating. She still thought about food constantly, and would cook elaborate meals for the family. Joan weighed just 45 kilos but still felt overweight and developed an overwhelming fear of getting fat. She felt her weight was the only thing in her life she could control.

Adapted from Oltmanns et al. (2011)

Check it

You have studied **one** disorder other than schizophrenia.

1. Describe **two** features of this disorder. [4]

2. Explain **one** practical issue relating to the diagnosis of this disorder. [2]

3. **Standard essay:** Evaluate the reliability and/or validity of the diagnosis of this disorder. [8] or [20]

4. **Methods essay:** Evaluate the use of **two** different research methods to investigate this disorder. You must include at least **one** comparison of the two methods in your answer. [8] or [20]

Anorexia nervosa: One biological explanation

Spec spotlight

5.1.3 For anorexia nervosa: One biological theory/explanation.

Genetic explanation for anorexia nervosa (AN)

AN runs in families – it is rare in first-degree relatives of people who never had an eating disorder, but 11.3 times more common in relatives of those who have had an eating disorder (Strober *et al.* 2000).

Heritability of AN as high as 70% (Gorwood *et al.* 2003).

EPHX2 and ITPR3 regulate aspects of eating behaviour and metabolism, and both are disrupted in AN – is this just a coincidence?

Genes and anorexia

EPHX2 gene

- Codes for the enzyme *epoxide hydrolase* which regulates cholesterol metabolism.
- Many people in the acute phase of AN (severe symptoms) have abnormally high levels of cholesterol.
- Scott-Van Zeeland *et al.* (2014) sequenced 152 candidate genes, EPHX2 significantly linked with AN.
- Inherited variant of EPHX2 gene may cause overactivity of epoxide hydrolase, disrupting metabolism of cholesterol and other fatty acids.

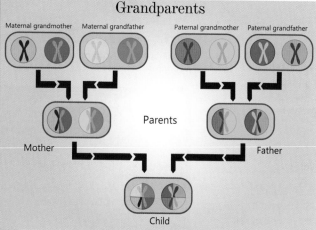

Could eating disorders like anorexia be inherited?

ITPR3 gene

- Encodes a protein which is a receptor for *inositol triphosphate* (detecting e.g. sweet and bitter tastes).
- May be a genetically-determined dysfunction of the taste pathway so people with AN indifferent to tastes that others enjoy and that partly motivate eating.

Genes and neurotransmitters

Genes and *dopamine*

- *DAT1* gene codes for a protein called the *dopamine transporter* (regulates movement of dopamine in reuptake).
- Mutation in the DAT1 gene disrupts this process, leaving abnormally high dopamine for transmission.
- Dysregulates the brain's reward systems (*mesocorticolimbic dopamine circuit*) so eating's normal rewarding function is impaired.

Apply it Concepts

Ekta has been testing candidate genes that may be involved in anorexia nervosa and believes she has found one that relates to the perception of body image, weight and shape. She wants to collect primary data by interviewing individuals with anorexia nervosa who have the candidate gene.

1. (a) Describe how Ekta can collect her primary data. (6)
   (b) Explain **one** benefit of using the procedure you described in part (a). (2)

2. Suggest **one** reason why using a questionnaire may be more suitable in Ekta's study. (2)

3. **Context/Methods essay:** Discuss how Ekta could collect her primary data. (8)

Genes and *serotonin*

- *5-HTR2A* gene codes for a subtype of postsynaptic serotonin receptor called the *5-HT2A receptor*.
- Mutation in the 5-HTR2A gene affects the structure of the 2A receptor – less binding between serotonin and receptor (appetite-related information is not transmitted normally).
- Kaye *et al.* (2005) found significantly decreased 5-HT2A activity in the serotonergic system throughout the brains of people with AN (especially in the *cingulate cortex*).

A strength of the genetic explanation is research support from twin studies.

For example, Holland et al. (1988) found AN concordance rates of 56% for MZs and 5% for DZs.

This study was replicated by Treasure and Holland (1995) and confirmed the earlier findings, with MZ concordance of 65% and 32% for DZs.

This provides good support as the twin study method is a convincing means of demonstrating genetic influences on disorders such as AN.

Identical treatment?

A weakness is twin studies depend on the equal environments assumption.

We assume MZ and DZ twins are treated with equal levels of similarity. But Joseph (2002) argues that MZs are treated more similarly than DZs.

MZs look more similar to each other and have more similar personality traits, so they elicit more similar behaviours from parents (e.g. dietary habits).

This greater environmental similarity means heritability estimates are inflated and genetic influences are not as great as studies suggest.

CA However, other psychologists argue there is little evidence that the equal environments assumption is violated in twin studies (Thornton et al. 2010). Are the ways in which MZs are treated more similar than DZs relevant to the causes of AN? Klump et al. (2000) found that MZ twins were no more likely to have similar attitudes towards eating than non-identical family members. The researchers concluded that their findings support the equal environments assumption for AN.

Another weakness is that AN is polygenic.

No one gene can explain the wide range of physical, cognitive and behavioural symptoms of AN (e.g. as defined by the DSM-5 or ICD-10).

AN is polygenic – many genes make modest but important contributions. It is likely that genes contribute to the various symptoms of AN to differing degrees.

This shows that the true picture of the causes of AN is complex, and any theory that seeks to explain the disorder in terms of one cause risks oversimplification.

Application: Understanding genes helps with prevention and treatment of AN.

Knowing someone's genetic profile could mean prevention and treatment (e.g. new drugs) are targeted more effectively at people most vulnerable to developing AN.

This is a long way in the future, but recent findings are a step in this direction and may help to improve current treatments.

This shows the value of the genetic explanation because treatments based on it may improve quality of life, reduce distress and avoid needless deaths.

I&D extra: Genetics throws light on the issue of nature and nurture.

Abraham (2008) argues that genes may create a diathesis (vulnerability) to AN that is only expressed when an individual tries to lose weight (a stressor).

Perhaps the diathesis (genes) makes the person vulnerable to disordered eating, but environmental factors influence the exact type of disorder.

Thus the effects of genes (nature) must be seen in the context of wider social, cultural and psychological influences (nurture).

Revision booster

You need to know 'one biological explanation' for anorexia nervosa. If genes are your chosen explanation then make sure that is what you stick to. If you mention neurotransmitters this could appear to be a second, different explanation. It is essential to make it clear to the examiner that you understand that neurotransmitters are part of the genetic explanation because genes underpin the action of neurotransmitters by controlling levels and receptors.

✓ Check it

You have studied **one** disorder other than schizophrenia.

1. Describe **one** biological explanation for this disorder. [3]

2. Explain **two** strengths of a biological explanation for this disorder. [4]

3. **Standard essay:** Assess **one** biological explanation for this disorder. [8] or [20]

4. **I&D essay:** Evaluate the role of nature and nurture as a cause of **one** disorder other than schizophrenia. [16]

Anorexia nervosa: One non-biological explanation

A01
Description

Spec spotlight

5.1.3 For anorexia nervosa: One non-biological theory/explanation.

Impaired global processing might be described as an inability to see the wood for the trees.

Cognitive explanation for anorexia nervosa (AN)	Core cognitive psychopathology is distorted perception of body shape/weight. Gives rise to all clinical features (Murphy *et al.* 2010).
Cognitive distortions and biases	People with AN are critical of their own body shape and misinterpret emotional states as 'feeling fat' – due to distorted body *schema* (Gadsby 2017): <ul><li>Mental representation of body size, shape, position.</li><li>Internal cognitive structure, continually updated.</li><li>Central to self-image but distorted in AN because it represents the body as bigger than it really is – affects how a person with AN interacts with their environment.</li></ul> Guardia *et al.* (2012) study (page 70) illustrates this: <ul><li>AN participants imagined walking through a doorway.</li><li>Compared with a control group, they overestimated their body size when imagining passing through a doorway.</li><li>But when asked to imagine the researcher walking through a doorway, they were accurate.</li></ul>
Irrational beliefs	Irrational beliefs and attitudes are a common feature of AN – giving rise to automatic negative thoughts (Beck 1991): <ul><li>*All-or-nothing thinking* – 'If I don't control my weight, I'm worthless'.</li><li>*Catastrophising* – putting the worst interpretation on events, 'I ate half a biscuit today, I've got no willpower'.</li></ul> For a minority of those with AN the fear of gaining weight (a dominant core belief) is so extreme it is 'delusional' (Steinglass *et al.* 2007) – this makes them highly resistant to treatment.
Impaired global processing	Ability to integrate details into a meaningful overall pattern (*global processing*) is impaired in people with AN. They find it hard to see the 'bigger picture', i.e. how details fit together – so they cannot perceive overall body shape accurately.
Enhanced local processing	At the same time, people with AN have a superior 'eye for detail' (enhanced *local processing*). An advantage in some situations, but works against the person with AN because they focus on tiny 'flaws' (e.g. 'fat eyelids'). *Weak central coherence* <ul><li>Combination of impaired global processing and enhanced local processing.</li><li>A cognitive deficit which may be an inherited vulnerability to developing AN, especially alongside other deficits.</li></ul>

Apply it Concepts

Cari writes a diary every day. It has entries such as 'Monday: I have fat toes. Tuesday: I imagined myself in a wedding dress and I looked like a white balloon. Friday: In a bikini I can see my blubber spilling out round the sides. It's because yesterday I ate celery AND lettuce.'

1. Explain how **one** of Cari's observations could be explained by **one** non-biological explanation. (2)

2. Identify **one** other symptom that Cari might experience and explain this using **one** non-biological explanation. (3)

3. **Context essay:** Discuss how **one** non-biological explanation would explain Cari's symptoms. (8)

A strength is research support for the role of cognitive distortions in AN.

Sachdev et al. (2008) used fMRI scanning to show that the same brain areas were activated in AN and non-AN participants when they were shown images of other people's bodies.

But when shown images of their own bodies, AN participants experienced less activation in areas of the brain thought to be involved in attention.

This confirms Gadsby's prediction that cognitive distortion is limited to the individual's own body image and does not extend to bodies in general.

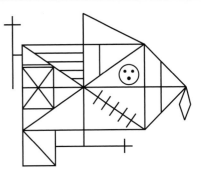

An item from the Rey–Osterrieth Complex Figures Test (ROCFT), used by Lang et al. (2016) in their study (see left). Participants have to copy the drawing from memory. People with AN often show poor memory of the overall pattern but strong recall of the details. This is evidence of weak central coherence, a cognitive deficit. But Lang et al. believe it is an outcome of AN and not a cause of it.

A weakness is that deficits could be outcomes of AN and not causes.

Lang et al. (2016) found no differences between recovered AN participants and non-AN controls on the ROCFT, a measure of local and global processing.

This showed that weak central coherence could be the result of starvation in AN (rather than a cause of AN), hence why it persists after recovery.

This suggests that cognitive theory lacks validity because it cannot explain the causes of AN (an alternative theory might be preferable).

CA However, Hamatani et al. (2018) found that AN participants' poor performance on the ROCFT remained even when the researchers statistically controlled for the effects of the symptoms (e.g. starvation, depression). So weak central coherence was not a consequence of the symptoms, and could be a cognitive cause of AN.

Another weakness is that there are conflicting findings.

Cornelissen et al.'s (2013) participants adjusted a computerised image of themselves until it matched their estimate of their body size.

There were no significant differences between AN participants and non-AN controls, so having AN did not worsen the ability to estimate body size.

This challenges the central role of body image distortion in cognitive theories of AN.

Revision booster

When answering a question about an explanation/theory, think about the different 'stages' or 'concepts' in the theory. Aiming to cover each of these will provide you with structure for your answer and cue you to find links between the explanation and the context if one is given.

Application: Several cognitive therapies have been developed to treat AN.

Cognitive-behavioural treatment (CBT) changes the client's distorted cognitions and irrational beliefs about food, eating, weight loss and body size/shape.

Dalle Grave et al. (2014) found that enhanced CBT led to a large increase in weight and a decrease in concerns about body shape in hospitalised AN participants.

This demonstrates the validity of predictions derived from the cognitive theory of AN as an explanation of the disorder.

✓ Check it

You have studied **one** disorder other than schizophrenia.

1. Describe **two** features of **one** non-biological explanation for this disorder. [4]

2. Compare **one** biological and **one** non-biological explanation for this disorder. [4]

3. **Standard essay:** Assess **one** non-biological explanation for this disorder. [8] or [20]

4. **I&D/Synoptic essay:** Assess **two** ways that psychological knowledge has developed over time. You must refer to **one** disorder other than schizophrenia and to social psychology in your answer. [20]

I&D extra: This research shows how psychological understanding has developed.

In their research, psychologists initially focused attention on body image distortions.

They eventually tried to explain them in terms of underlying deficits in cognitive processing (e.g. weak central coherence).

The next step is to formulate theories that integrate these factors and show how they are affected by non-cognitive influences (e.g. mood).

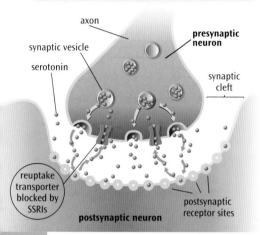

axon

presynaptic neuron

synaptic vesicle

serotonin

synaptic cleft

reuptake transporter blocked by SSRIs

postsynaptic neuron

postsynaptic receptor sites

Diagram showing how SSRIs work, blocking the reuptake of serotonin at the presynaptic neuron. This increases the amount of serotonin in the synaptic cleft so there is more there to stimulate the postsynaptic neuron, thus improving mood.

Apply it Concepts

Klee has been diagnosed with anorexia nervosa (AN) and his parents are worried about his drug therapy. He is taking SGAs and is gaining weight but they think this is not solving the real problem. He is unhappy because he feels greedy as he cannot ignore feeling hungry.

1. (a) Give an explanation to Klee's parents to tell them how SGAs should work. (4)
   (b) Explain why SGAs may not work well for Klee. (3)
2. Justify the use of a different drug for Klee. (3)
3. Context essay: Discuss possible biological treatments for Klee. (8)

Drug treatments for anorexia nervosa (AN)

Biochemical mechanisms underlie AN (e.g. abnormal levels of *dopamine* and *serotonin*), therefore altering neurotransmitter activity may benefit AN symptoms.

Antidepressants

Serotonin levels low in AN.

Drug increases serotonin in the synapse.

SSRIs (*selective serotonin reuptake inhibitors*):

- Low serotonin may be a direct cause of AN or may be because AN is co-morbid with depression.
- Serotonin molecules remaining in the synapse are normally removed by the process of reuptake.
- They are taken back into the presynaptic neuron through the serotonin transporter.
- This process is blocked by SSRIs – therefore excess serotonin is not recycled, instead it stays in the synapse and repeatedly binds with postsynaptic receptors.
- Extends the appetite-enhancing effects of serotonin.

SNRIs (*serotonin-noradrenaline reuptake inhibitors*):

- Work in a similar way to SSRIs but target *noradrenaline* as well as serotonin (inhibiting reuptake of both).
- Suggests that low serotonin is not the only neurotransmitter dysfunction in AN.

Antipsychotics

Dopamine abnormally high in AN.

Drug decreases dopamine in the synapse.

Mostly dopamine antagonists, e.g. *chlorpromazine*, block postsynaptic dopamine receptors without activating them, reducing overall dopamine activity.

- Counter distorted cognitions about fatness (similar to delusions experienced in schizophrenia).
- Counter reduced appetite resulting from disrupted dopamine system.

SGAs (atypical second-generation antipsychotics) e.g. *olanzapine*:

- Causes weight gain when used to treat schizophrenia and bipolar disorder (a form of depression where there are alternating periods of being manic).
- May reduce 'anorexic ruminations' in people with AN (obsessive thoughts about food, body size and shape).
- Is a powerful dopamine antagonist but also a weak serotonin antagonist.
- May influence AN symptoms by blocking *D2* or *D3 dopamine receptors* and serotonin *5-HT2A receptors*.
- May increase secretion of the hormone *ghrelin* (increased ghrelin linked to decrease in feelings of fullness after eating, encouraging further food intake, van der Zwaal et al. 2012).

A strength is supporting evidence from case studies of SGAs.

Boachie et al. (2003) used olanzapine to treat four children with AN.

They gained weight (average of under one kilo per week) and also experienced less anxiety at mealtimes, with few side effects.

This highlights the potential of olanzapine, suggesting an effective drug treatment may finally be within reach.

CA However, case studies are limited because they have no control group. The gold standard for effectiveness testing is the randomised controlled trial (RCT). The findings from RCTs have been mixed. Kafantaris et al. (2011) found that 15 adolescents given olanzapine gained weight and showed improved eating attitudes. But so did the participants in the control group, and at the same rate.

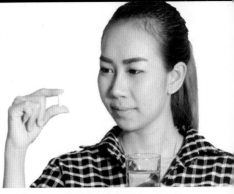

The current state of drug treatment for AN is neatly summed up by the National Institute for Clinical Excellence (NICE 2017): 'Do not offer medication as the sole treatment for anorexia nervosa'.

A weakness is contrary evidence of poor effectiveness from a meta-analysis.

Lebow et al. (2013) found that people with AN who take SGAs showed increases in BMI and body satisfaction.

But the AN participants did not significantly differ from placebo participants. The drugs were linked with *greater* anxiety and *worse* overall symptoms.

These negative outcomes cast doubt on the effectiveness of the most promising class of drugs to treat AN.

Another weakness is that drugs focus on symptoms of AN and not causes.

Drugs may reduce symptoms of AN that maintain the disorder by stabilising dysfunctional neurotransmitter systems in the brain.

But a temporary and reversible reduction in symptoms is not the same as treating the cause (ultimately genetic or psychological).

Therefore, a psychological therapy such as CBT might be preferable (with fewer side effects).

Application: Drugs for AN have side effects but they can be managed.

Most side effects are mild to moderate (e.g. dry mouth and headache), some are serious but rare (e.g. type 2 diabetes).

Side effects can be controlled and/or reduced through monitoring, adjustment of dose and in some cases additional medication.

This knowledge of side effects increases acceptability of medication for people with AN, so they are more likely to continue treatment.

Check it

You have studied **one** disorder other than schizophrenia.

1. Explain how symptoms of this disorder may be treated using a biological treatment. [2]

2. Explain **one** ethical issue relating to the use of biological treatments for this disorder. [2]

3. **Standard essay:** Evaluate **one** biological treatment for this disorder. [8] or [20]

4. **Methods essay:** Assess the use of case studies and meta-analyses as research methods in clinical psychology. Refer to biological treatments in your answer. [8] or [20]

I&D extra: Drug treatment for AN illustrates important ethical considerations.

An ethical benefit of drug treatment is that it encourages a perception that AN is a medical disorder and not a result of psychological weakness.

The ethical benefit is that the disorder becomes less stigmatised as more people realise that the symptoms of AN are not the person's 'fault'.

This encourages more affected individuals to seek treatment without fear of being blamed.

Anorexia nervosa: One non-biological treatment

Spec spotlight

5.1.4 For anorexia nervosa: One non-biological treatment.

Not all people with AN suffer from low self-esteem. But the broad type of CBT-E can help those who do.

Cognitive-behavioural treatment (CBT) for AN

CBT is the leading evidence-based therapy of choice for anorexia nervosa (AN).

Makes sense as core psychopathology of AN is cognitive (an overevaluation of the importance of body shape and weight).

Enhanced CBT (CBT-E)

Fairburn (2008), outpatient therapy for all eating disorders.

'Enhanced' as it uses newer strategies rooted in cognitive theory.

Two types

- *Broad* type (CBT-Eb) – treats core pathology of AN (overevaluation of body shape/weight) plus other symptoms 'external' to the core. Suitable for e.g. clients with low self-esteem or perfectionism.
- *Focused* type (CBT-Ef) – does not tackle external symptoms (default treatment for most clients).

Two intensities

- 40 sessions over 40 weeks for BMI < 17.5.
- 20 sessions over 20 weeks for BMI > 17.5.

Stages of CBT-E

Four stages (Murphy et al. 2010).

Stage 1 'Start well' – intensive (good start predicts success):

- Client and therapist together identify main AN-related cognitions and behaviours.
- Two elements introduced – 'weekly weighing' (only weighing time, recorded on a graph) and 'regular eating' (client and therapist devise specific times for eating).

Stage 2 Brief stage – client and therapist review progress:

- Identify barriers to change and plan stage 3.
- Switch to broad CBT-E if 'external' symptoms appear.

Stage 3 – How self-evaluation depends on body weight/shape:

- Client learns to focus instead on other areas of their lives.
- Dietary rules identified (e.g. avoiding certain foods).
- Therapist helps client break rules using behavioural experiments (and then learn that breaking rules doesn't have to lead to weight gain).

Stage 4 'End well' – maintain progress and prevent relapse:

- Weekly weighing continues at home.
- Client and therapist plan next 20 weeks before a follow-up session.
- Client continues with rule-breaking and avoiding body-checking, realistic about relapse (inevitable but can overcome).

Apply it Concepts

Beth feels she is a failure. She is sure it is possible to be perfect but she seems unable to get everything exactly right. Her BMI is under 17.5. She has a rule that she can eat white, red or green food but not yellow or brown food. Her therapist sets her homework to replace her small portions of (white) rice with the same amount of pasta.

1. (a) Suggest **one** reason why a non-biological treatment could help Beth. (2)

   (b) Explain how **one** of Beth's physical symptoms could affect her non-biological treatment. (1)

2. Explain **one** way in which Beth's therapist is using a non-biological treatment. (3)

3. **Context essay:** You will have studied **one** disorder other than schizophrenia.

   Discuss how Beth could be helped by **one** non-biological treatment for anorexia. (8)

A strength is research support for CBT-E as an effective therapy.

Fairburn *et al.* (2015) randomly allocated 130 participants with eating disorders to either CBT-E or interpersonal psychotherapy (IPT).

After 20 weeks, 65.5% of CBT-E and 33.3% of IPT participants were 'in remission'. After 60 weeks, 69.4% for CBT-E and 49% for IPT.

This shows CBT-E is more effective (and quicker) for the majority of people with AN than the well-established IPT.

CA However, all of the participants had a BMI above 17.5 so were not seriously underweight. It is unclear whether CBT-E is as effective for severely underweight people. On the other hand, the UK's National Institute for Clinical Excellence (NICE 2017) considers CBT-E effective enough to recommend it for adults with AN.

'Normalisation of eating' procedures may be more effective than cognitive elements of CBT.

A weakness is research challenging the cognitive element of CBT.

Södersten *et al.* (2017) compared CBT and a 'normalisation of eating' procedure giving clients feedback at mealtimes to encourage normal eating behaviour.

The remission rate was 75% and relapse was just 10% over five years for normalisation (compared with a remission rate of 45% and relapse of 30% for CBT).

This strongly implies that the behavioural elements of therapy are sufficient and the cognitive element is not necessary to improve AN symptoms.

Another weakness is lack of treatment adherence for CBT.

CBT dropout rates are high because it is a demanding therapy, especially the intensive form of CBT-E (in terms of attendance and homework).

Clients have to make difficult changes to their behaviour and thought processes. Carter *et al.* (2012) found 45% dropout for a CBT-E programme.

This means that, overall, the effectiveness of the therapy is considerably enhanced in research results as only 'completers' are included in any research sample.

✓ Check it

You have studied **one** disorder other than schizophrenia.

1. Longitudinal studies are a research method that is used in clinical psychology.

   Explain how you could use this research method to determine the success rate of a non-biological treatment for a disorder other than schizophrenia. [3]

Application: Research participants with AN require extra ethical care.

People with AN experience intense fear of becoming 'fat' and their perception of 'fat' is distorted.

So 'improvement' (gaining weight) creates anxiety for them – successful therapy represents a step towards something they are very frightened of.

Therefore, understanding the experience of AN helps researchers to support vulnerable participants taking part in research.

2. Explain **two** strengths of **one** non-biological treatment for this disorder. [4]

3. **Standard essay:** Evaluate **one** non-biological treatment for this disorder. [8] or [20]

I&D extra: CBT-E to treat AN illustrates the issue of gender in psychology.

Research participants (diagnosed with AN) are nearly always female, so there are too few males for any meaningful conclusions to be drawn about gender differences.

For example, in Fairburn *et al.*'s (2015) study, only three out of 130 participants were males.

There are implications for therapy because the female therapists are better for female clients (provide role model), but this may be problematic for male clients.

4. **I&D essay:** Assess the use of psychological knowledge in society. You must refer to **one** disorder other than schizophrenia in your answer. [20]

Contemporary study on anorexia
Scott-Van Zeeland et al. (2013)

Spec spotlight

5.3.5 One contemporary study: Scott-Van Zeeland et al. (2013) Evidence for the role of EPHX2 gene variants in anorexia nervosa.

She's an example of an SNP! Different kind though, obvs.

SNP stands for single nucleotide polymorphisms. These are genetic markers (small variations) on a person's DNA.

A person's phenotype is their characteristics as determined by both genes and the environment. 'Genotype' refers to their genes only.

 **Concepts**

Dr Rose has conducted a genetic study of males with anorexia nervosa (AN) and a control group. She has identified some gene variants that appear to be important, but her findings show that, in males, these gene variants are not the only factor contributing to AN.

1. Dr Rose's study was an experiment. Describe the independent variable. (4)

2. (a) Justify **two** characteristics that would be important in selecting the control group. (3)

   (b) Explain the potential effect of **one** other extraneous variable that could have affected Dr Rose's study. (2)

3. **Context/Methods essay:** Evaluate the use of experiments, including Dr Rose's, to study **one** disorder other than schizophrenia. (8)

Aims

Genome-wide association study (GWAS) to identify genes related to anorexia nervosa (AN).

Identify those SNPs more frequent in people with AN than in controls.

Procedure

Initial sequencing study ('discovery phase'):

- Sample – 300 women with AN + 100 controls, psychological tests for depression, anxiety and eating disorder symptoms.
- Only high-quality DNA used (so 262 AN, 80 controls).

1. Pooling-based replication study:
   - Sample – 500 AN + 500 controls + data from earlier GWAS.
   - Created 50 'pools' each containing DNA from 20 individuals (= 1000 participants). Half were participants with AN, half were control participants.
   - After exclusions for quality, 4,798 variants were left.

2. Single-locus replication study:
   - Replicated procedures again to 'fill in' missing data.
   - Used sequenced genotypes from the *Bogalusa Heart Study* and the *Scripps Genomic Health Initiative*.

3. Other analyses:
   - Longitudinal – SNP impact on AN symptoms (phenotype).
   - Links between SNPs and BMI and e.g. cholesterol levels.
   - *Allen Brain Atlas* – used to identify brain areas in which genes associated with AN were under- or over-expressed.

Findings

Initial sequencing, two significant sets of variants:

- 35 in *ITPR3*, encodes protein detecting tastes e.g. sweet.
- 14 in *EPHX2*, encodes *epoxide hydrolase*, metabolises fats.

Pooling-based replication:

- 8 of the 14 EPHX2 variants also identified at this stage.
- Variants of *ESR2* identified, encodes oestrogen receptors.

EPHX2 variant highly expressed in brain areas related to:

- Feeding (e.g. *hypothalamus*) and anxiety (e.g. *amygdala*).
- Male/female differences (*corpus callosum, hippocampus*).

Conclusions

AN likely to be caused by complex interacting influences, including genetic variants and environmental/social factors.

Rare variants of the EPHX2 gene involved in AN, expressed in cholesterol functioning and key brain areas.

EPHX2 also regulates expression of epoxide hydrolase in liver and kidney tissues (fats and carbohydrates disrupted in AN).

A strength is that this was a highly reliable study.

It used standardised procedures at all stages, including a common and well-established GWAS protocol.	All procedures were carried out consistently and all DNA samples subjected to the same processes.	This means enough detail is provided for other researchers to replicate the study and support the validity of the findings.

CA That said, the researchers themselves point out that their study is exploratory, so the findings are provisional. The key to establishing the EPHX2 gene's involvement in AN is replication. It is important to replicate the study to show that the findings are not a 'one off'. But replicating GWASs is hard because it requires many resources.

A weakness of the study is its lack of functional significance.

GWASs discover genetic variants by identifying which occur more frequently in people with AN than in a control population.	But this is not the same as identifying the systems and processes involved in making someone susceptible to AN (e.g. neural pathways affected by the variants).	This means that, although GWASs are a crucial first step, further research is needed using methods such as brain scanning and animal models.

Anorexia nervosa is a complex puzzle, with many missing pieces.

Another strength is that the study used stringent quality control procedures.

Samples with more than 10% missing SNPs were excluded. The DNA of participants was compared to a database (the *International HapMap Project*).	This meant the study included only participants of European descent, making the sample genetically homogenous (similar) and easier to spot differences in DNA.	These procedures ensured the researchers were working with high-quality samples that gave them the best chance to identify genetic variants.

Application: The study could lead to improved treatments for AN.

For example, the study highlighted the link between the EPHX2 gene and cholesterol metabolism in AN.	By identifying genetic variants, researchers can focus on this link to develop an effective drug treatment (potentially targeting an individual's cholesterol profile).	These new treatments could bring greater quality of life to individuals with AN, especially as it has the highest mortality rate of any mental disorder.

I&D extra: The study illustrates psychology as a science.

It used standardised and quality-controlled procedures to test hypotheses about which genetic variants might be involved in AN.	It also took into account previous findings about links between AN, anxiety and depression (to explain the full AN phenotype). Also used objective measures.	This shows how using an objective scientific approach makes studying the genetics of AN possible.

Check it

You have studied **one** contemporary study of **one** disorder other than schizophrenia.

1. Justify **one** design decision in the procedure of this contemporary study. [2]

2. Explain **one** weakness of this contemporary study. [4]

3. **Standard essay:** Assess this contemporary study. [8] or [20]

4. **Standard plus essay:** Evaluate this contemporary study with reference to reliability and validity. [20]

Contemporary study on anorexia: Guardia *et al.* (2012)

Spec spotlight

5.3.6 One contemporary study: Guardia et al. (2012) Imagining one's own and someone else's body actions: Dissociation in anorexia nervosa.

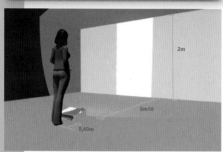

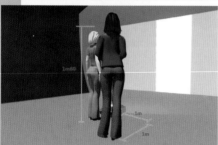

The 1PP condition is shown at the top and the 3PP condition is below.

Concepts

Dr Ross is measuring imagined and actual passability ratios in participants diagnosed with anorexia nervosa (AN). Relative to controls, he found they had higher ratios on both tests: they believed they were wider than they really were and behaved as if this was true (by turning sideways). Dr Ross was surprised because the passability ratios of the participants with AN correlated positively with their weight recovery.

1. (a) Explain the AN participants' high passability ratios. (4)
   (b) Explain why the correlation with weight recovery was a surprising result. (2)

2. Explain which of Dr Ross' tests was more valid. (3)

3. **Context essay:** Discuss how **one** contemporary study of **one** disorder other than schizophrenia could help to explain the findings of Dr Ross' study. (8)

Aims

To see if people with anorexia nervosa (AN) overestimate body size even in action.

To see if AN overestimation of body size extends to bodies in general or is limited to their own.

Procedure

Sample – 25 females with AN (12 *restricting*, 13 *binge-eating/purging* subtypes), and a matched control group of 25 healthy female students.

Body weight (measured six months and one month before the study and again at the start).

Body Shape Questionnaire (BSQ, assesses body dissatisfaction), *Eating Disorder Inventory-2* (EDI-2, assesses weight and shape concerns).

Image of 2-metre high door projected on a wall (see left). Width varied 30–80 cm. 51 images altogether, each shown four times.

Independent variable represented in two experimental conditions, completed by both groups:

- 1PP (1st-person perspective) – participant stood 5.9 m from wall and imagined walking through a 'door' (decided if she could do so at normal speed without turning sideways).
- 3PP (3rd-person perspective) – experimenter stood 5.9 m from wall and participant decided if experimenter could walk through the 'door' without turning sideways.

'Perceived passability ratio' (PPR) calculated for participants' perceived body size (high ratio = larger apparent body size).

Findings

No significant differences between the groups in age, educational level and height.

Mean BMI and median shoulder width significantly greater in controls.

AN participants scored significantly higher than controls on median EDI-2 total score, median drive for thinness score, median body dissatisfaction score and median BSQ score.

1PP condition, mean PPRs were significantly higher in AN group (1.321 compared to 1.106 for control group).

3PP condition, mean PPRs were higher for AN group but not significantly (1.227 compared to 1.128).

Conclusions

'Passability ratio' findings support clinical findings that people with AN feel their body is bigger than it really is.

Differences between 1PP and 3PP ratios suggest that people with AN overestimate their own body size but their *schema* for bodies in general is not disrupted.

Overestimation of body schema in AN may be linked to an impaired ability to integrate conflicting sensory inputs (e.g. seeing a thin body but feeling inside as if it is much bigger).

A strength is that the study is supported by other research.

Case et al. (2012) studied size-weight illusion (if you compare two objects of equal weight but different size, people tend to judge smaller object as heavier).	This is the result of normal integration of two senses, visual and tactile (touch). But people with AN are less affected by the illusion.	This supports Guardia et al.'s conclusion that the ability to integrate information from multiple senses is disturbed in AN.

CA However, research on the rubber hand illusion (RHI, see right) doesn't support this. Eshkevari et al. (2012) showed that participants with AN had a stronger RHI than controls. Perception of RHI depends on ability to integrate information from multiple sensory inputs but there was no sign of an AN-related impairment in this study.

A weakness is that the body-action task lacks ecological validity.

It is a simulation in which participants *imagine* performing the actions involved in passing through an aperture.	The researchers recognised that this is not identical to the real activity of passing through a doorway and changing position if necessary.	This means the perceived passability ratio (PPR) is not an ecologically valid measure of the participants' true behaviour.

Another weakness is that there is an important confounding variable.

The experimenter's body in the 3PP condition more closely resembles the size of the control participants' bodies than the AN participants' bodies.	This makes it 'easier' for the control participants to imagine the experimenter passing through the 'door' (or not).	This variable may affect the experience of the AN and control participants in the 3PP condition, so the differences between the groups may not be valid.

Application: The study could lead to improvements in how AN is treated.

The findings imply that a cognitive impairment underlies AN (disrupted self-body schema). If true, forms of cognitive therapy could be more effective.	For instance, virtual reality could be used to counter distorted cognitions by demonstrating 'own' and 'other' body sizes passing through doorways.	This is especially valuable because such a treatment would address an underlying cause of AN.

I&D extra: The study illustrates the role of reductionism in psychology.

The researchers acknowledged that visual perception in the real world is influenced by psychological and social factors (e.g. emotions).	But these influences have been stripped away in the experimental procedure used in the study.	This is an issue because reductionist explanations do not account for the true complexity of the causes of AN and thus may be misleading.

The rubber hand illusion (RHI) – a researcher strokes a rubber right hand and also strokes the person's own right hand, which is out of sight, in the same direction at the same time. The person comes to feel the rubber hand is their own. If the rubber hand is stabbed with a needle the person reacts as if it were their own hand being stabbed. A strong response to this illusion suggests high sensory integration.

Revision booster

Although the formulae for statistics are given to you in the examination paper, there are other mathematical procedures you need to understand, such as passability ratios for this study. Although you cannot be asked to calculate a passability ratio, you must be able to remember how they are measured.

✓ Check it

You have studied **one** contemporary study of **one** disorder other than schizophrenia.

1. Describe **one** aim and **one** conclusion from this contemporary study. [2]

2. Explain **one** strength of this contemporary study. [4]

3. **Standard essay:** Assess this contemporary study. [8] or [20]

4. **Standard plus essay:** Assess this contemporary study with reference to the way in which the data was collected and analysed. [8] or [20]

Obsessive compulsive disorder (OCD): Symptoms and features

Spec spotlight

Students study schizophrenia and one other disorder from anorexia nervosa, obsessive compulsive disorder and unipolar depression.

5.1.3 For obsessive compulsive disorder (OCD): Description of symptoms and features.

Schizophrenia is a compulsory topic to study but the remaining three mental disorders (anorexia nervosa (AN), obsessive compulsive disorder (OCD) and unipolar depression) are options – you must study one of these three.

Although technically a disorder, OCD is all about order.

Apply it Concepts

Kat is 8 years old and has been diagnosed with obsessive compulsive disorder (OCD). She has scary thoughts about horrid things happening to her mum if she doesn't put her dolls in exact height order. She worries about whether the dolls are just right and spends a lot of time swapping the dolls around to be sure.

1. (a) Explain Kat's obsession. (2)
   (b) Explain Kat's compulsion. (2)

2. Explain the effect of putting the dolls in order on Kat's anxiety. (2)

3. **Context/Methods essay:** Kat's doctor intends to conduct a case study on Kat. Evaluate the use of a case study to find out about Kat's OCD. (8)

Obsessive compulsive disorder (OCD)

OCD is an anxiety disorder involving extreme or pathological worries.

Anxiety comes from *obsessions* or *compulsions* and is diagnosed if a person experiences either or both.

Obsessions

Repetitive thoughts.

Obsessions are cognitive and usually catastrophic.

Themes include:

• Ideas (e.g. that germs are everywhere).

• Doubts (e.g. worrying something important overlooked).

• Impulses (e.g. to shout out obscenities).

• Images (e.g. fleeting sexual images).

Individual is aware their obsessions are irrational (necessary for a diagnosis).

The DSM-5 defines obsessions on the basis of two key characteristics:

1. Recurrent and persistent thoughts or impulses experienced as intrusive and unwanted.

2. Person tries to suppress such thoughts, or neutralise them with another thought or action (i.e. using a compulsion).

Compulsions

Repetitive behaviours.

The DSM-5 defines compulsions as:

1. Repetitive behaviours (e.g. handwashing, ordering, checking) or acts with a mental element (e.g. praying, counting). Person driven to perform these in response to an obsession or according to 'rules'.

2. The behaviours or mental acts are aimed at preventing or reducing anxiety, or preventing some dreaded event – but they are not realistically connected with what they are designed to neutralise/prevent, or are excessive.

Further criteria

Obsessions/compulsions are time-consuming (more than an hour a day) and/or significantly interfere with normal life, work, relationships.

No other mental disorder is present and disturbance is not due to the direct physiological effects of a substance.

If a child has OCD they may have little recognition that their obsessions/compulsions are unreasonable.

Features

OCD-UK (2017) estimates that 1.2% of the UK population experience OCD at any time (slightly higher rates in the US).

Lifetime prevalence is 2.3% (Ruscio *et al.* 2010), affects males and females equally.

Bimodal distribution of onset – some cases appear around 10 years of age and another peak at around 21 (Menon 2013).

A strength is that reliability of OCD diagnosis has been demonstrated.

López-Pina et al. (2015) conducted a meta-analysis of 144 studies using the Y-BOCS scale (based on the DSM criteria).

Mean +.866 for coefficient alpha (a measure of internal consistency) and +.848 for test-retest correlations (same person tested again after a reasonable time interval).

These very high values show that diagnosis using Y-BOCS is reliable.

A weakness is that diagnosis may lack validity.

Diagnosis may be biased because people don't give honest answers in questionnaires about their obsessive/compulsive symptoms.

This may be due to a fear of ridicule or because rating symptoms requires subjective judgements, e.g. Y-BOCS requires an estimate of how many hours a day are spent having thought intrusions.

This means a questionnaire may not be measuring what it intended to measure, reducing the internal validity of diagnosis.

The ritualistic behaviour displayed by people with OCD may have no obvious connection with the obsessive thoughts they are designed to neutralise.

Y-BOCS (*Yale-Brown Obsessive Compulsive Scale*) is the most common diagnostic scale used to measure OCD symptoms. It is a semi-structured interview. The first two sections ask people to identify which obsessions and compulsions are being experienced now or have been in the past. The final section consists of ten short questions (referred to as Y-BOCS-10), for example concerning the extent that obsessions/compulsions interfere with everyday life.

CA On the other hand, some assessments of validity have been more positive. Co-morbidity is an important issue for the validity of diagnosis (the extent that two or more conditions co-occur). Rosenfeld et al. (1992) found that people diagnosed with OCD had higher Y-BOCS scores than those with other anxiety disorders and normal controls (i.e. it distinguishes people with OCD from others). But not all research has supported this. Woody et al. (1995) found that OCD was often diagnosed alongside depression. Co-morbid conditions make it difficult to decide on the best treatment.

Revision booster

Remember that you can be asked to apply any method from Year 1 to any situation in a Year 2 topic.

A case study of OCD

My earliest memory of the illness was when I was about eight years old. The symptoms were a fear of stepping on the pavement cracks. I don't know why, but it made me feel physically uncomfortable if I did it.

Another ritual, a compulsion, was the fear that if I didn't say my prayers respectfully and sincerely, my mother might be killed in a car accident. I took on this huge responsibility as a child for another person's life.

A lot of people know about the handwashing and the checking of things, but many people are unaware that OCD can take a sinister angle, where you have a fear that you may harm your own children violently. When I had my fourth child I had intrusive thoughts at bedtime that I would go to the children's bedrooms in my sleep, take out their dressing gown cords and strangle each one. This was horrendous to go through.

People with OCD are not dangerous and they do not harm, but I was permanently exhausted. That was because of the obsession. The compulsion was to try to relieve some of the terror that came from those thoughts. I would get out of bed, find their dressing gowns, take the cords out and tie them into as many knots as possible, so that I wouldn't be able to put the cords around their necks. Then I'd go back to bed, but I still couldn't sleep. I would get out of bed again, get the cords, put them in a bag, seal the bag, and put the bag in a high cupboard.

Adapted from tinyurl.com/yx9h8n8g

Check it

You have studied **one** disorder other than schizophrenia.

1. Explain how the concepts of 'deviance' and 'danger' may be linked to the symptoms of this disorder. [4]

2. Describe **one** feature of this disorder. [2]

3. **Standard essay:** Evaluate the diagnosis of this disorder. [8] or [20]

4. **Methods essay:** Assess how qualitative **and** quantitative data might be used when gathering information about a client's symptoms. You must refer to a disorder other than schizophrenia in your answer. [8] or [20]

Obsessive compulsive disorder (OCD): One biological explanation

Spec spotlight

5.1.3 For obsessive compulsive disorder (OCD): One biological theory/explanation.

GWAS (genome-wide association studies) look at the entire human genome for candidate genes of interest rather than focusing on specific genes.

Apply it **Concepts**

Seb has been diagnosed with obsessive compulsive disorder (OCD), as have his uncles Clive and Phil. Seb is in a volunteer pool for studies on OCD. A brain scanning study found Seb had disrupted brain functioning. The next study is on neurotransmitter levels.

1. **(a)** Explain why knowing his uncles have OCD may help to understand Seb's disorder. (3)

   (b) Suggest **one** reason why this may not be helpful in explaining Seb's disorder. (2)

2. Describe how **one** biological explanation would account for **either** the results of Seb's brain scan **or** the potential findings of the next study. (3)

3. **Context essay:** Discuss **one** biological explanation for Seb's OCD. (8)

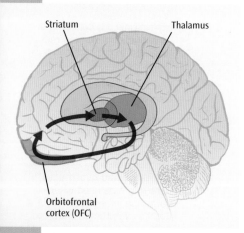

Striatum   Thalamus

Orbitofrontal
cortex (OFC)

A proposed 'worry circuit' (brown arrows).

Genetic explanation for OCD

OCD is unlikely to be caused by a single gene but by several, i.e. polygenic, multiple genes each make small contributions to OCD.

These contributions are incremental (the more of the genes you have, the more likely you are to have the disorder).

Taylor (2013) reviewed 113 GWASs (*genome-wide association studies*) and found that up to 230 different genes may be involved in OCD.

There were significant associations between OCD and genes related to the neurotransmitter *serotonin* and there is some association (not significant) between OCD and both *dopamine* and *glutamate*-related genes.

Candidate genes

SERT gene (also called 5-HTT gene):

- Organises transport of serotonin within the synapse.
- Ozaki et al. (2003) found a mutation of SERT in two unrelated families with OCD.
- The mutation led to a different form of the gene which produced lower levels of serotonin.
- Low serotonin prevents normal transmission of mood-relevant information from taking place.

COMT gene:

- Regulates production of *catechol-O-methyltransferase*.
- One allele of the COMT gene is more common in people with OCD than in people without the disorder.
- This variation produces lower activity of the COMT gene and higher levels of dopamine (Tükel *et al.* 2013).

What is inherited?

Genetic factors may lead to abnormal neurotransmitter levels but may also lead to abnormal functioning of areas of the brain.

The 'worry circuit' involves the *orbitofrontal cortex* (OFC), a region in the *frontal lobe* concerned with decision-making.

Brain scans have shown higher activity in the OFC of people with OCD (e.g. Kwon *et al.* 2003).

The OFC sends signals to the *thalamus* via the *striatum* about things that are worrying.

The striatum normally suppresses minor 'worry' signals, but when damaged it fails to suppress these signals and alerts the thalamus (sends signals back to OFC, amplifying the worry).

Serotonin has been linked to the operation of the OFC and the striatum, so it appears that lower levels of serotonin might cause these areas to malfunction (Walker *et al.* 2009).

Dopamine is linked to this 'worry circuit' as it is the main neurotransmitter of the *basal ganglia*, one part of which is the striatum – high levels of dopamine lead to overactivity of this region (Sukel 2007).

A strength is supporting evidence for genetics from twin and family studies.

Nestadt *et al.* (2010) reviewed twin studies and found that 68% of MZ twins shared a diagnosis of OCD as opposed to 31% of DZ twins.

Nestadt *et al.* (2000) found that people with a first-degree relative with OCD (parents or siblings) had a five times greater risk of OCD at some time, than general population.

These findings strongly suggest a genetic influence on OCD.

Twins.

CA The problem with twin and family studies is that the role of shared environment is not excluded. Similarities may be due to shared genes or shared environment. It is now recognised that MZ twins share more similar environments than DZ twins – their genetic similarities make their environments more similar than DZ environments.

A weakness is criticisms from the diathesis-stress model.

According to the model, environmental factors trigger or increase the risk of developing OCD. Environmental factors may be biological as well as non-biological.

Cromer *et al.* (2007) found that over half their participants with OCD had a traumatic event in their past, and that OCD was more severe in those with more than one trauma.

This suggests that genes are not the only factor to consider, so it may be more productive to focus on environmental causes because we can do something about these.

Another weakness with the worry circuit explanation is that support is mixed.

PET scans show heightened activity in the OFC of people with OCD and a decrease in activity after treatment (Kang *et al.* 2003).

But there is a wide range of other potential components of the worry circuit (e.g. *anterior cingulate cortex*) and there may be several different worry circuits.

This means that the explanation as yet lacks clarity and therefore lacks usefulness.

Application: The explanation may help identify suitable drug treatments.

Some antidepressants aim to raise levels of serotonin which is low in people with OCD.

Such drugs have been shown to reduce OCD symptoms (Pigott *et al.* 1990), whereas antidepressants that have less effect on serotonin do not reduce symptoms (e.g. Jenicke 1992).

This shows that biological explanations can offer potential treatments, the same might be true for *transcranial magnetic stimulation* (TMS) where an electrical current might modify the OFC pathway.

I&D extra: The explanation illustrates practical problems in designing research.

Much of the evidence comes from research on animals (e.g. Welch *et al.* 2007).

Mice lacking the COMT gene compulsively groom themselves and show greater anxiety than normal mice.

This raises concerns about whether such data can be reasonably applied to OCD or just applies to OCD-like behaviours.

Revision booster

When answering context/scenario questions, it is not enough to just mention the names given, you need to go through and find all the 'hooks' in the scenario, i.e. what are you being told about the people, their disorder or symptoms? You need to really engage with the information and think about how it connects to the concepts, theories and studies you have learned about.

✓ Check it

You have studied **one** disorder other than schizophrenia.

1. Compare **two** explanations for this disorder. [6]

2. Explain **one** strength and **one** weakness of **one** biological explanation for this disorder. [4]

3. **Standard essay:** Evaluate **one** biological explanation for this disorder. [8] or [20]

4. **Context essay:** A politician gives a speech about the biological origins of mental disorders. Mrs E. writes to the politician saying more attention should be paid to non-biological factors.

   To what extent is the politician right that biological factors are more important than non-biological ones with reference to **one** disorder other than schizophrenia? [20]

Obsessive compulsive disorder (OCD): One non-biological explanation

Spec spotlight

5.1.3 *For obsessive compulsive disorder: One non-biological theory/explanation.*

In the Year 1 chapter on learning theories we looked at explanations of phobias. Like OCD, phobias are an anxiety disorder. Therefore, the same behaviourist explanation that was used for phobias can be used for OCD.

Some situations trigger a feeling of helplessness.

Apply it
Concepts

When Gill was six she was playing with big building blocks. Beth said her block tower was rubbish as it wasn't straight. Then Gill's tower fell over, hurting Gill, and Beth laughed. At 27, Gill has been diagnosed with obsessive compulsive disorder (OCD). She finds it hard to cook as she keeps stacking the pans up evenly and at work she often leaves meetings to check that the boxes on her desk are tidy.

1. (a) Explain how Gill could have acquired OCD in childhood. (3)
   (b) Explain how Gill may be maintaining her OCD. (3)

2. Describe how **one** non-biological explanation could account for **one** of Gill's symptoms. (3)

3. Context essay: Discuss **one** non-biological explanation for Gill's OCD. (8)

A behaviourist explanation for OCD

The two-process model.

Mowrer's (1960) *two-process model* is based on learning theory (i.e. behaviourist).

Part 1

• Acquisition of fears begins when a neutral stimulus is associated with anxiety through classical conditioning.

> e.g. a child is told that eating food dropped on the floor is disgusting and this creates anxiety for the child.

• Whenever the child thinks of any dirty object, feelings of anxiety are now associated with that object (classical conditioning) – these feelings become obsessions.

Part 2

• Obsessions (thoughts) are maintained by avoidance.

• Any action that enables the individual to avoid a negative event is *negatively reinforcing* (operant conditioning).

Compulsive rituals

Compulsions are learned because a link is formed between anxiety-associated obsessions and the reduction of that anxiety, for example:

• A person who is worried about germs experiences relief when they wear gloves to touch a dirty door knob.

• The behaviour (wearing gloves) is then linked with relief, negatively reinforcing the behaviour.

• This is operant conditioning.

Accidental associations form, becoming compulsive, when the person faces thoughts or situations that provoke anxiety:

• Every time a behaviour is repeated it becomes harder to resist because of the temporary relief it provides.

• Over time, people become more convinced that these intrusive thoughts are dangerous, so fear increases.

• This pattern of behaviour is like an addiction – the more you do it, the more you have to do it again.

Learned helplessness

Seligman (1975) proposed that people learn to be helpless:

• They experience negative situations in childhood from which escape is not possible.

> e.g. an abusive parent or overprotective mother displays anger and the child cannot escape.

• The child eventually gives up trying to escape and a pattern of behaviour develops – they deal with any difficult situation by accepting it instead of trying to escape.

• This is classical conditioning – learning to associate an aversive stimulus with no escape and acceptance.

• Such acceptance creates anxiety and this may be dealt with by creating compulsive rituals.

A strength is research support for Mowrer's two-process model.

Tracy et al. (1999) gave students a checklist of OCD symptoms and categorised them from their responses as more or less OCD-like.

Those who were identified as more OCD-like were more rapidly conditioned on an eye-blink task than those who were less OCD-like.

This supports a prediction of the two-process model that people with OCD are predisposed to rapid conditioning.

CA It is questionable as to whether findings from a non-clinical sample of people who just have 'OCD-like' symptoms can really be generalised to understanding people with a disorder. So this research does not offer much support for the model, though it is an attempt to study some aspects of the explanation.

A weakness is that conditioning may not be the real explanation.

Learning theory (two-process model) assumes that explanations for human and animal behaviour are the same, ignoring cognitive, social or emotional influences.

The model ignores the meaning of behaviours to the individual. Obsessions may be symptoms of underlying distress, not the consequence of classical conditioning.

This means that the learning explanation may prevent understanding the real issue for the person and may block successful treatment.

Blinking: winking with both eyes.

The eye-blink task involves a puff of air being blown into the eye, the unconditioned response is to blink. If a bell (neutral stimulus) is rung along with the puff, a person acquires a conditioned response of blinking to the sound of the bell (now a conditioned stimulus).

Another strength is research shows compulsions do reduce anxiety.

If the performance of compulsive rituals relieves anxiety associated with obsessions, then blocking these rituals should cause a rise in anxiety.

Rachman and Hodgson (1980) found that delaying compulsive rituals did lead to anxiety, though this anxiety did gradually decline.

This shows that compulsions provide quicker relief from anxiety than would be the case with spontaneous decay alone.

Application: Behaviourist explanations lead to straightforward treatments.

Exposure and response prevention (ERP) is a therapy based on behaviourist (learning theory) principles.

Individuals perform 'forbidden' acts but not compulsive rituals, so anxiety levels decrease naturally. The stimulus-response link is relearned so the obsession is not associated with anxiety.

This shows that the behaviourist explanation can account for why a particular therapeutic approach is successful.

I&D extra: The behaviourist and biological explanations can be compared.

A biological explanation would suggest that genetic factors cause obsessive behaviour. This can be combined with the behaviourist model.

The anxiety associated with obsessions may be reduced by performing various rituals (i.e. compulsive acts). Such rituals are thus rewarding and will be repeated.

This shows that it is more productive to take a broader view of explanations rather than focusing on biological or non-biological approaches alone.

✓ Check it

You have studied **one** disorder other than schizophrenia.

1. Describe **one** non-biological explanation for this disorder. [4]

2. Explain **two** strengths of **one** non-biological explanation for this disorder. [4]

3. **Standard essay:** Assess the strengths of **one** non-biological explanation for this disorder. [8] or [20]

4. **I&D essay:** Evaluate the role of nurture in determining human behaviour. You must give examples from **one** disorder other than schizophrenia in your answer. [16]

Obsessive compulsive disorder (OCD): One biological treatment

Spec spotlight

5.1.4 For obsessive compulsive disorder: One biological treatment.

Diagram showing how SSRIs work, blocking the reuptake of serotonin at the presynaptic neuron. This increases the amount of serotonin in the synaptic cleft so there is more there to stimulate the postsynaptic neuron, thus improving mood.

Drug treatments for OCD

Antidepressants

Low *serotonin* is associated with both OCD and depression – so antidepressant drugs which increase serotonin activity are commonly used by people with OCD.

Selective serotonin reuptake inhibitors (SSRIs), e.g. *fluoxetine* (Prozac) and *paroxetine* (Paxil)

- Useful to treat co-morbid depression (which occurs alongside OCD in many people).
- But also reduce symptoms of OCD directly.
- Reduce reuptake of serotonin in the synapse (it is normally drawn back into the presynaptic neuron via serotonin transporters).
- Block the transporters, so excess serotonin cannot be recycled – increases serotonin in the synapse.
- Serotonin continues to stimulate the postsynaptic neuron leading to reduction in anxiety.

Tricyclics (TCAs)

- Older type of antidepressant used to treat OCD.
- Affect *noradrenaline* as well as serotonin (so also more noradrenaline left in the synapse).
- Jointly these neurotransmitters improve mood.
- TCAs not the preferred treatment because there are serious side effects (such as heart-related problems) but continue to be used in treatment-resistant cases.

Anti-anxiety drugs

Anxiety is created by obsessions – so anti-anxiety drugs are used.

Benzodiazepines (BZs), e.g. Valium, Librium

- Enhance activity of *GABA* (gamma-aminobutyric acid), a neurotransmitter that has a general quietening effect on many of the neurons in the brain.
- GABA reacts with GABA receptors on receiving neurons.
- It is an inhibitory neurotransmitter so when it locks into these receptors it makes it harder for the neuron to be stimulated by other neurotransmitters.
- Slows down activity, making person feel more relaxed.

D-cycloserine

- Antibiotic drug developed to treat tuberculosis, also has a sedative effect on people with OCD.
- It can be combined with a non-biological treatment so that anxiety levels can be controlled and allow new patterns of learning to develop (Kushner *et al.* 2007).

Apply it Methods

Lotty is leading a study which is evaluating a new drug for obsessive compulsive disorder (OCD). She wants to compare participants using the drug against a control group given a placebo. She intends to measure symptoms of OCD after six weeks and also assess any problems with side effects.

1. **(a)** Describe how Lotty could select and treat her client group and control group. (4)

   (b) Suggest **one** advantage and **one** disadvantage of testing participants once after six weeks. (4)

2. Describe **one** way to measure change in symptoms. (3)

3. **Context/Methods essay:** To what extent is testing drug therapy using experiments useful? You must refer to the context in your answer. (20)

A strength is evidence that drug therapy is effective.

Soomro et al. (2008) reviewed 17 studies and found that all showed significantly better findings for SSRIs than for placebo conditions.

Typically symptoms declined significantly for around 70% of those taking SSRIs (also found in the POTS study described on page 84).

This is strong evidence because it suggests drugs can improve quality of life for people with OCD because symptoms are reduced.

CA However, this meta-analysis and the POTS study concluded that effectiveness was greatest when SSRIs were combined with a psychological treatment, usually cognitive-behavioural treatment (CBT). Therefore, the evidence only offers some support for drugs as an effective therapy (and also they are not a lasting cure).

A weakness of drug therapies is the potential side effects.

For SSRIs these include nausea, insomnia, headaches and low sex drive (many temporary). Less common side effects include hallucinations and suicidal thoughts.

BZs also have side effects but most importantly have been linked to addiction (Ashton 1997), so it is recommended that they should not be taken for more than four weeks.

Therefore, the effectiveness of drug treatments is reduced because people stop taking the drug (or don't start in the first place).

During insomnia, the mind works the night shift.

Another strength of drug treatments is that they are cheap and easy.

A person can just take a drug until their anxiety subsides and this will enable them to resist obsessions and lead a normal life (go to work, look after their family).

By contrast, psychological therapies require high levels of motivation as the person with OCD has to expose themselves to their anxieties and resist their compulsions.

This makes drug treatments more appealing to many people.

Revision booster

When you are tackling a question on treatments, try to relate your descriptive points directly to the symptoms of the disorder the treatment is for. This is particularly important to remember if you have learned the same treatment for two different disorders. Your answers must always be shaped to the disorder.

Application: Drugs combined with another therapy is an effective treatment.

The best solution is a combined therapy using drugs plus non-biological treatment – in this way drug treatments make an important contribution to eventual recovery.

Drug treatment alone just removes symptoms but can help people with OCD engage more effectively with CBT (reduce anxiety which otherwise blocks ability to think rationally).

This shows that drugs ultimately have an important role in effective therapy.

I&D extra: One issue with all research on mental disorders is social sensitivity.

There are implications for people who have OCD – research showing drugs are an effective therapy may be 'abusing' the people they claim to help.

This is because drugs may simply be a kind of 'chemical cosh', i.e. using a drug just to keep someone quiet so they do not intrude on society.

This is not in the best interests of the person with OCD and therefore shows there are socially-sensitive matters related to drug treatments.

✓ Check it

You have studied **one** disorder other than schizophrenia.

1. Describe **one** biological treatment for this disorder. [4]

2. Explain **one** practical issue relating to the use of biological treatments for this disorder. [2]

3. **Standard essay:** Assess **one** biological treatment for this disorder. [8] or [20]

4. **I&D essay:** Evaluate the issue of social control in relation to the use of biological treatments. Your answer must include examples from **one** disorder other than schizophrenia in your answer. [16]

Obsessive compulsive disorder (OCD): One non-biological treatment

Spec spotlight

5.1.4 For obsessive compulsive disorder: One non-biological treatment.

There are, apparently, more germs on a computer keyboard than a toilet seat. That's my excuse for not doing any work anyway.

Apply it Methods

Whittal *et al.* (2005) compared two therapies (treatment 1 and treatment 2) for obsessive compulsive disorder (OCD). Participants were randomly allocated to 12 weeks of one treatment only. No significant differences were found in Y-BOCS scores immediately after treatment or after three months.

1. Explain why the participants were randomly allocated. (1)

2. (a) Explain the experimental design used in this study. (1)
   (b) Suggest **one** strength of this design in this study. (1)

3. **Context/Methods essay:** Discuss how psychologists can ensure studies testing treatments are valid. You must refer to the context in your answer. (8)

A behaviourist therapy

Exposure and response prevention (ERP).

Obsessions and compulsions acquired through conditioning, so recovery should involve unlearning behaviours.

In everyday life:

- Obsessions negatively reinforced by avoidance, prevents relearning taking place.
- Compulsive rituals are associated with anxiety reduction, again preventing relearning.

Thus ERP therapy reconditions these two elements:

- E (exposure) – allows relearning and anxiety reduction.
- RP (response prevention) – relearning about compulsions.

Exposure (E)

- Individual is repeatedly presented with the feared stimulus until anxiety subsides ('habituation').
- Exposures may be at first imagined and later experienced *in vivo* (e.g. actually touching dirty objects).
- Exposures may move gradually from least to most threatening (like a hierarchy is used in systematic desensitisation).

Avoidance response persists because the individual has no opportunity to re-experience the feared stimulus due to the associated anxiety.

The client is 'forced' to experience the stimulus and learn a new association between it and relaxation rather than anxiety.

Relaxation techniques can be learned and practised in anxiety-provoking situations.

Response prevention (RP)

At the same time as exposure, the client is prevented from engaging in the usual compulsive response.

The client should learn that obsessions that previously created anxiety no longer produce this response.

For example:

- A woman obsessed with cleanliness is given a list of rules to accept, such as not cleaning her house for a week and then only spending half an hour vacuuming it.
- Clinician devises a routine to restrict compulsive behaviours such as the toilet can only be flushed twice.

ERP in action

Clinician identifies target symptoms using Y-BOCS (see page 73), client ranks these from least to most anxiety-provoking.

ERP typically involves 13–20 weekly sessions, but severe cases need longer and/or more frequent sessions (March *et al.* 1997).

Once a person has made progress, they are encouraged to continue applying ERP techniques in new situations.

Monthly booster sessions can be added to prevent relapse.

A strength of ERP is evidence of its effectiveness.

Fisher and Wells (2005) used a standardised procedure (Jacobson method) to compare methods of therapy.

Different studies use different methods of determining 'recovery' so using a standardised method is important.

This study showed that ERP is the most effective treatment of all, with a 50–60% reduction in all OCD symptoms.

CA However, ERP combined with drug therapy may be better. For example, Foa *et al.* (2005) found that a combination of an antidepressant and ERP was more effective than either alone. Wilhelm *et al.* (2008) also found that simultaneous administration of *D-cycloserine* (a *glutamate* agonist) substantially improved effectiveness of ERP.

A weakness is that ERP targets symptoms rather than causes.

Genetic factors and/or conditioning experiences may act as a vulnerability but such factors alone are not usually sufficient. Usually a further event triggers OCD (e.g. a new baby).

Any therapy really needs to address the feelings about the event (often traumatic) whereas ERP just targets symptoms. ERP + drugs + CBT may produce the best results by targeting underlying 'triggers'.

This may explain why the long-term effectiveness of ERP was improved when integrated with discussions of dysfunctional beliefs, i.e. a form of CBT (Huppert and Franklin 2005).

Another weakness is that ERP requires effort.

Success of ERP depends on the client's effort, e.g. exposing themselves to their anxieties and consciously resisting the obsessions.

This takes time and determination, especially as exposure and resistance can make the person extremely distressed.

This may be beyond the willpower of many people and means that the therapy cannot offer help to everyone.

Application: ERP can be used as a form self-help.

Self-directed ERP is a reasonably effective alternative to therapist-led ERP, especially for mild OCD.

A computer-based programme (*BT Steps*), was more effective than relaxation alone (but less effective than therapist-led ERP, Greist *et al.* 2002).

This means ERP offers wider treatment options for people with OCD, at least for those experiencing milder symptoms.

I&D extra: ERP illustrates how psychological knowledge is used in society.

ERP may simply target symptoms but it does improve the well-being of people with OCD and may help them contribute more fully to society.

ERP is quite reliant on psychologists, even when used in a self-help situation, to guide the steps that need to be followed to recovery.

This contribution to society is one of the core aims of psychology.

Did I touch that keyboard?

✓ Check it

You have studied **one** disorder other than schizophrenia.

1. Meta-analyses are used to determine the effectiveness of treatments in clinical psychology.
    Suggest how meta-analysis could be used to research **one** non-biological treatment for a disorder other than schizophrenia. [3]

2. Compare **one** biological and **one** non-biological treatment for this disorder. [6]

3. **Standard essay:** Assess **one** non-biological treatment for this disorder. [8] or [20]

4. **Standard plus essay:** Evaluate **two** treatments for this disorder in terms of practical and ethical issues. [8] or [20]

Spec spotlight

5.3.7 One contemporary study:
Masellis et al. (2003) Quality of
life in OCD: Differential impact
of obsessions, compulsions and
depression co-morbidity.

Does OCD affect it?

Apply it
Concepts

Imagine three people diagnosed
with obsessive compulsive disorder
(OCD). Jenny is young and married,
with severe compulsions. Merv is old
and depressed after losing his wife.
Chloe is single and middle-aged, with
severe obsessions and depression.

1. (a) Using the findings of Masellis et al.
   (2003), explain whether Jenny, Merv
   or Chloe's gender or marital status
   will affect intrusiveness of
   symptoms. (1)

   (b) Also explain whether Jenny, Merv
   or Chloe's intrusive symptoms
   will be the worst. (3)

2. Explain **one** reason why predictions
   about Jenny, Merv or Chloe's
   experience of illness intrusiveness
   may be invalid. (2)

3. **Context essay:** Discuss the
   usefulness of Masellis et al.'s
   (2003) study for understanding
   the individual differences
   related to a mental
   disorder, as illustrated
   by Jenny, Merv
   or Chloe. (8)

Aims

To find the extent to which the quality of life (QoL) of people
with OCD is affected by obsessions and compulsions.

To find out how co-morbid depression affects QoL.

Procedure

Correlational study using *hierarchical linear regression
analysis*. This aims to predict QoL (quality of life) from
clinical and demographic variables and symptoms of
depression, obsession and compulsion.

Sample – 18 males and 25 females who met the DSM-IV
criteria for OCD.

Three reliable and valid scales measured symptoms:

- *Y-BOCS* (see page 73) – severity of obsessions and
  compulsions (e.g. distress, time spent).

- *Illness Intrusiveness Rating Scale* (IIRS) – measures the
  effects of OCD on QoL in 13 areas of life (e.g. work,
  health, finances). Gave total score from 13 (minimal
  intrusiveness) to 91 (extreme intrusiveness).

- *Beck Depression Inventory* (BDI) – severity of depression
  symptoms (e.g. sadness, loss of pleasure, suicidal
  thoughts).

Findings

Clinical and demographic variables (e.g. age, marital status)
did not significantly correlate with illness intrusiveness
scores.

Significant positive correlations between intrusiveness and
obsession and between intrusiveness and compulsion.

Ability to significantly predict illness intrusiveness:

- Obsession, compulsion and depression scores entered 'as
  a block' – together predicted illness intrusiveness.

- Depression and obsession separately predicted illness
  intrusiveness (greater severity = greater intrusiveness).

- Compulsion severity alone did not predict intrusiveness.

Conclusions

QoL of people with OCD is affected by the severity of their
obsessional symptoms.

Clinical symptoms of compulsion did not influence QoL.

May not support the behaviourist explanation (i.e.
obsessions create anxiety and compulsions are a way of
managing it).

Intrusive and uncontrollable obsessions have a bigger
effect on QoL than compulsions (perceived as necessary
to cope).

Therapies that emphasise reducing compulsions are
unhelpful for people with OCD with mostly obsessional
symptoms.

The researchers recommend therapies (e.g. CBT) that
focus on reducing obsessional thoughts to improve quality
of life.

A strength is that the conclusions are supported by previous research.

The suggestion that therapies should focus primarily on reducing obsessional thoughts is supported by Freeston et al. (1997).

They found that between 17% and 44% of people with OCD do not experience any clinically significant compulsions.

This supporting research strengthens the validity of the conclusions drawn by Masellis et al. and the confidence we can place in them.

CA However, the Freeston et al. study is cross-sectional rather than longitudinal, so the findings give only a 'snapshot' at one point in time. Therefore, the researchers could not infer causal links between symptoms and QoL. This means an alternative conclusion is that having a poor quality of life makes OCD and depression symptoms worse.

A weakness of the study is a lack of validity.

The IIRS is assumed to assess the relatively permanent ways in which OCD symptoms intrude (i.e. these are unchanging and stable over time).

But it is just as likely that it measures temporary intrusions that depend on how the participant feels at the time they complete the scale (i.e. the ratings are state-dependent).

This means the researchers cannot be sure what the real relationships are between symptoms and QoL, especially in the longer term.

Freeston et al.'s study may only provide a 'snapshot' at one point in time.

Another weakness is that the study raises ethical issues.

OCD participants completed scales to assess highly personal experiences of matters close to most people's hearts – some may have found this stressful.

On the other hand some people completing questionnaires may not be distressed by the experience – they may find it therapeutic or even enjoyable.

This means that ethical safeguards (consent, debriefing) are especially important when dealing with vulnerable people sensitive to questions about their disorder.

Application: The study has important consequences for OCD therapies.

The findings favour cognitive therapies that focus on reducing obsessions and addressing co-morbid depressive symptoms.

The researchers also suggest that therapies focusing on compulsion-reduction are less effective.

This offers the real prospect of enhancing the quality of life of people with OCD by improving the therapies available to them.

I&D extra: Practical issues in design and implementation of research.

The conclusions of the study stand or fall on the quality of the scales the researchers used.

Apart from a validity issue with the IIRS, several studies (e.g. Bieling et al. 2001) have established that the validity and reliability of the other scales used are high.

This means we can be fairly sure that the scales measured the variables the researchers wished to measure, and did so in a consistent way so others can replicate the study.

Spec spotlight

5.3.8 One contemporary study: The Paediatric OCD Treatment Study (POTS) team including March et al. (2004) Cognitive-behaviour therapy, sertraline and their combination for children and adolescents with obsessive compulsive disorder.

Apply it  Methods

Dr Benn is testing a new drug for obsessive compulsive disorder (OCD). He is comparing its effectiveness under four conditions: drug alone (D), drug plus non-biological therapy (D+T), a placebo where the participants believe they are receiving the new drug (PD) and one condition combining the placebo and non-biological therapy (PD+T).

1. (a) Explain the role of each of Dr Benn's **four** conditions. (4)
   (b) Explain **one** other condition that Dr Benn could include. (1)

2. Explain how Dr Benn should allocate participants to the different groups. (2)

3. Context/Methods essay: Discuss the importance of randomisation and controls in studies of treatments in clinical psychology. (8)

Table showing comparisons of CY-BOCS scores between groups.

Comparison	Outcome	Significance
Combined vs CBT	Combined superior	$p = 0.008$
Combined vs sertraline	Combined superior	$p = 0.006$
Combined vs placebo	Combined superior	$p < 0.001$
CBT vs sertraline	No difference	$p = 0.80$
CBT vs placebo	CBT superior	$p = 0.003$
Sertraline vs placebo	Sertraline superior	$p = 0.007$

Graph showing the mean CY-BOCS scores for each treatment group at each assessment point.

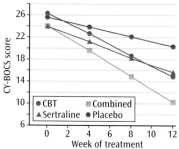

The scores have been statistically adjusted to take account of all variables (e.g. time, site) and interactions between them.

Aims

The Paediatric OCD Treatment Study (POTS) team aimed to evaluate three treatments for OCD for young people.

Procedure

12-week randomised controlled clinical trial.

Sample – 112 volunteer OCD outpatients aged 7 to 17 years were randomly allocated to one of four groups:

1. CBT alone – 14 individual one-hour sessions. Each session e.g. set goals, reviewed previous week, gave practice, set homework.

2. Medical management with SSRI drug (sertraline) – parents filled in medication diary.

3. Combined treatment – CBT plus sertraline began at same time. Intensity of each treatment increased independently.

4. Control (placebo) – treated same as group 2, except no active ingredient in tablets given.

Outcome measures:

• Assessments were at baseline (start) and in the 4th, 8th and 12th weeks.

• Same independent assessor each time, 'masked' (blinded) to treatment group membership.

• CY-BOCS (children's Y-BOCS, see page 73) used to diagnose OCD at baseline and to monitor changes later – remission was defined as a score of 10 or below.

• Responses to medication monitored using a checklist completed by children and parents.

Findings

	CBT	Sertraline	Combined	Placebo
Dropout rates	2.7%	1.8%	2.7%	6.3%
CY-BOCS Wk 12	14.0	16.5	11.2	21.5
Remission	39.3%	21.4%	53.6%	3.6%

Remission in combined treatment was significantly better than in sertraline and placebo.

Regression analysis found OCD symptoms were significantly better at the end of the study compared with the start.

Improvement over time was not equal in all groups.

Conclusions

CBT (either alone or combined with medication) is superior to treatment with medication alone and also to placebo.

As sertraline was superior to placebo, this shows that medication can be an effective treatment for OCD in children.

The sample was generally representative so the findings suggest that children and adolescents with OCD should be treated with CBT or with CBT alongside an SSRI drug.

A strength is that the study used several techniques to ensure high reliability.

Procedures were standardised so increase in drug dose was guided by a strict schedule and CBT sessions followed established protocols.

Also, all groups had regular meetings with a professional and both the sertraline and placebo groups took tablets they believed were likely to help them.

This means that variations *within* a group were likely due to genuine individual differences (and due to variations *between* groups to the treatment), not to procedural differences.

CA However, not all procedures were rigorously standardised. 12 participants and clinicians knew that combined-treatment participants were receiving medication rather than placebo (the 'masking' in the study was imperfect). So knowledge of group membership may have affected the outcomes by influencing expectations.

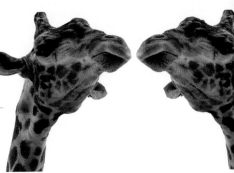

Two heads are better than one. It would appear to be the same with treatments.

A weakness is that the study used non-equivalent groups.

Combined-treatment participants completed more CBT sessions than those in the CBT-only group (mean of 14 and 12 respectively).

Also, combined group participants had a lower daily dose of medication, than participants in the sertraline-only group (133 mg versus 170 mg).

This makes it more difficult to make valid comparisons when some participants receive 'more' of a treatment than others.

Revision booster

When trying to evaluate a study you can always develop a point related to the methods or findings. What strengths or weaknesses are there in terms of generalisability, reliability applications, validity or ethics?

Another strength is that researchers were sensitive to ethical issues.

The lead researcher (John March) was responsible for the confidentiality and security of the data.

All participants gave written consent, and those who received the placebo were able to choose a 'genuine' treatment at the end of the study.

The key point is that concern about ethical issues improves the value of the study because it is more respected by the public and participants.

Application: There are implications for management of OCD in young people.

The researchers argue that the CBT-medication treatments used in their study were acceptable to the participants and well-tolerated.

The treatments were also highly practical, using protocols that are well-established and easily available to clinicians.

This should lead to routine use of combined CBT-medication treatment and would have benefits for young people with OCD as well as wider society.

I&D extra: The study illustrates different ways of explaining behaviour.

Greater success in treating OCD using both CBT and medication implies that their effects are additive rather than alternatives (they work together).

This may be because they affect different processes (CBT affects obsessive thoughts, drugs tackle neurotransmitters). Or they may work together (e.g. drugs may help a person cope with CBT).

This shows how a combination of explanations can produce the best result.

✓ **Check it**

You have studied **one** contemporary study of **one** disorder other than schizophrenia.

1. Suggest **one** improvement that could be made to this contemporary study. [2]

2. Explain **one** strength of this contemporary study. [4]

3. **Standard essay:** Assess **one** contemporary study of a disorder other than schizophrenia. [8] or [20]

4. **Methods essay:** Assess this contemporary study with reference to the type of data collected (e.g. primary or secondary, qualitative or quantitative). [8] or [20]

Unipolar depression: Symptoms and features

Spec spotlight

Students study schizophrenia and one other disorder from anorexia nervosa, obsessive compulsive disorder and unipolar depression.

5.1.3 For unipolar depression: Description of symptoms and features.

Schizophrenia is a compulsory topic to study but the remaining three mental disorders (anorexia nervosa (AN), obsessive compulsive disorder (OCD) and unipolar depression) are options – you must study one of these three.

Depression. No joke.

Apply it Concepts

Poppy is nine and used to enjoy dancing and riding lessons. She doesn't want to go any more and her mum often finds her sobbing in her bedroom but Poppy can't explain why. Her mum is worried as Poppy always seems tired but used to be really lively.

1. (a) Describe **three** symptoms of depression that Poppy is showing. (3)
   (b) Explain how **one** of these relates to distress or dysfunction. (1)

2. Explain why **either** the features of Poppy's depression are common **or** why they are unusual. (2)

3. **Context essay:** Discuss the symptoms and features of Poppy's depression. (8)

Unipolar depression Also called major depressive disorder (MDD).	Depression is classed as an affective disorder, i.e. a disorder related to 'affect' (emotions, feelings). The term *unipolar* distinguishes 'depression' from *bipolar disorder* where depression alternates with mania. The DSM-5 and ICD-10 both: • Identify single or recurrent depressive episodes. • Recognise mild, moderate and severe forms. • Require symptoms to be present for at least two weeks. The DSM suggests a person's subjective distress and social/occupational functioning must also be considered.
Affective symptoms Mood.	Key symptom – depressed mood and loss of interest/pleasure. People with depression may feel sad, empty or hopeless and may be tearful (children and adolescents may be irritable). The term *anhedonia* describes a lack of enjoyment or pleasure found in previously enjoyed activities, events or places.
Bodily symptoms Physical.	Key symptom – reduced energy levels/fatigue. Knock-on effect – depressed people tend to withdraw from work, education and social life. Changes in appetite – decrease/increase leading to significant weight loss/gain (change of >5% of body weight in one month). Sleep is disrupted nearly every day – insomnia (difficulty sleeping) or hypersomnia (excessive sleep).
Cognitive symptoms Thought.	People with depression experience negative thoughts – blame themselves for events outside their control, feel guilty/unworthy. Lack self-confidence, feel incompetent/incapable, pessimistic. May experience recurrent thoughts of death or thoughts of suicide (but without a specific plan).
Behavioural symptoms	Fatigue and loss of pleasure and enjoyment can lead to social withdrawal and diminished activity. Some people show signs of psychomotor retardation or agitation (must be observable by others).
Features	Prevalence in the *Adult Psychiatric Morbidity Survey* in 2014 was 3.3 people per 100 population (up from 2.7 in 2007) – more common in women than in men. Highly prevalent partly because it is co-morbid with many other mental disorders, e.g. anorexia nervosa. Also linked to many physical illnesses, e.g. found in 23% of women undergoing treatment for ovarian cancer (Watts *et al.* 2015). Linked to many chronic physical illnesses.

Issues with the diagnosis of depression

A weakness is that depression is difficult to diagnose.

Field trials of the DSM-5 (Regier *et al.* 2013) used a measure of agreement between diagnostic practitioners called the *kappa statistic*.

This agreement was just 0.28 for MDD ('questionable' reliability). There was full agreement for only 4–15% of diagnoses (Lieblich *et al.* 2015).

This questions the value of research and treatment if even highly-trained and experienced specialists cannot make reliable diagnoses using the DSM-5.

There are wounds that never show on the body that are deeper and more hurtful than anything that bleeds.

CA Nevertheless the DSM-5 can be used in a more reliable way. Real-world clinical diagnosis is usually based on a semi-structured interview (e.g. *Structured Clinical Interview for DSM-5* (SCID-5). Shankman *et al.* (2018) found 'substantial' reliability when using the SCID-5 to diagnose severity of MDD. However, such interviews usually go well beyond criteria specified in the DSM-5.

Another weakness is that cultural differences can make diagnosis difficult.

Many cultures do not recognise depression and do not even have a word in their language which fully matches the English connotation.

This does not mean depression does not exist in these cultures, just that it is experienced in different ways. In different cultures depression is manifested through different symptoms (Watters 2010).

This means that a Western clinician might not diagnose depression in some people because the symptoms have a specific cultural form.

CA This said, the DSM-5 includes a section on how to conduct a *Cultural Formulation Interview* which gives information about how a person's cultural identity may affect the expression of signs and symptoms. This should help clinicians to make more valid diagnoses for disorders subject to significant cultural variation.

A case study of depression

Sofia has started to find it hard to wake up in the mornings. She wakes up every night, worrying about exams and her university applications. She doesn't seem to realise that the reason she did badly in her mocks may have been because she missed a lot of school the previous term due to glandular fever.

Sofia's friends are concerned. She is tearful and snappy, she can't make up her mind about anything, even the smallest decisions, and she has lost weight. She used to walk her dog every day but now she leaves it to her parents and she has stopped going to the usual rounds of parties, sleepovers and nights out.

Sofia has been letting homework pile up, her teachers have noticed that she has stopped going to the extra study skills sessions for her upcoming A level exams. She cancelled her last two driving lessons and has been ignoring texts from her boyfriend as she thinks that he is going to dump her because she has been so miserable lately.

Note: This is not a real case history but one based on real descriptions.

✓ Check it

You have studied **one** disorder other than schizophrenia.

1. Explain how **two** symptoms of this disorder may affect a person in their day-to-day life. [4]

2. Explain **one** weakness related to the validity of the diagnosis of **one** disorder other than schizophrenia.

3. **Standard essay:** Assess **one** disorder other than schizophrenia. [8] or [20]

4. **Context essay:** Dr. Sutton is collecting information about his client, Ms. A's symptoms with a view to making a diagnosis.

   Discuss **two** or more HCPC guidelines that he must bear in mind when working with Ms. A. You must refer to a disorder other than schizophrenia in your answer. [8]

Unipolar depression: One biological explanation

Spec spotlight

5.1.3 For unipolar depression: One biological theory/explanation.

Make sure you present all three hypotheses as one explanation – it is jointly the *neurochemical* explanation of depression.

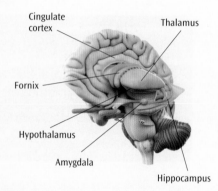

Cingulate cortex

Thalamus

Fornix

Hypothalamus

Amygdala

Hippocampus

Components of the limbic system. The effect of monoamine neurotransmitter depletion on these structures (and of BDNF in the hippocampus) is a key factor in the neurochemistry of depression.

Apply it Concepts

Drew is depressed. His doctor says his serotonin levels must be too low and has given him a drug to raise them. Drew is worried the drug isn't working as his symptoms haven't changed after three weeks. Drew feels that even if the drug works it doesn't mean the doctor was right about serotonin being the cause.

1. (a) Explain why Drew was given the drug using **one** theory of depression. (4)
   (b) Explain **one** weakness of Drew's doctor's explanation. (2)

2. Give an alternative biological explanation for Drew's lack of progress. (2)

3. **Context essay:** Discuss Drew's depression using **one** biological explanation. (8)

Neurochemical explanations	Some disruption of synaptic transmission is the cause of mental disorder. (See page 92 for diagram of synapse.)
Monoamine depletion hypothesis Schildkraut (1965)	Early version • Depression caused by an abnormally low level (depletion) of the *monoamine* neurotransmitter *serotonin* (monoamines are a class of proteins). • This regulates the brain's *limbic system* (*amygdala, hypothalamus, hippocampus*, etc.). • These are the brain's emotional centres, forming many connections with other brain areas (e.g. *frontal cortex*). • Ignored evidence for the role of *noradrenaline*. Later version – permissive hypothesis • Depression caused by imbalance of serotonin *and* noradrenaline. • Serotonin level normally controls noradrenaline level. • But abnormally low serotonin 'permits' noradrenaline to decrease as well – the outcome is depression. • Low serotonin is necessary for depression but not enough on its own.
Receptor sensitivity hypothesis Challenged the monoamine hypothesis as too simplistic.	Some drugs had antidepressant properties but did not increase availability of monoamine neurotransmitters. Therefore, there is more to depression than monoamine depletion. Depression caused by changes in the sensitivity of postsynaptic receptors. Normal response of receptors to neurotransmitter depletion is *upregulation* – neurons compensate for reduced stimulation by increasing receptor sensitivity and (long-term) producing more. Serotonin and noradrenaline postsynaptic receptors even more sensitive (supersensitivity) to reduced stimulation than normal.
BDNF hypothesis Brain-derived neurotrophic factor.	BDNF is not a neurotransmitter but a chemical which 'feeds' neurons the nutrients they need to survive, grow and function. Key role in *neuronal plasticity* (brain forms new synapses). BDNF in the hippocampus and *prefrontal cortex* is abnormally low in people with depression. Also close relationship between BDNF level and symptom severity (lower level, more severe symptoms). Hypothesis links depression with stress: • Gene for BDNF may be 'switched off' under stress. • Neurons fed by BDNF are vulnerable to atrophy (shrinkage) or apoptosis (cell death). • Both of these are observed in depression.

A strength is support for the role of BDNF from two main sources.

Sen et al. (2008) found a negative correlation between blood serum BDNF and the severity of depressive symptoms.

Post-mortems of people who had depression have found abnormally low BDNF in the hippocampus and prefrontal cortex.

This evidence from Martinowich et al. (2007) shows a clear association between BDNF level and depressive symptoms.

A weakness is research evidence against monoamine depletion.

There is a therapeutic delay when people with depression start taking antidepressant drugs.

It often takes as long as four to six weeks before there is any improvement in symptoms.

This is hard to explain when levels of serotonin and noradrenaline increase immediately and within a week are normal.

CA However, this can be explained by receptor sensitivity (another biochemical explanation). Antidepressants increase availability of serotonin and/or noradrenaline. This leads to a downregulation in postsynaptic receptors (fewer are produced) to compensate for the greater stimulation, but the process takes several weeks.

Another weakness relates to the treatment aetiology fallacy.

Early observations of how medication affected depression noted that postsynaptic receptors were downregulated by antidepressants that increased serotonin.

People assumed that if a biochemical treatment improved the symptoms of depression, then this implied that depression must have a biochemical cause (aetiology).

This is not necessarily true – a drug could work by correcting a biological process that is disturbed by a psychological factor (e.g. stress), so treatment is biological but the cause is psychological.

Application: Better understanding of neurochemistry improves treatments.

Recent drug treatments target both serotonin and noradrenaline levels (e.g. duloxetine) as opposed to serotonin only (e.g. fluoxetine).

GABA and dopamine are also becoming targets for medication and BDNF offers yet another route involving a different type of biological treatment (transcranial magnetic stimulation of the brain).

This is a strength of biochemical explanations because treatments based on them may improve quality of life and reduce distress.

I&D extra: The explanation sheds light on nature and nurture in psychology.

A dysfunctional biochemical mechanism makes the individual vulnerable to developing depression (it is a diathesis).

But the dysfunction has to be triggered by a 'lifetime' factor such as stress caused by a trauma.

This relationship is two-way – the experience of stress can trigger the biochemical dysfunction. But the dysfunction affects the individual's experience of stress.

OH, MY GOD... I FORGOT I HAD CHILDREN

A stress trigger?

Revision booster

You have also learned about a biological explanation for schizophrenia, so take care to note any similarities or differences between the explanation for depression and for schizophrenia. Which neurotransmitters are involved with both disorders and which are different? What is their site of action? Spending time thinking about similarities and differences may stop you being muddled.

✓ Check it

You have studied **one** disorder other than schizophrenia.

1. Describe how **one** biological explanation accounts for the symptoms of this disorder. [4]

2. Explain **two** strengths of the biological explanation for this disorder. [4]

3. **Standard essay:** Evaluate **one** biological explanation for this disorder. [8] or [20]

4. **I&D/Synoptic essay:** Assess the development of psychological knowledge over time with reference to **one** disorder other than schizophrenia. [20]

Unipolar depression: One non-biological explanation

A01
Description

Glass-half-empty thinking is characteristic of depression.

Apply it Methods

A study looked at attention to negative stimuli such as words like 'loser' or 'misery'. There were three groups of participants: (a) depressed group (people diagnosed with depression), (b) vulnerable group (people who scored high on a test of vulnerability to depression) and (c) non-depressed group (participants listened to sad music so they would experience a low mood). The depressed group found it hard to avoid noticing negative stimuli. This was not true for the other two groups.

1. (a) Suggest **one** positive word and **one** further negative word that could have been used as stimuli in the study. (2)

   (b) Explain how attention to the stimuli could be measured. (2)

2. Explain which **two** groups were control groups. (2)

3. **Context essay:** Discuss how **one** non-biological explanation could account for the findings of this study. (8)

Cognitive explanations for unipolar depression

Faulty/irrational thinking is a symptom of depression but also may be the cause, and becomes a downward spiral.

e.g. if a person believes everyone dislikes them, they may develop negative feelings about themselves which in turn reinforce their perception that everyone dislikes them.

Beck's cognitive explanation for depression

Focuses on faulty cognitions (Beck 1967).

The *negative cognitive triad* – depressed people make three types of cognitive error, pessimistic/irrational thoughts about:

• The self – believes they are worthless, unattractive, a failure, etc. Confirms their feelings of low self-esteem.

• The future – views the future in unavoidably negative ways (e.g. 'I will never… get a job, be happy', etc.).

• The world – perceives the world (people, situations, events) as hopeless.

Faulty cognitions stem from childhood (criticism and rejection), unrealistic expectations and experiences of loss.

Ellis' ABC theory

Focuses on irrational thinking (Ellis 1962).

'Rational' thinking = thinking that allows us to be happy and free of (psychological) pain.

Anything else is clearly irrational.

A – Activating event

• Irrational thoughts are triggered by situations.

• Depression occurs when negative external events (e.g. failing an exam) activate irrational thoughts and beliefs.

B – Beliefs

• Person's irrational beliefs about the event cause depression, not the event itself. For example:

   Musterbation ('I must be perfect, I must be successful, I must be the most attractive.').

   Utopianism ('Life should always be fair.').

   I-can't-stand-it-itis (something not going perfectly is a major disaster).

• The beliefs are mostly self-defeating, so the person interprets the event in the most negative way.

C – Consequences

• Irrational beliefs have emotional and behavioural consequences.

   e.g. someone who believes life should always be fair may become depressed when things do not turn out that way, or a person who 'must always be successful' could react particularly badly to failure.

A strength of Beck's theory is research support.

Evans et al. (2005) measured self-beliefs of 12,003 women who were 18 weeks pregnant.	Those with the most negative beliefs were more likely to eventually become depressed than women with positive self-beliefs. A negative self-schema is a risk factor for depression in women.	These cognitions occurred before the onset of depression, supporting Beck's view that negative beliefs cause the disorder.

CA However, other studies do not support causation. For instance, Dohr et al. (1989) found that negative self-beliefs expressed during a depressive episode usually become positive afterwards. According to Brown (2007), there is much evidence that negative thinking accompanies depression but little evidence it causes depression.

You can if you think you can!

A weakness is that Beck's and Ellis' explanations are incomplete.

Depression is a complex disorder – not all of the symptoms are experienced by everyone, and there are individual differences in severity.	Some depressed people experience extreme symptoms such as hallucinations and delusions.	This makes it hard to see how the cognitive triad and dysfunctional beliefs can account for the variety of experiences of depression.

Revision booster

This is an explanation based on the idea that depression arises from faulty *cognition*. You therefore could think about ideas from Year 1, such as information processing to help to show that you understand how it is a cognitive theory.

Another weakness is that Beck's theory has validity issues.

Eysenck (1997) argues the theory does not explain depression, mainly because there is no independent way of establishing the existence of negative *schemas*.	This means the theory lacks predictive validity because it does not identify risk factors for depression and cannot predict who is likely to become depressed.	This suggests that Beck's theory may be a better explanation for how depressive episodes are triggered and maintained over time rather than how depression is caused.

Application: Both theories have led to effective treatments for depression.

Lipsky et al. (1980) support Ellis' view that challenging the irrational beliefs of depressed people can improve their symptoms.	Beck's CBT identifies the components of the negative triad, and the therapist encourages the depressed client to test whether they are true.	This evidence shows that cognitive techniques successfully treat depression, implying faulty information processing may be at the root of the disorder.

I&D extra: Cognitive explanations illustrate reductionism in psychology.

Beck's and Ellis' theories seek to reduce the complex experience of depression to cognitive dysfunctions such as negative self-schemas.	The theory leads to treatments that target cognitions rather than wider socioeconomic factors (e.g. social inequality).	This lack of a more holistic perspective may be a weakness of the cognitive approach.

✓ Check it

You have studied **one** disorder other than schizophrenia.

1.   Describe **one** non-biological explanation for this disorder. [4]

2.   Compare **one** biological and **one** non-biological explanation for this disorder. [4]

3.   **Standard essay:** Assess **one** non-biological explanation for this disorder. [8] or [20]

4.   **Standard plus essay:** Evaluate **one** non-biological explanation for this disorder. Make at least **one** comparison with **one** biological explanation in your answer. [8] or [20]

Unipolar depression: One biological treatment

A01
Description

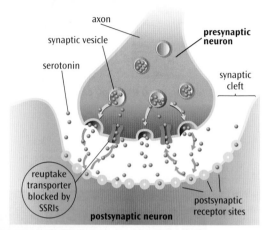

Diagram showing how SSRIs work, blocking the reuptake of serotonin at the presynaptic neuron. This increases the amount of serotonin in the synaptic cleft so there is more there to stimulate the postsynaptic neuron, thus improving mood.

Labels in diagram:
axon
synaptic vesicle
presynaptic neuron
serotonin
synaptic cleft
reuptake transporter blocked by SSRIs
postsynaptic receptor sites
postsynaptic neuron

 **Methods**

Ava is taking antidepressants. She felt much better when her doctor explained that her symptoms were typical of depression, that she wasn't to blame for how she felt and that there were good biological treatments available for depression. However, she is already thinking that she wants to discontinue the treatment.

1. Explain **one** reason why Ava may have benefited from her doctor's advice, other than his advice about the best treatment. (2)

2. (a) Suggest how **one** drug could help Ava. (4)
   (b) Explain **one** reason why Ava may want to discontinue the biological treatment. (2)

3. **Context essay:** Discuss how Ava's visit to her doctor may help her. (8)

Drug treatments for unipolar depression	Antidepressants work mainly by influencing the activity of the neurotransmitter *serotonin* as well as the brain circuits that produce and use serotonin.
MAOIs Monoamine oxidase inhibitors. Introduced in 1950s.	After normal neurotransmission and reuptake: • Excess neurotransmitter in the synapse is removed by an enzyme. • This 'degrades' the neurotransmitter into chemical components, which are reabsorbed by the presynaptic neuron. MAOIs: • Weaken this mechanism by inhibiting the activity of the enzyme *monoamine oxidase*. • Serotonin remains in the synapse for further use because it escapes degradation. • Also raise levels of *dopamine* and *noradrenaline*.
SSRIs Selective serotonin reuptake inhibitors. Introduced in 1980s.	Most common UK antidepressants, e.g. *fluoxetine* (Prozac). SSRIs interact with fewer compounds than MAOIs (so are safer in overdose). Serotonin transporter in the synapse pumps serotonin molecules back into the presynaptic neuron. SSRIs block the serotonin transporter, so serotonin cannot be recycled and remains in the synapse for further use. Prolongs antidepressant effects of serotonin through repeated binding with receptors on the postsynaptic neuron.
SNRIs Serotonin-noradrenaline reuptake inhibitors.	Newer generation (e.g. *duloxetine*) developed due to increased understanding that noradrenaline also regulates mood. Work in a similar way to SSRIs, but target noradrenaline as well as serotonin, inhibiting reuptake of both neurotransmitters.
NaSSAs Noradrenergic and specific serotonergic antidepressants.	Useful for people who do not benefit from SSRIs/SNRIs (e.g. if they were ineffective or side effects were intolerable). NaSSAs have a complex action, working in two main ways: • Inhibit reuptake of serotonin and noradrenaline (but much less than SSRIs/SNRIs). • Antagonists of serotonin and noradrenaline receptors. Seems counterintuitive to increase serotonin by blocking the receptors but there are 14 types of receptor: • NaSSAs block the serotonin receptors *5-HT2* and *5-HT3*, increasing activity of the key *5-HT1A* receptor. • NaSSAs also block a noradrenaline receptor (*a2-adrenergic* receptor).

A strength of antidepressants is research support for their effectiveness.

Cipriani *et al.* (2018) reviewed high-quality published and unpublished studies of 21 antidepressants.

In 522 double-blind trials involving 116,477 randomly-allocated people with depression, drugs were found to be more effective than placebo.

This is the most ambitious demonstration yet that antidepressants can improve mood in clinically diagnosed individuals.

CA However, the same study also found that some of the most effective drugs were also the ones with the worst compliance rates (i.e. people were more likely to stop taking them). Effect sizes were also 'mostly modest'. Any antidepressant will lift mood more than doing nothing, but factors such as individual differences mean antidepressants are not universally useful.

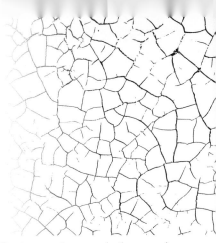

Drugs are not a cure, do they merely paper over the cracks?

A weakness is that drugs relieve symptoms but do not tackle causes.

Effective antidepressants stabilise the dysfunctional serotonin circuits in the brain, but only for as long as the person takes the drug.

Symptoms such as low mood improve (although not always), but the cause of the depression (genetic or environmental) remains.

This means the benefits of drugs are limited in the long-term (so a psychological therapy may be more useful).

Revision booster

Being able to explain the action of antidepressants clearly depends on a thorough understanding of synaptic transmission from Year 1. Before revising the topic on this spread, ensure that you can remember events such as release of neurotransmitters into the synapse and their movement across the synapse, attachment to receptors and breakdown/reuptake of neurotransmitters.

Another strength is ethical issues in treating depression as a medical disorder.

A common belief about depression ('just pull yourself together') implies the cause is a lack of motivation or other 'psychological weakness'.

The fact that drugs are effective helps people see that the condition is related to physical changes and not the individual's 'fault'.

This is beneficial because, by removing the stigma linked to depression, more people are willing to seek treatment.

Application: Knowing about side effects helps to manage them.

Most side effects are common and mild but some are rare and severe. Also, MAOIs interact with other drugs and with chemicals in food (e.g. tyramine).

These issues can be controlled with careful monitoring of the individual's diet and additional medication.

This ability to manage the side effects increases the credibility and acceptability of the treatment, so people are likely to continue with it.

I&D extra: Treatment shows how psychological knowledge is useful in society.

Depression is the world's leading cause of disability (WHO). Biological psychologists have made a significant contribution to understanding, preventing and treating it.

As there are biological/medical treatments, then depression is a medical condition and not a personal failing.

This demonstrates how psychology can help to reduce the personal and economic burden of depression on individuals, families and societies.

Check it

You have studied **one** disorder other than schizophrenia.

1. Describe how a biological treatment may reduce the symptoms of this disorder. [4]

2. Explain **one** strength of **one** biological treatment for this disorder. You must refer to research evidence in your answer. [3]

3. **Standard essay:** Assess **one** biological treatment for this disorder. [8] or [20]

4. **Standard plus essay:** Assess practical and ethical issues relating to the use of **one** biological treatment for this disorder. [8] or [20]

Unipolar depression: One non-biological treatment

Clients may have to convince themselves to keep up with their homework (do you know that feeling?).

Apply it Concepts

Bryn has an appointment to see a therapist about his depression. A colleague, Nick, has had a non-biological treatment for depression. Nick tells Bryn that this kind of treatment is really tough. He says that sessions may involve Bryn being told what to think, making Bryn do things he doesn't want to do and questioning Bryn's beliefs in a threatening way.

1. (a) Explain why Nick says Bryn will be made to do things he doesn't want to do. (2)
   (b) Explain **two** types of questions a therapist may use that Nick may have perceived as threatening. (4)

2. Nick says nothing positive about non-biological treatment. Suggest **one** comment he could make to encourage Bryn to attend his appointment. (2)

3. **Context essay:** Discuss Nick's beliefs about **one** non-biological treatment for depression. (8)

Beck's cognitive-behavioural treatment (CBT) for depression	Cognitive – corrects faulty cognitions by addressing the *negative cognitive triad* with a range of therapeutic techniques.
	Behaviourist – uses learning theory techniques to help the client develop skills to function effectively (e.g. coping with everyday life).
Assessment	Therapist and client assess aspects of the client's functioning (severity, past treatments, personal coping resources, etc.).
	Questionnaires and interviews measure depression and co-morbid disorders (e.g. anxiety and substance abuse).
	Therapist and client identify specific issues, list the goals for therapy and construct a plan.
	A key task is to identify the client's negative thoughts and re-evaluate them to avoid relapse.
Role of education	Client has an active role in the therapy plan, so needs to clearly understand their symptoms (learn about the role of faulty thinking).
	Therapist is a valuable source of information and also provides other resources (e.g. printed or online materials).
	Therapist suggests and explains techniques to help the client, who can then express their views from a position of knowledge.
Role of homework	Therapy sessions identify and challenge faulty cognitions.
	Client also carries out the plan in real life – homework tests the reality of negative beliefs (like a scientist tests a hypothesis).
	e.g. client writes down the details of an event they enjoyed or an occasion when someone was nice to them.
	When client later says 'Everyone hates me', the therapist can use written evidence to show the client's negative beliefs are wrong.
A typical session Clinical psychologist Keith Dobson (2008).	Client's current functioning is assessed (e.g. *Beck Depression Inventory*), changes since last session can then be discussed.
	Discussion moves on to recent homework – what the client learned or perhaps why it was not completed.
	Client chooses the most important issues to discuss.
	Therapist might use the *three questions technique* to challenge the client's *automatic negative thoughts* (ANTs):
	• Three questions – What's the evidence? What are the alternatives? So what?
	• Helps client address cognitive distortions, such as jumping to conclusions.
	• Can explore possibility that ANTs may not be the only interpretations of an event.

A strength is research support for the effectiveness of CBT.

Elkin *et al*. (1989) randomly allocated 239 participants diagnosed with depression to one of four treatment groups.	CBT was as effective in reducing symptoms as interpersonal therapy, antidepressants, or a placebo pill. Effectiveness continued after 18 months (Shea *et al* 1992).	This shows that CBT is a successful treatment for mild to moderate depression in the short- and longer-term.

CA However, both studies also showed that CBT was not a very useful therapy for severely depressed people. Antidepressants were significantly more effective, as was interpersonal therapy. CBT was also not especially effective in preventing relapse. After 18 months, 36% of CBT clients relapsed, a higher rate than in the interpersonal therapy group. On the other hand, later studies (e.g. DeRubeis *et al*. 2005) showed that CBT can be equally effective for mild, moderate and severe depression.

A weakness of CBT concerns the therapeutic relationship.

Easterbrook and Meehan (2017) suggest that CBT practitioners have downplayed the importance of the therapeutic relationship.	They concluded that a collaborative relationship established before using CBT encouraged more open communication.	Therefore, CBT practitioners might improve outcomes if they additionally focus on the quality of the therapeutic relationship.

Another weakness is that treatment adherence is an issue in CBT.

CBT is very challenging, especially for severely depressed clients who may not benefit without the aid of antidepressant medication.	CBT requires commitment to therapy and homework tasks. Some find it hard to have well-established negative thoughts challenged.	This results in high dropout rates which are costly for the NHS and make it difficult to assess the true effectiveness of therapy.

Application: CBT can help prevent relapses into depression.

Unlike biological treatments, clients in CBT learn skills and techniques they apply for themselves (e.g. ways of combating ANTs).	This does not require a therapist in the longer term as homework develops independence. It respects clients' dignity, giving them control.	Thus the client becomes their own therapist which makes it less likely that depression will recur.

I&D extra: CBT illustrates how psychological understanding has developed.

Beck originally felt that the outcomes of psychodynamic therapy were poor, mostly because of its focus on the client's past and the unconscious mind.	But ultimately – like the psychodynamic approach – Beck acknowledged that it was important to explore the meaning of the client's experiences.	This shows how approaches to treatment build on each other to become increasingly effective – keeping some ideas, removing others and adding new ones.

Interpersonal therapy is a therapy used specifically for depression that focuses on the person and their relationships with other people.

Combat those ANTs!

Revision booster

Look for similarities and differences of the two treatments for depression that you have learned. This will not only help you to answer short answer 'compare' questions, but can also provide you with advantages and disadvantages for an essay question asking you to evaluate one or the other. For example, think about whether one but not the other has side effects, or takes a long time to work.

✓ Check it

You have studied **one** disorder other than schizophrenia.

1. Longitudinal studies can help determine the effectiveness of non-biological treatments.

   Suggest how a longitudinal study could be used to research **one** non-biological treatment for this disorder. [3]

2. Compare **one** biological and **one** non-biological treatment for this disorder. [6]

3. **Standard essay:** Assess **one** non-biological treatment for this disorder. [8] or [20]

4. **I&D essay:** Evaluate ethical issues arising from human research into **one** disorder other than schizophrenia. [16]

Contemporary study on depression: Kroenke *et al.* (2008)

Spec spotlight

5.3.3 One contemporary study on depression: Kroenke et al. *(2008) The PHQ-8 as a measure of current depression in the general population.*

Methods

Wormwood *et al.* (2018) used the PHQ-8 to assess depressive symptoms in participants in the laboratory. The researchers reassessed the same participants two weeks later, after they had read various news items (all items were assessed in terms of positive or negative content). Those participants who read more negative news reported more physical and depressive symptoms.

1. Explain **two** ethical issues raised in this study and how they could be solved. (4)

2. **(a)** Draw a graph to illustrate the correlational findings of this study. (3)

   (b) Explain why the PHQ-8 is a good choice to use if the researchers wished to widen the study to an online survey. (2)

3. **Context/Methods essay:** Discuss the ethical issues raised in studies on depression such as Wormwood *et al*'s. (8)

Graph showing the number of self-reported days of impaired HRQoL in the 'past 30 days' of the study.

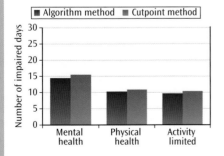

| ■ Algorithm method | ■ Cutpoint method |

Aims

To assess the PHQ-8 as a method of measuring depression in a large population.

To compare two methods of defining depression (diagnostic algorithm and cutpoint).

Procedure

BRFSS = Behavioural Risk Factor Surveillance Survey.

PHQ = Patient Health Questionnaire.

BRFSS – monthly phone survey in the US on health-related behaviours, 38 states included in this study.

Sample – 198,678 randomly-selected adults.

Interviewees completed PHQ-8 (lists eight DSM-IV symptoms related to depression). For each symptom, they stated the number of days each symptom was experienced in the past two weeks. Produced a score of 0–24.

PHQ-8 assessed 'current depression' using:

- Diagnostic algorithm method – symptoms apparent on more than half the days for at least 5 out of 8 items.
- Cutpoint method – PHQ-8 score of 10 or more.

The *Health-related quality of life* (HRQoL):

- Analysed three questions from the BRFSS measuring mental and physical health in previous 30 days.
- Had five additional questions (e.g. sleep problems, pain limitations) which were asked in three US states only.

Findings

PHQ-8 distribution

- Diagnostic algorithm method – MDD prevalence of 4.3%.
- Any depression – diagnostic algorithm method prevalence 9.1%, cutpoint method prevalence 8.6%.

HRQoL and depression

- Depressed respondents had more days of impaired HRQoL (all types) than nondepressed people.
- No difference between algorithm and cutpoint methods in number of impaired HRQoL days (depressed and nondepressed).

Conclusions

Prevalence rates using the PHQ-8 are generally 'accurate or slightly conservative estimates of depression in the US'.

The PHQ-8 is useful in research contexts – it portrays depression as a dimension along which people vary in severity.

This gives the PHQ-8 an advantage because the DSM-5 (which was not yet produced at the time of this study) was likely to introduce a dimensional element to diagnosis.

PHQ-8 is just as good at measuring severity as other scales and is superior for diagnosing depression under the DSM-IV.

A strength of the study is it used standardised procedures.

Kroenke *et al.*'s data from the BRFSS used a standardised questionnaire and was administered by trained interviewers by phone.

Interviewers followed a detailed protocol, so procedures were carried out consistently. Also no face-to-face cues that could affect responses.

This means that the study had good reliability as the experience of the survey was similar for all respondents.

A weakness is that the study had sampling issues.

The BRFSS did not include people in institutions (e.g. treated for a mental illness) or anyone who did not have or could not use a phone.

These characteristics may apply to people with higher depression rates, resulting in an unrepresentative sample of the US adult population.

This means the sample would have been biased and the study underestimated (or overestimated) the true prevalence of depression.

All of the phone interviewers were highly trained.

Another strength is that the study considered ethical issues carefully.

BRFSS respondents complete a detailed consent form and their data is kept confidential and protected by law (in the US this is primarily the US Privacy Act).

But the questions (e.g. about depression and anxiety) are personal and may cause stress. Surveillance of the nation's health raises questions of privacy.

On balance, the BRFSS is carried out in an ethically responsible way which means people are more likely to participate, contributing to the validity of the survey.

Application: The PHQ-8 could be used to help prevent depression.

As a 'quick and easy' instrument, it could be used to screen large numbers of people.

This would improve the chances of identifying the early signs and symptoms of depressive disorders.

This is a strength because early identification is cost-effective and helps avoid personal distress, as depression is linked to poor quality of life.

CA However, application of the PHQ-8 is limited. This is because it is based on the PHQ-9 but leaves out item 9 on suicidal thoughts (inappropriate in a phone survey). So the PHQ-9 is more useful in clinical situations to diagnose and treat depression because it can identify the symptom of suicidal thoughts, whereas the PHQ-8 cannot.

I&D extra: The study shows the benefits of psychological knowledge to society.

Large-scale population-based surveys such as the BRFSS can reveal valuable information about depression and who is affected by it.

This includes how depressed and nondepressed people differ in terms of quality of life, differences in prevalence and factors influencing severity of depression.

The result is that these issues help us to understand depression and its possible causes better and thus direct resources appropriately within society.

✓ Check it

You have studied **one** contemporary study of **one** disorder other than schizophrenia.

1. Justify **one** design decision from the procedure of this study. (2)

2. Suggest **one** improvement to this contemporary study. (2)

3. **Standard essay:** Assess this contemporary study of a disorder other than schizophrenia. (8) or (20)

4. **Methods essay:** Evaluate this contemporary study, including the way in which the data was collected and analysed. (8) or (20)

Contemporary study on depression: Williams *et al.* (2013)

Spec spotlight

5.3.4 One contemporary study on depression: Williams et al. *(2013) Combining imagination and reason in the treatment of depression: a randomised control trial of internet based cognitive bias modification and internet-CBT for depression.*

The following questionnaires were used in Williams *et al.*'s (2013) study:
- BDI-II = Beck Depression Inventory (measured depression).
- K10 = Kessler Psychological Distress Scale (measured distress).
- AST-D = Ambiguous Scenarios Test–Depression (measured positive interpretation of ambiguous scenarios).

Apply it Methods

Yang *et al.* (2018) conducted a meta-analysis of web-based intervention studies including Williams *et al.* (2013). The outcome of the meta-analysis supported Williams *et al.*'s findings. All the studies in the meta-analysis included both genders, and had a control group who were either given their usual treatment (treatment as usual, TAU) or put on a register to await treatment (a wait-list control, WLC).

1. Explain **one** reason why Yang *et al.*'s meta-analyses could be more useful than Williams *et al.*'s study. (2)
2. **(a)** Suggest why it was desirable that all studies included both genders. (2)
   (b) Explain **one** advantage and **one** disadvantage of a TAU group compared to a WLC. (4)
3. **Context/Methods essay:** Discuss the use of meta-analyses such as Yang *et al.* in clinical psychology.

A table comparing mean scores for the different groups of participants.

Measure	Group	T1	T2	T3
BDI-II	Intervention	27.97	18.96	10.40
	WLC	28.00	24.82	20.54
K10	Intervention	29.26	24.11	17.40
	WLC	28.62	28.33	24.45
AST-D	Intervention	4.18	4.67	N/A
	WLC	4.60	4.32	N/A

Aims

To study the impact of 'imagery-based cognitive bias modification' (CBM-I) on negative thinking bias, distress and symptoms.

To see whether this intervention would improve the effectiveness of online CBT (iCBT).

Method

Sample – clients recruited by an Australian clinic. Participants completed an online screening questionnaire and diagnostic interview by phone, resulting in 69 participants, randomly allocated to intervention group or wait-list control group (WLC).

- Time 1 (T1) – baseline measures of depression symptoms, distress, degree of disability, anxiety, negative thinking.

  Intervention group – seven days CBM-I.
  WLC – no intervention.

- Time 2 (T2) – all clients complete questionnaires again.

  Intervention group – 10-week iCBT course.
  WLC – no intervention.

- Time 3 (T3) – all clients complete questionnaires again.

  WLC group – 10-week iCBT (*without* initial week of CBM-I).

All clients rated satisfaction with the programme on a five-point scale.

CBM-I ('bottom up'):
- Daily 20-minute sessions for one week.
- Shown ambiguous scenarios resolved in a positive way, to train clients to think positively about events in everyday lives.

iCBT ('top-down'):
- *Sadness Program* is six online lessons showcasing 'best practice CBT' (includes homework, access to resources).

Findings

CBM-I (T2) – mean BDI-II score dropped 9 points (from T1) for intervention group, 3 points for WLC.

iCBT (T3) – mean BDI-II score dropped nearly 18 points (from T1) for intervention group, only 7.5 points lower for WLC.

Mean K10 score decreased nearly 12 points (from T1) for intervention group, 4 points for WLC.

Following CBM-I, mean AST-D score increased by 0.5 for intervention group, and dropped by 0.3 for WLC.

Conclusions

Brief online CBM-I has significant symptom effect in one week.

Combined intervention significantly reduces depressive symptoms, distress, disability, anxiety and rumination in people diagnosed with a major depressive episode.

The integration of a 'bottom-up' approach into more traditional 'top-down' iCBT may be a useful addition.

A strength is that a wait-list control group (WLC) was included.

The WLC group completed the same set of questionnaires as the intervention group over the course of the 11-week study period.	The study could establish the extent to which changes in symptoms and distress were due to the interventions and not just the passing of time.	This was an important practical consideration which increased the overall validity of the study.

CA This said, the study could have been improved by collecting further data from the WLC group following their 10-week course of iCBT (without CBM-I). This would have allowed the researchers to determine how much the additional week of CBM-I contributed to the reduction of symptoms. Furthermore, it would have been helpful if the researchers had followed up both groups several months later.

A weakness is that there were problems with quantitative data.

People often do not give honest answers on self-report scales (intervention participants may over-estimate improvements as they were aware of being in therapy).	Furthermore quantitative data tells us nothing about why symptoms have improved, whereas a semi-structured interview using open questions might have done this.	This means that the data collected might be biased and the research fails to provide more than a superficial understanding of how the therapy works.

Something told the researchers that Jane's self-report answers weren't altogether genuine.

Another weakness is that there was no 'active' control group.

No comparison was made in the study to an alternative therapy (e.g. an active control group).	This means clinical change might be due to other factors (e.g. attention from a therapist) instead of the techniques used.	This was tested in a further study (Williams *et al.* 2015) but the control condition was not effective as it had similar ingredients to CBM.

Revision booster

When deciding how to answer a question it is important to develop the skill of 'selectivity'. Try not to write the first thing that comes into your head. Instead decide what best matches the question that is being asked. For example, if you are asked an extended response methods question, make sure your answer is about the method, using the context for examples.

Application: The study can help to improve clinical practice.

Symptoms and distress can be significantly reduced without costly face-to-face time with a clinician (just seven extra days of CBM-I led to further gains).	Online services could mean that people on NHS waiting lists may be able to access critical and potentially life-saving support at home.	This is clearly a useful application of psychology as users are once again able to enjoy life at work and with their families.

✓ Check it

You have studied **one** contemporary study of **one** disorder other than schizophrenia.

1. Describe this contemporary study. (5)

2. Explain **one** weakness of this contemporary study. (2)

3. **Standard essay:** Assess **one** contemporary study of a disorder other than schizophrenia. (8) or (20)

4. **I&D essay:** Evaluate a classic and contemporary study of a disorder other than schizophrenia with reference to the development of psychological knowledge over time. (20)

I&D extra: The study illustrates the importance of considering culture.

Cultural barriers and increased stigma towards mental health often preclude Chinese people from seeking treatment.	But Choi *et al.* (2012) adapted iCBT so it would be relevant to Chinese-Australians. Zheng (2017) found improvements six months later.	This shows that iCBT can be modified to reflect the culturally-specific experiences of differing populations.

Explanations of crime and anti-social behaviour: Biological explanations

Spec spotlight

Explanations of crime and anti-social behaviour, with consideration given to gender differences.

6.1.1 Biological explanations, including brain injury, amygdala and aggression, XYY syndrome.

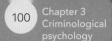

Apply it Concepts

Sara had two boys, Toby and Arlo who are now in their 30s and in prison. Both were very sporty but Arlo had two severe accidental head injuries as a child which stopped him playing football. Toby used to be utterly fearless and crash into things, hurting his arms and legs. Now Arlo is the risk-taker.

1. Explain how Arlo's childhood may have affected:
   (a) His adult thinking. (2)
   (b) His adult temperament. (2)

2. Suggest **one** biological reason why Toby may have been reckless as a child. (2)

3. **Context essay:** Discuss biological explanations for Toby and Arlo's criminal behaviour. (8)

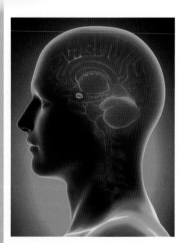

The amygdala – if you wondered where to find it.

Brain injury

Link between brain injury (especially in childhood) and offending.

Williams *et al.* (2010) studied inmates from a single UK prison, 60% recalled one or more head injuries in their youth.

This 60% were younger at first offence, engaged in more reoffending, spent more time in prison in the previous five years than the rest of the sample.

Acquired brain injuries (ABIs) result from e.g. sports accidents.

Connection between ABIs and offending:

- Brain is not fully mature until mid-20s. Cognitive abilities (e.g. impulse control, forward planning) are among the last functions to develop.
- ABI can disrupt development, so the person fails to move beyond the reckless and risk-taking behaviour of childhood.
- Brain injury may also destabilise mood, concentration and decision-making, making offending behaviour more likely.

Amygdala and aggression

Almond-shaped structure in the *temporal lobe* of both brain hemispheres.

The *amygdala* is part of the *limbic system* which directs how we react to threatening situations (part of the brain's 'startle response').

Raine *et al.* (1997) found reduced metabolic activity in several brain areas of psychopathic murderers, including the left amygdala.

Gao *et al.* (2010) conducted a study looking at the role of abnormal amygdala functioning:

- Sample – 1,795 children aged 3, conditioned to fear certain sounds (one tone followed by a loud unpleasant sound, and another followed by silence). Whether the child developed a conditioned fear response to the first tone was assessed using measures of skin conductance.
- 20 years later, those who went on to commit crimes were less likely to have shown a fear response to the first tone.
- Abnormal amygdala functioning (lack of fear at age 3).

Pardini *et al.* (2014) conducted neuroimaging scans:

- 26-year-old men were grouped according to whether they had normal-volume or reduced-volume amygdala.
- Three years later, the reduced-volume men were three times more likely than the others to be aggressive, violent and show psychopathic traits.

XYY syndrome

About 1 in 10,000 genetic males are born with an additional Y chromosome.

Testosterone levels and sexual development are unaffected, but XYY males are taller than average, have lower intelligence, can be impulsive and may experience behavioural difficulties.

Jacobs *et al.* (1965) reported a connection between XYY syndrome, aggression and crime:

- Chromosome survey of male patients in a Scottish hospital.
- Men with XYY chromosomal pattern were over-represented in prison populations (around 15 per 10,000) compared to the general population.

A strength is supporting evidence for the link between brain injury and crime.

Fazel *et al.* (2011) studied the link between brain injury and convictions for violent crime, including murder, sexual offences, robbery and assault.

Of those who experienced a brain injury, 8.8% had committed a violent crime compared to 3% in a matched control group of similar size.

This suggests that physical trauma to the brain may be a precursor to violent crime.

CA The relationship between brain injury and offending is not necessarily causal, other variables may have an influence. People with serious head injury are also more likely to experience mental illness, or be alcohol- or drug-abusers. It is these factors that may create the predisposition to offend, rather than the brain injury itself.

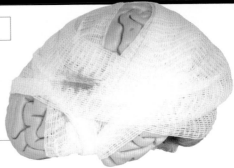

Do broken brains lead to broken laws?

'CA' stands for 'competing argument'.

OFC = orbitofrontal cortex

A weakness is the complex relationship between the amygdala and crime.

The amygdala does not operate alone but is influenced by the OFC (part of the frontal lobe, not the limbic system).

The OFC regulates self-control, and reduced functioning is associated with increased aggression and violent outbursts.

This suggests that the influence of the amygdala (and all brain areas) on aggression (and crime) is difficult to disentangle.

A weakness of the XYY syndrome explanation is the lack of evidence.

Re and Birkhoff's (2015) meta-analysis considered 50 years of evidence and concluded that there is no link between XYY and offending behaviour.

Prevalence of XYY males within prison populations, might be explained by social factors (e.g. XYY characteristics make it harder to integrate into society and find work).

Therefore, the XYY syndrome is not a credible explanation for crime.

Application: Biological research may lead to new ways to assess culpability.

Williams *et al.* (2010) argue for more awareness of brain injuries in the criminal justice system, including standard screening of young people when they first offend.

Neural injury should be viewed in the same way as mental health and taken into account in sentencing (punishment should be reduced as the person is less responsible for their crime).

This shows that biological explanations may come to have an important influence on decision-making during criminal trials.

I&D extra: Biological explanations of criminal behaviour are reductionist.

The idea of explaining crime as the result of a single biological factor is appealing because it suggests that there are simple solutions for dealing with crime.

But this ignores the fact that offending is more likely to occur in a context of social deprivation, poor education and dysfunctional role models (Farrington *et al.* 2006).

This means that biological explanations may distract us from a truer understanding of crime.

Revision booster

Although the heading here of 'biological explanations' sounds quite general, you need to know some very specific concepts as these are named in the specification – make sure that you can respond to direct questions about brain injury, the amygdala and aggression, XYY syndrome and gender differences in crime and anti-social behaviour.

 Check it

1. Explain the link between XYY syndrome and crime and/or anti-social behaviour. [4]

2. Austin is in prison for a violent assault. His parole officer believes an abnormality of the amygdala may be responsible.

   Explain **one** strength of this explanation for Austin's behaviour. [2]

3. **Standard essay:** Evaluate **one** biological explanation for crime and/or anti-social behaviour. [8] or [16]

4. **Prompt essay:** Biological explanations for crime call criminal responsibility into question.

   Evaluate biological explanations for crime with reference to how society responds to crime and offenders. [16]

Explanations of crime and anti-social behaviour: Personality

A01
Description

Crimes against dancing? Looks like it.

Apply it Concepts

Luke is a quiet boy who hates being told off for doing something wrong. He is talking with his friends about who is most likely to get arrested. Jake is popular as he is loud and craves excitement – and because he is so reliable. If he says he will do something, he does. Gary has a sharp sense of humour, though his jokes are often hurtful and he can fly into a rage apparently over nothing.

1. (a) Describe **one** example of a boy's neurotic behaviour. (2)
   (b) Describe **one** example of a boy's psychotic behaviour. (2)

2. Explain extraversion and introversion using **two** of the boys as examples. (2)

3. **Context essay:** Discuss why some of the boys' personalities might put them at risk of criminality. (8)

Eysenck's theory of the criminal personality

Two dimensions of personality related to the criminal type.

Extraversion (E)–Introversion

- Extraverts crave excitement and stimulation, so are prone to engage in dangerous, risk-taking behaviour.
- They also tend not to condition easily (they do not learn from their mistakes).
- This means an extravert engaging in criminal behaviour would not be affected as strongly by punishment as an introvert would.

Neuroticism (N)–Stability

- Neurotic individuals are easily agitated and anxious.
- Their general instability means their behaviour is difficult to predict.

According to Eysenck, the typical criminal personality is an *extravert–neurotic*.

Biological basis

Eysenck's theory is essentially biological in nature.

The personality traits we develop throughout our lives are explained by the type of nervous system we inherit:

- Extraverts have a constant need for excitement. This may be caused by an underactive nervous system which requires unusually high levels of arousal.
- Neurotics are volatile and react strongly to situations others would find less stressful or even neutral.

A third dimension – psychoticism

Eysenck later added another dimension to the criminal type.

Psychoticism (P) is seen in people who are self-centred, cold and lack empathy for others (Eysenck was less clear about the link with the nervous system).

The criminal type scores highly on all three dimensions.

Eysenck developed the *Eysenck Personality Questionnaire* (EPQ), a questionnaire which places respondents along E, N and P dimensions to determine personality type.

The socialisation process

The theory has a biological emphasis but Eysenck acknowledged that the socialisation process in childhood determines whether a person becomes law-abiding or not.

However, the fact that extraverts are natural reward-seekers makes them less receptive to operant conditioning and therefore less affected by punishment for wrongdoing.

Similarly, high neuroticism interferes with efficient learning which may relate to difficulty taking on board social rules.

These factors make extravert–neurotics more likely to behave anti-socially.

A strength is empirical evidence supporting the existence of a criminal type.

Boduszek et al. (2013) investigated Eysenck's personality traits in repeat offenders (133 violent and 179 non-violent males in a high-security prison).	A criminal thinking 'style' correlated with high psychoticism, neuroticism and extraversion (also linked to criminal friends and criminal identity).	This suggests that Eysenck's theory has validity as the personality types he identified are associated with repeat offending.

CA However, evidence for the criminal personality is not conclusive. Farrington et al. (1982) found little evidence that Eysenck's questionnaire (EPQ) was an adequate measure for predicting offending, in juveniles or adults. This suggests that Eysenck's original ideas about the nature of the criminal personality may lack validity.

A weakness is that there is not just one single criminal personality type.

The five-factor model of personality accepts Eysenck's concepts of extraversion and introversion, but adds openness, conscientiousness and agreeableness (= OCEAN).	Low levels of conscientiousness and agreeableness are related to offending. Also Lipsey and Derzon (1998) claim impulsivity is a better predictor of anti-social behaviour.	This research suggests that the criminal personality may be more complicated than Eysenck suggested.

Another strength is support for the biological basis of criminal personality.

Raine et al. (1990) took physiological measures from participants aged 15 years and related these to later criminal status.	24 years later those who had a criminal record had shown more signs of nervous system under-arousal when aged 15 than non-criminals (e.g. lower resting heart rate).	This suggests a link between biological factors and offending, but the researchers pointed out that there are also social variables that influence criminal behaviour.

Application: Eysenck's theory may help with early crime prevention.

The theory argues that criminal tendencies (e.g. lack of response to conditioning and inability to learn from mistakes) can be identified in early childhood.	Early intervention could modify the socialisation experiences of high-risk people to prevent them becoming offenders (in school or at home with support).	This would suggest that early interventions for vulnerable individuals, based on Eysenck's theory, may be beneficial.

I&D extra: Eysenck's theory integrates different ways of explaining behaviour.

It acknowledges genetic and physiological factors as well as individual differences in personality, and early socialisation.	This is a more integrated and interactionist approach than some of the other explanations discussed in this chapter.	This recognises that crime is a complex social activity that is likely to have different influences.

Unusually for him, Crooked Stan had decided honesty was the best policy.

Revision booster

The details on the specification for 'personality' are not very prescriptive compared with the other biological explanations on the previous spread. You still need to know a range of information thoroughly, but you cannot be asked specific questions about, for example, personality types, although you could be asked about gender differences.

✓ Check it

1. Compare personality with **one** other biological explanation for crime and/or anti-social behaviour. [4]

2. Explain **one** strength of personality as an explanation for crime and/or anti-social behaviour. [2]

3. **Standard essay:** Evaluate personality as an explanation for crime and/or anti-social behaviour. [8] or [16]

4. **Methods essay:** When studying crime, psychologists are interested in the links between personality and anti-social behaviour.

   Evaluate the validity and reliability of research in this area. [8] or [16]

Explanations of crime and anti-social behaviour: Social explanations

Spec spotlight

Explanations of crime and anti-social behaviour, with consideration given to gender differences.

6.1.2 Social explanations, including labelling, self-fulfilling prophecy.

Don't mess with the office workers. They've got spreadsheets and everything.

Apply it Methods

Eve is studying the effect of having an older brother or sister who is naughty. She believes that younger children with naughty older siblings will be labelled as anti-social at school whereas younger siblings of well-behaved children will not.

1. Write a directional hypothesis for Eve's study. (2)

2. (a) Describe **one** way that Eve could collect a representative sample for her study. (2)

   (b) Explain **one** reason why Eve may choose to use **one** named alternative sampling technique. (2)

3. **Context essay:** Discuss **one** social explanation for anti-social behaviour which would explain Eve's hypothesis. (8)

Social learning theory (SLT) proposes that behaviour is learned through both direct and indirect conditioning. The latter involves observation, vicarious reinforcement and modelling.

Social explanations

Crime may be learned as a result of social circumstances. However, criminal behaviour is still determined, but the source of the influence is social (i.e. other people), rather than biological.

Labelling

Labels people are given let us judge what must be going on inside, the kind of people they are.

If a person is labelled as 'criminal' or 'deviant', that will define them and affect how society behaves towards them.

Becker (1963) asked how and why are some actions labelled criminal in the first place?

- Powerful groups in society create deviance by making up rules and applying them to people they see as 'outsiders'.

- What counts as criminal behaviour only becomes so when labelled by others – crime is a *social construct*.

Self-fulfilling prophecy

Takes the idea of labelling a step further.

Research shows how describing students as 'disobedient', 'clever', etc. can have consequences for achievement:

- Teacher expectations based on a label are communicated to student, student then internalises their label (Rosenthal and Jacobson, 1968).

- Label becomes 'real' – it influences the student's perception of themselves and the teacher's behaviour.

This can equally be applied to the label 'criminal':

- The 'deviant' sees themselves in this way because of the stereotyped response of others towards their label.

- Stigmatised and isolated from society, the offender seeks support from deviant groups and subcultures.

- This draws the individual further into crime, confirming their criminal identity and deviant status.

Social learning

Assumptions of social learning theory that you studied in Year 1 can be applied to criminal behaviour.

Observational learning

- Criminal behaviour is learned indirectly by observing and imitating the actions of deviant others.

- To learn a criminal act, the behaviour must be attended to, recalled, and the would-be offender must have the skill and capacity to perform the behaviour successfully.

Vicarious reinforcement

- If criminal behaviour is to be imitated, it must be seen to be rewarded (vicarious reinforcement).

- Offending behaviour is rewarded through acquisition of money, increased status in a criminal gang, etc.

Role models

- Identification – a young offender may look up to and want to be like a gang leader (high status and respect, glamorous and attractive lifestyle).

A strength is that evidence supports the self-fulfilling prophecy.

Jahoda (1954) studied the Ashanti of Ghana (boys named after day of birth). Monday boys (*Kwadwo*) are thought to be even-tempered compared to 'aggressive and volatile' *Kwadku* (Wednesday boys).	Jahoda observed (over a five-year period) that Kwadku were three times more likely to be involved in violent crime than Kwadwo.	This suggests that a self-fulfilling prophecy based on cultural expectations had been formed and had influenced the boys' behaviour.

CA In contrast, a study by Zebrowitz *et al.* (1998) found that boys with a 'baby face' were more likely than their mature-faced peers to be delinquent and involved in crime. Perhaps the baby-faced boys were overcompensating for the perception they may be 'weak' or 'childlike', rather than living up to the 'baby/innocent' label.

Serving (bed)time.

A weakness is that labelling theory is only a partial explanation for offending.

Labelling theory implies that without labelling, crime would not exist (someone who commits an offence, but is not labelled, is not a criminal).	Most people would agree that serious offences (e.g. murder) are more than social constructs, and that murderers are criminals whether labelled or not.	This would suggest that labelling theory is too simple to be a single explanation for crime.

Another weakness is lack of evidence for labelling as applied to crime.

Most studies of labelling and self-fulfilling prophecy have been confined to educational settings (e.g. Rosenthal and Jacobson).	The teacher–student relationship may be unique in expectations having a major influence on a child's attainment (hard to replicate in the context of crime).	There are too many factors that affect the relationship between labelling and crime to study the phenomenon effectively.

Application: Knowledge of labelling may help with reintegrative shaming.

According to Braithwaite (1989), societies have lower crime rates and reoffending rates if they communicate shame about crime effectively.	In *reintegrative shaming*, the offender is supported back into society with guidance from family and prison staff, so are less likely to offend again.	This suggests that how offenders are labelled may affect how well they retake their place in society.

I&D extra: Social explanations contribute to the nature–nurture debate.

The explanations on this spread are supportive of the nurture side of the debate.	Supports the view that criminal behaviour is acquired through interaction with society and the immediate environment.	That said, crime is a complex social activity which is likely to be explained by a number of different influences (including nature, innate).

'Shaming' is an approach to offender punishment to communicate disapproval for a crime. *Reintegrative shaming* aims to do this in a way that makes the criminal feel they are a good person who has done a bad thing.

Check it

1. Explain self-fulfilling prophecy as an explanation for crime and/or anti-social behaviour. (3)

2. Compare **one** social and **one** biological explanation for crime and/or anti-social behaviour. (4)

3. **Standard essay:** Evaluate social explanations for crime and/or anti-social behaviour. (8) or (16)

4. **Context essay:** Arun was caught shoplifting clothing and hair straighteners.

   To what extent is Arun's behaviour likely to have resulted from social factors? (16)

Cognitive interview and ethical interview techniques

A01
Description

Never mind whether I nicked this coat, the question you should be asking is why are we stuck in the 1940s?

Revision booster

Take care with questions about interviewing! The cognitive and ethical interviews are described here but these are not research methods – for research methods you have learned about unstructured, semi-structured and structured interviews.

Methods

DC Quinn is collecting data about interview techniques. He wants to plot a graph to show how many facts were recalled correctly when a standard interview (SI) was used and when a cognitive interview (CI) was used. He believes CI is better and wants to know if there is a significant difference between the number of facts correctly recalled by his 11 witnesses in SIs and 12 witnesses in CIs.

1. Name the type of graph DC Quinn should draw to display his findings. (2)

2. **(a)** Name the statistical test DC Quinn should use. (1)

   (b) Name **two** pieces of information that DC Quinn will need to find the critical value for this statistical test. (2)

3. **Context/Methods essay:** Evaluate the use of field experiments in criminal psychology. (8)

Cognitive interview (CI)

Fisher and Geiselman (1992), four main techniques.

The cognitive interview is designed to improve witness' recall by using research into how memory works.

1. *Report everything* – the witness is encouraged to report every detail (even if it seems unimportant or irrelevant).

2. *Reinstate the context* – the witness imagines all aspects of the crime scene (e.g. the weather, time of day, how they felt). These context cues help by triggering more recall.

3. *Reverse the order* – the witness describes what they saw in a different chronological order (e.g. from end to beginning, or from midway). This avoids witnesses relying on their expectations of what they thought happened.

4. *Change perspective* – the witness 'tells the story' of the event from someone else's viewpoint (e.g. a different witness or someone directly involved).

Enhanced CI

Develops the original technique.

This pays more attention than standard CI to the interaction between interviewer and interviewee.

The interviewer maintains eye contact with the witness, reduces distractions, asks open-ended questions and gets the witness to speak slowly (Fisher *et al.* 1987).

Ethical interviewing techniques (EI)

Focused on suspects' rights.

The Royal Commission on Criminal Justice (1991) concluded that many false confessions and miscarriages of justice resulted from police using unethical interview techniques (with suspects rather than eye-witnesses).

Their report was very critical of police making threats and false promises and using physical force to extract confessions, etc.

There has since been more emphasis on 'ethical interviewing', teaching officers to keep an open mind and behave less aggressively towards suspects.

The PEACE model of ethical interviewing

1990s collaboration between law enforcement agencies and psychologists in England and Wales.

This is based on the idea that suspects cooperate better (and are more likely to give a true confession) if they feel relaxed, secure and not threatened.

There are five principles:

1. **P**reparation and planning – identifying key objectives.

2. **E**ngage and explain – active listening to promote rapport.

3. **A**ccount, clarification, challenge – using open-ended questions to elicit information.

4. **C**losure – giving the suspect a chance to ask questions.

5. **E**valuate – reflecting on the interviewer's performance.

All interviews that adopt the PEACE model are recorded to maintain transparency and ensure that guidelines for proper police conduct are being adhered to.

A strength of CI is supporting evidence for its effectiveness.

Geiselman *et al.*'s (1985) participants saw a film of a violent crime and were later interviewed by an officer either using the CI, standard interview (SI) or an interview with hypnosis.

The average number of correctly recalled facts were 41.2 for the CI, 29.4 for the SI, 38.0 for hypnosis.

This suggests that the CI leads to superior recall compared to alternative interviewing techniques.

A weakness is that CI can also lead to recall of more inaccurate information.

Köhnken *et al.* (1999) recorded an 81% increase in correct information using CI techniques.

But this was offset by a 61% increase in *incorrect* information, compared with SIs.

Thus the real strength of CIs is that more information is produced overall, but it may be inaccurate.

A strength of EI is evidence that it produces higher success rates.

Holmberg and Christianson (2002) studied murderers' and sexual offenders' experiences of police interviews and their inclination to admit or deny crimes.

Interviews featuring intimidation by the interviewer were associated with denials. Interviews marked by respect and a positive attitude towards the suspect were associated with confessions.

Therefore, EI may result in more cooperative interviewees and ultimately preferable outcomes.

In 1992, Colin Stagg (above) was falsely accused of murdering Rachel Nickell. Police tried to extract a confession using a female officer to befriend him. Under the rules of ethical interviewing, such police coercion would no longer be allowed. Stagg's case was dismissed due to lack of evidence.

CA Although EI means police are unlikely to engage in the questionable practices that led to the wrongful arrest of Colin Stagg (see right), some commentators remain wary of EI. Gudjonsson (1992) argues that some EI techniques are naïve, and that the 'social skills' approach to questioning should not entirely replace more traditional methods which might be more persuasive.

Application: Research shows which interview techniques are most effective.

Milne and Bull (2002) found that any of the individual elements of CI are more effective in getting accurate information than SIs.

However, the researchers also noted a combination of report everything and context reinstatement particularly was most fruitful.

This means police can use shortened versions of the CI in some situations because it is widely acknowledged that CI is too time-consuming.

I&D extra: Illustrates how psychological understanding has developed.

Main CI techniques are based on the view that memory is reconstructive and influenced by *schemas* (Bartlett, Loftus and Palmer in relation to EWT).

By understanding the frailty of human memory, cognitive psychologists have helped transform questioning techniques with eye-witnesses.

This has been important in reducing miscarriages of justice.

✓ Check it

1. Ethical interviewing has been shown to improve cooperation of suspects.
   Describe **two** examples of good practice with regard to ethical interviewing. [2]

2. Explain **one** strength and **one** weakness of using the cognitive interview to collect information from witnesses to a crime. [4]

3. **Standard essay:** Evaluate the use of cognitive and/or ethical interviewing. [8] or [16]

4. **I&D essay:** Evaluate the use of psychological knowledge in society. You must refer to **one** application of psychology in your answer (e.g. clinical, criminological, child and/or health). [16]

The use of psychological formulation

Read about BPS code of ethics and HCPC principles on page 176.

That'll teach you to wee on the couch.

Psychological (case) formulation aims to explain the causes of a person's difficulties by constructing an individual summary or story of a person's life. This is jointly constructed by the person and their therapist.

Apply it Concepts

Kim was arrested for shoplifting again. She steals soft toys, although she is 45 with no children. A psychologist building her case formulation asks how stealing makes her feel. She tells him it's scary but that each toy makes her feel special. When he asks about her childhood she says she was the youngest of nine, so never had anything of her own.

1. Explain which phase of case formulation the psychologist is working on with Kim. (2)

2. Explain whether Kim's case could be applied to other thieves. (1)

3. **Context essay:** Discuss how psychological formulation would assist in understanding Kim's behaviour. (8)

Psychological formulation

A form of diagnosis used with mental disorders and also criminals.

Forensic psychologists assess and treat offending behaviour.

To do so, they produce a *psychological formulation* of individual offenders after they are sentenced (sometimes called a 'case formulation' because it applies to an individual, i.e. one 'case').

A psychological formulation analyses the offence to try to understand why the offender did it, and if they may reoffend.

A treatment plan is drawn up to minimise reoffending risk.

Phase 1 – Offence analysis

Analyse the offence to gain insight into the offender's motivations.

This is likely to be difficult as there could be many complex reasons why an offender turned to crime.

The psychologist/therapist may consider similar offences committed by others to see if there are general factors relevant.

But psychological formulation is *idiographic* – it relates specifically to the offender who is the subject of the formulation, it is not about an average 'type' of offender.

Identifying reasons for the offence allows the psychologist to assess the risk of reoffending, and what possible causes can be removed or changed to reduce the risk.

Phase 2 – Understanding the function of offending

What purpose does offending serve for the individual?

For some offenders, criminal behaviour may be like an addiction, fulfilling a craving or need (Hodge *et al.* 2011), for example:

• A rapist may compensate for their own feelings of worthlessness by exercising power over their victims.

• This does not excuse their behaviour but may help to understand what compels them to do it.

Psychological theory could be useful here:

• Behaviourist perspective – crime is reinforced as it is rewarding for the individual (e.g. the rapist).

• Psychodynamic perspective: crime may hint at early issues or abuse within the family.

Phase 3 – Application to treatment

Establish intervention based on conclusions drawn.

Psychological (case) formulation has its roots in the field of mental health treatment – there may be overlap here, as many offenders also have mental health problems.

The recommended rehabilitative programme should reflect:

• How the offending started in the first place.

• The risk of reoffending.

• How likely the offender is to stick with the programme (level of motivation).

The psychological formulation is a 'work in progress' and is reassessed and adapted based on the success of diagnosis and treatment.

A strength is that psychological formulation is useful in complex cases.

It brings together many professionals within the criminal justice system, (e.g. probation service, police, psychologists).

Pooling expertise helps when deciding the best options for the offender, and the range of treatments available.

This ensures that a case is managed effectively in order to work towards the best outcome.

CA There may be a practical problem when trying to make sense of the wealth of information that is made available. Some of the evidence gained about the offender from different sources may be contradictory. This means there may be no obvious rehabilitative programme that suggests itself, and it may be difficult for the psychologist to work this into a clear and structured formulation.

A weakness is that there are sources of bias in the process.

Information related to offence analysis and the function of offending usually comes from semi-structured interviews with the offender.

The offender's recall of life events (e.g. family circumstances) may be unreliable. Also conclusions are based on the psychologist's subjective interpretation.

This introduces bias within the formulation process which may impact upon the effectiveness of diagnosis and treatment.

Another weakness is that it is difficult to measure success.

Success of psychological formulation is usually assessed in terms of whether the offender goes on to reoffend (*offender group reconviction score*, OGRS).

But as most reoffending is undetected, reconviction rates are measured instead. Success may be better judged by whether the person changes their sense of identity or social circumstances.

This suggests that the effectiveness of psychological formulation should be based on different, and perhaps more valid, criteria.

Application: The approach offers a different way to reduce reoffending.

Psychological formulation does at least try to tackle offending at its source – the function it serves for the offender.

This means educating the offender as to how they arrived in their current predicament, which could lead to reduced reoffending in the future (currently around 70%).

This suggests that widespread adoption of psychological formulation methodology may help to reduce reoffending.

I&D extra: There are ethical issues related to use of psychological formulation.

Professional psychologists working in the field of formulation are subject to the *Health and Care Professions Council* (HCPC) ethical guidelines.

15 Proficiency Standards are followed by forensic and clinical psychologists working with offenders (e.g. exercising competent judgements, up-to-date knowledge).

This ensures that offenders are dealt with in a manner that is safe, appropriate and involves professional expertise.

Stalemate following a gruelling four-hour interview, there was now only one way for Simon and Keith to decide who would take the senior management role.

Revision booster

Case formulation and case studies share some features. However, make sure that you don't mix up the two. Psychological (or case) formulation always has a specific purpose and is more organised than a case study – with phases, each of which serves a different purpose.

Check it

1. Describe **one** offending behaviour which serves a specific function for the individual. (2)

2. Jacqui is working on a psychological formulation for Oona, a convicted drug-dealer and single mother.

   Explain **two** ways that the HCPC standards affect Jacqui's work with Oona. (4)

3. **Standard essay:** Evaluate the use of psychological formulation for understanding offending behaviour. (8) or (16)

4. **I&D/Synoptic essay:** Evaluate issues presented by socially sensitive research. You must use examples from **two** applications of psychology (e.g. clinical, criminological, child and/or health). (20)

Treatments for offenders: Cognitive-behavioural treatment

Spec spotlight

Two treatments for offenders, including strengths and weaknesses and one study for each that considers their effectiveness.

6.1.5 One cognitive-behavioural treatment e.g. CBT, social skills training, anger management, assertiveness training.

You'd be annoyed if you had no nose. Or fingers. And your head wasn't attached to your body.

Apply it Concepts

Jack, a therapist, is using cognitive-behavioural treatment (CBT) with an inmate called Ryan, who was arrested for being violent when he was frustrated in stationary traffic. Jack says, 'You're in a busy pub and have just reached the bar when another man pushes in front of you. How might you feel?' Ryan says he'd want to thump him. Jack asks what music Ryan finds calming and suggests he plays it to help him relax in busy places. At the next session, Jack is deliberately 10 minutes late.

1. Explain **one** way that CBT might help Ryan. (2)

2. Explain **one** reason why CBT might not help Ryan. (2)

3. **Context essay:** Discuss **one** cognitive-behavioural treatment for Ryan. (8)

A cognitive-behavioural treatment (CBT)

The offender's inability to control anger is the root cause of offending.

Novaco (1975) suggests some offenders see certain situations as threatening and stressful, so they react aggressively.

- Cognitive – the offender's appraisal of a situation acts as the *trigger* for anger.

- Behaviourist – anger is *reinforced* by the offender's feelings of control that anger gives them in that situation.

Therefore, anger results from cognitive and behavioural problems, so treatment needs to tackle both.

---

1. Cognitive preparation

The first of three phases in anger management.

With a trained therapist, the offender reflects on past triggers of anger and whether they could have reacted differently.

  e.g. someone who is violent after physical contact at a busy bar redefines the situation as non-threatening, so events that may once have been 'flashpoints' are perceived more rationally.

---

2. Skill acquisition

Offenders learn behavioural techniques to help them cope.

May involve just simple ways of coping.

  e.g. counting to ten when feeling stressed.

'Self-talk' promotes calmness rather than aggression, and becomes an automatic response if practised regularly.

Some strategies deal with physiology of anger (e.g. meditation), aim to control emotions, not be controlled by them.

---

3. Application and practice

The offender demonstrates their new skills.

Reconstruct past events when the offender lost control.

  e.g. offender simulates queuing at a bar for a drink while therapist provokes them (e.g. shoves them).

This tests whether the new techniques have been internalised.

Research study – Ireland (2004)

Procedure	Sample – offenders randomly allocated to either: • Treatment group (CBT anger management programme, 12 sessions). • Wait-list control group (no treatment until later). Measures to assess progress taken two weeks before and eight weeks after treatment: • Interview and questionnaire (for participants). • Behaviour checklist (for prison staff).
Findings	92% of treatment group showed significant improvement on at least one measure, 48% showed improvement on questionnaire and behaviour checklist (most improvement was in offenders judged to be 'violent' before the investigation began). Control group showed no improvement on any measure.
Conclusions	Anger management is more effective than no treatment at all, and is most effective for those with a history of violence.

A strength is evidence the treatment reduces the urge for revenge.

Holbrook (1997) studied 26 male prisoners with a history of aggression chosen for anger management training.

They completed a vengeance scale (desire for revenge) which showed a significant reduction in scores after treatment.

This suggests that anger management may have positive long-term outcomes, including decreasing the desire for revenge.

CA However, Blackburn (1993) argued that anger management may help offenders control their conduct in the short-term, but may have little impact on long-term reoffending rates. One explanation for this may be that there isn't a causal relationship between anger and offending (Loza and Loza-Fanous 1999).

Morris' anger was not alleviated by being forced to wear an orange jumpsuit for the rest of the day.

A weakness is that anger management is not suitable for all.

After an enquiry into the murder of John Monckton in 2006, Home Secretary Charles Clarke insisted anger management in prisons be scaled back as it was counter-productive for some offenders.

Monckton was murdered by Hanson who received anger management therapy. It is possible this improved his ability to control situations and was able to convince a parole board to release him.

This suggests that anger management therapy may assist some prisoners to become more manipulative.

Another strength is it is an eclectic approach to offending.

Anger management addresses different aspects of offending behaviour.

It's an interdisciplinary approach that works on different levels in the context of role play – phase 1 cognitive, phase 2 behavioural, phase 3 social.

This acknowledges the fact that offending is a complex psychological activity that requires an eclectic approach to treatment.

A methodological weakness of the study is its short-term nature.

In Ireland's investigation, the assessment was after eight weeks.

This may not be enough time to evaluate the effectiveness of programmes, especially once an offender is released from the institutional setting.

This means it is questionable whether Ireland's study is a good indicator of how effective anger management would be in the long term.

I&D extra: Anger management may be seen as a form of social control.

Success depends on the offender's ability to adopt the new forms of thinking and ways of behaving that the therapist deems acceptable.

A key feature of the therapist's job is to make judgements about what aspects of the offender's behaviour require adjustment.

Thus anger management is arguably a form of social control involving forced compliance to the therapist's way of seeing the world.

Check it

1. Describe **one** cognitive-behavioural treatment for offenders. [4]

2. Explain **one** strength of a cognitive-behavioural treatment for offenders. [2]

3. **Standard essay:** Evaluate **one** cognitive-behavioural treatment for offenders. [8] or [16]

4. **Methods essay:** Evaluate research into treatments for offenders with reference to sample selection and objectivity. [8] or [16]

Spec spotlight

Two treatments for offenders, including strengths and weaknesses and one study for each that considers their effectiveness.

6.1.6 One biological treatment, e.g. improved diet, hormone treatment.

'I have a bit of chocolate on my face? Oh really, where?'

 **Methods**

Carl is in prison for a violent crime and still behaves aggressively. He has been selected by Dr Gray to participate in a dietary programme. At mealtimes the participants will have a choice of salad or a healthy hot option but not chips or other junk food. Prison officers will rate the behaviour of the participants on a 10-point scale.

1. Explain which measure of central tendency Dr Gray should use. (1)

2. Justify an effective way for Dr Gray to select participants. (2)

3. Carl thinks any changes in participants' behaviour are due to extra attention. Explain why this would matter. (2)

4. **Context/Methods essay:** Assess the use of field experiments in criminal psychology. You must refer to the context in your answer. (8)

High sugar diets and crime Sugar may not cause violent crime, but they are linked.	Moore *et al.* (2009) found that 69% of a group of violent offenders reported eating 'confectionary' (sweets or sugary snacks) almost every day during childhood. • High-sugar diet causes changes in blood sugar levels. • Junk food creates high glucose levels which trigger major insulin secretions to soak these up. • This leads to a shortage of glucose (called *hypoglycaemia*) which is associated with irritability, difficulty making judgements and violent outbursts (in extreme cases). Benton *et al.* (1996) found that children playing a video game became more aggressive as their blood sugar level decreased.
Vitamins, minerals and fatty acids Brain function relies on vitamins and minerals.	Deficiencies in unsaturated fatty acids (omega 3), magnesium, zinc, iron, vitamins B, C and D have been linked to crime. The more junk food that people consume, the less space there is in their diet for healthier nutritional content. Lack of nutrients has been linked to mental illnesses (e.g. depression) and behavioural problems (e.g. aggression).
Diet changes as a treatment for crime	Diet improvement starts with a baseline measure of diet – this ascertains which minerals and vitamins an offender is lacking and how this can best be addressed. In most cases, a multi-vitamin is added to the offender's diet, then effects on behaviour are monitored over a given period.

Research study – Gesch *et al.* (2002)

Procedure	Sample – 231 inmates in a young offender's institute randomly allocated to: • Experimental group (daily vitamin, mineral and fatty acid supplement). • Placebo control group (placebo pill), matched on disciplinary incidents and progress in prison regime. Double-blind procedure – prison staff gave out pills but did not know who was allocated to which group, all pills (supplement or placebos) arrived in blank packaging. A baseline measure of diet and assessments of anger, anxiety and depression were taken at the beginning of the study.
Findings	Experimental group – 35.1% reduction in disciplinary incidents per 'thousand-person days' (just 6.7% in placebo group), 37% reduction in serious violent incidents (10.1% in placebo).
Conclusions	Supplementing offenders' diets with vitamins, minerals and fatty acids is linked to a decrease in incidents of anti-social behaviour, including violent behaviour.

A strength of improving diet is support from research evidence.

Schoenthaler (1983) found a 48% reduction in formal disciplinary incidents among 276 young offenders (similar study to Gesch et al.).	The study took over two years and saw a reduction in sugar consumed rather than supplements (sugary drinks, etc. were replaced by low-sugar alternatives).	This suggests that a high-sugar diet is associated with anti-social behaviour which can be controlled if sugar consumption is reduced.

CA However, Gesch et al.'s and Schoenthaler's studies were conducted in institutional settings where behaviour is highly controlled. We cannot know from these studies alone whether the effects of diet would generalise to real-life settings.

A weakness is that the cause-and-effect link between diet and crime is unclear.

Linked to the competing argument above, crime is a complex social activity that is unlikely to be addressed by treating a single factor alone.	People with the poorest diets are also most likely to be living in socially- and economically-deprived circumstances. These factors (not diet) may be the causes of offending.	Therefore, the positive effects of a change in diet may be short-lived if offenders are returned to the same circumstances following their sentence.

'Two of these three times a day with water? Are you having a laugh?'

Another weakness is that most outcome studies focus on violence.

Dietary treatments for offending tend to focus mostly on controlling aggressive urges.	Not all crimes are linked with aggression and acts of violence – offenders in prison for financial crime (e.g. fraud) are not helped by a change of diet.	This means that the benefits of an improved diet may only apply to particular types of offender.

A strength of Gesch et al.'s study is that it is well-controlled.

Double-blind procedure minimised the effect of demand characteristics on prisoners, and also experimenter effects on staff administering pills.	Groups were matched on key variables so differences in outcome between groups could not be explained by other factors (e.g. nature of disciplinary incidents and progress whilst in prison).	This control exercised within the study increases the validity of its findings.

Revision booster

When you are presented with a question that has a context (a short answer question or an extended response question), take a little time to see how much of the context you can use in your answer. You can underline parts of the context and make notes around it to help you.

I&D extra: Improved diet is a reductionist approach to treating offenders.

An approach to treating offenders that focuses solely on a physiological, chemical level (as improved diet does) is reductionist.	This obscures the fact there are cognitive factors in offending which should be addressed. Also, other biological therapies (e.g. hormones) are successful in treating offenders.	Therefore, successful approaches to crime prevention and treatment are likely to be those that take a more holistic approach to the problem.

✓ Check it

1. Describe the findings of **one** study of **one** biological treatment for offenders. [4]

2. Compare **one** biological and **one** cognitive-behavioural treatment for offenders. [4]

3. **Standard essay:** Evaluate **one** biological treatment for offenders. [8] or [16]

4. **Standard plus essay:** Evaluate **two** treatments for offenders with reference to practical and ethical issues. [8] or [16]

Factors influencing EWT: Reliability

Spec spotlight

6.1.7 Factors influencing eye-witness testimony, including consideration of reliability (including post-event information and weapon focus).

Bartlett used the folk tale War of the Ghosts *to illustrate how memory is shaped (reconstructed).*

Concepts

Jody and Mary were at different checkouts when a woman raided the store. Mary is 80 and was shocked that a woman would do such a thing and was scared. Jody, a teenager, wasn't surprised but was terrified when the woman ran at her with a knife. After the woman had run out of the shop with the money, another shopper said 'She was about 50, she should know better!'

1. Explain how post-event information might affect Mary's memory of the event, when asked what she witnessed. (3)

2. Explain how weapon focus might affect Jody's memory of the event, when asked what she witnessed. (3)

3. **Context essay:** Discuss factors affecting the reliability of Mary and Jody's eye-witness testimony. (8)

Graph showing the inverted-U relationship between anxiety and recall.

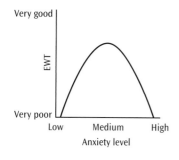

Eye-witness testimony (EWT)	This is a legal term which refers to the account given by a witness of a crime or other dramatic event (e.g. car crash).
	Research addresses the issue of whether eye-witness accounts are reliable or not, and the different factors affecting this.
	Reliability = consistent, i.e. consistent with the real events.

Post-event information Information arriving after an event that may affect an eye-witness' memory of what happened.	Human memory is *reconstructive* (see Bartlett's theory in our Year 1 Revision guide, page 58): • Memory does not record events in exact detail (e.g. like a camera). • Instead, it fits memories within pre-existing frameworks of expectations and past knowledge (*schemas*). A person's ability to recall a crime may be based more on their schema of the event than on what actually occurred. Bartlett called this 'effort after meaning'.

Leading questions A form of post-event information that triggers schemas.	A *leading question* (or statement) suggests a particular answer because of the way it is phrased and may point an eye-witness towards a specific answer (see Loftus and Palmer, page 118). e.g. 'Was the man in the green coat holding a knife?' – this may suggest a more vivid (but not necessarily correct) account than 'Was there a weapon involved?'. The witness may incorrectly access the information provided in the first question, rather than what they actually remember.

The influence of anxiety	Witnessing a dramatic event creates stress and anxiety which may affect the person's ability to register and recall the event. Deffenbacher (1983) reviewed 21 studies and concluded that: • Moderate anxiety helps memory (like an athlete produces their best performance when 'pumped up' before a crowd). • If an eye-witness' anxiety continues to rise (and becomes extreme), this creates a decline in recall (see inverted-U graph on left).

Weapon focus	*Weapon focus* is one way anxiety is pushed 'over the edge': • In violent crimes when the perpetrator is carrying a weapon, the brain's natural tendency is to zoom in on that as the main source of stress. • So an eye-witness' recall is relatively poor and other important details (e.g. what the perpetrator looked like or what s/he was wearing) are not noticed or distorted. Weapon focus is explained by *tunnel theory*: • Presence of a weapon leads to selective attention. • This excludes or ignores competing bits of information.

A strength is that research evidence shows the effect of leading questions.

Loftus and Palmer (1974) showed participants video clips of car accidents and asked them to estimate how fast the cars were travelling.	Participants who heard 'smashed' gave higher estimates. In a follow-up, those hearing 'smashed' were more likely to report seeing broken glass (there was none).	This suggests that post-event information in the form of leading questions has a significant effect on recall.

A weakness is that evidence from real-life crimes is contradictory.

Yuille and Cutshall (1986) assessed recall of 13 witnesses to a real-life shooting who rated themselves as very anxious at the time. Each witness was initially interviewed by the police.	About five months afterwards the witnesses produced accurate accounts despite researchers including two leading questions in this second interview.	This suggests that the effects of leading questions and weapon focus may be less pronounced when applied to real-life events.

A strength of the weapon focus explanation is supporting evidence.

Johnson and Scott (1976) arranged for half of their participants to overhear an argument and see a man with greasy hands carrying a pen (control). The other half saw a man with a blood-stained knife (experimental condition).	49% of controls later correctly identified the man (from 50 photos) compared to 33% in the experimental condition. (Participants were not aware of being studied so this had high ecological validity.)	This suggests that participants' attention had been drawn towards the weapon and away from other peripheral details.

CA However, Pickel (1998) found a similar effect when a man pulled out a raw chicken or a Pillsbury Dough Boy to pay a cashier rather than presenting his wallet. This suggests that 'weapon focus' is related to surprise as much as anxiety.

Application: EWT research has brought about changes in the legal system.

EWT research has led to the introduction of *social framework evidence*. In US courts psychologists may be called to provide some 'context' to juries.	This is often in the form of relevant psychological evidence that demonstrates the unreliability of such testimony.	This suggests that research which recognises the fallibility of human memory is useful in reducing miscarriages of justice in legal cases.

I&D extra: EWT studies illustrate practical issues in research design.

Lab studies of EWT exercise a high level of control of the environment in order to establish cause and effect.	However, such studies lack real consequences (e.g. no one goes to prison) and participants don't experience the anxiety of a real crime.	This means that research should include real-world observations to support the findings of laboratory studies (e.g. Yuille and Cutshall, above).

'You won't get away with this,' said the dog. 'Psychological research suggests that the anxiety created by this situation will enhance my recall of the event.'

'That's as maybe,' replied the sheep, but you'll never pick me out of a line-up.'

Schemas affect memories at the time they are stored *and* at the time they are recalled.

Revision booster

You have learned about several different factors affecting EWT – however, you can only be asked specific questions about 'post-event information' and 'weapon focus' as these terms are in the specification.

Check it

1. Explain **one** way that weapon focus can influence the reliability of eye-witness testimony. [3]

2. Give **one** example of post-event information that might affect the reliability of eye-witness testimony. Your example can be from real life or psychological research. [2]

3. **Standard essay:** Evaluate factors that influence the reliability of eye-witness testimony. [8] or [16]

4. **I&D essay:** Evaluate whether psychology can be considered a science with reference to **one** application of psychology (e.g. clinical, criminological, child or health). [16]

Factors influencing jury decision-making

AO1
Description

My client was found at the scene, his fingerprints are all over the stolen painting, and when discovered he is reported as saying, 'It's a fair cop, guv'nor, it was me wot done it'…but, in his defence, can you let him off, as he is really nice to his Mum?

Characteristics of the defendant

Attractiveness	Abwender and Hough (2001) asked 207 participants to judge an imaginary drunk and reckless driver who killed a pedestrian:
	• Female participants were more lenient towards an attractive female defendant, less towards an unattractive defendant – male participants showed the opposite tendency.
	• Provides partial support for *Attractiveness Leniency Hypothesis* (ALE) – attractive defendants favoured by juries.
Race	Bradbury and Williams (2013) analysed real US criminal cases:
	• Juries comprised mostly of white jurors (and Hispanic jurors) were more likely to convict black defendants.
	• In both cases, the effect was more marked for certain crimes (e.g. drug offences).
	Pfeifer and Ogloff's (1991) participants read a transcript of a trial in which the race of victim and defendant were varied:
	• Participants rated the guilt of the defendant.
	• Participants rated black defendants guiltier than white defendants, especially when the victim was white.
Accent	Dixon *et al.* (2002) played a recorded conversation between a male suspect and a male policeman to 119 participants:
	• The suspect's accent was varied so participants heard either a Birmingham accent or a 'standard British' accent.
	• Guilt ratings were significantly higher for the suspect with a Birmingham accent (another factor influencing juries).

Pre-trial publicity (PTP) – Steblay *et al.* (1999)

Procedure	Meta-analysis of 44 mock-jury trials or questionnaires. Negative information given to experimental group (not to control group). All asked to decide on defendant's guilt.
Findings	Experimental participants were significantly more likely to return guilty verdicts than controls (59% vs 45%).
	PTP effect greater e.g. for murder or sexual abuse.
	PTP effect reduced e.g. for disorderly conduct.
Conclusions	PTP produces a greater likelihood of guilty judgements (to prevent this, Steblay *et al.* suggested that trials attracting extensive PTP could be held overseas).
	PTP creates *schemas* in the minds of jurors which are hard to shift – the more publicity, the more entrenched the schemas.

Apply it Methods

Dr Ali is conducting a meta-analysis of studies on race and jury decisions. He finds 75 studies that are relevant and selects 25 to use in his meta-analysis.

1. Calculate the percentage of the original studies that Dr Ali selected. Give your answer to **two** significant figures. (1)

2. **(a)** Explain **one** measure of the influence on jury decision-making that Dr Ali could look for in his chosen sample. (2)

   (b) Dr Ali rejected some studies because of the way they measured jury decisions. Suggest **two** other reasons why Dr Ali might reject studies. (2)

3. **Context/Methods essay:** Evaluate the use of meta-analyses in criminal psychology. You must refer to the context in your answer. (8)

AO3
Evaluation

The new Strictly Come Dancing *judges rarely agreed on anything.*

A strength of research in this area is that it is ethical.

Mock juries and 'imaginary' cases allow us to manipulate variables that would not be practical or ethical in real trials.

Bradbury and Williams (2013) did use real-trial data, but this was secondary data from trials that had already occurred.

This means that extra-legal factors can be analysed without prejudicing the outcome of a real trial.

A weakness is that other untested factors may influence real juries.

Research (e.g. Abwender and Hough) studies characteristics of defendants, but there may be other important influences on jury decision-making.

Such as jurors' personal experience of the offence, charismatic leaders who can sway opinion, or whether characteristics of jurors and defendant match (greater empathy).

Thus, the failure to include some key factors such as these may limit the usefulness of mock or even real jury research.

Another weakness is that research findings are often inconsistent.

Patry (2008) found mock jurors who discussed the case were more likely to find an attractive defendant guilty, those who discussed less were more likely to find a plain defendant guilty.

This was inconsistent with the findings of Abwender and Hough (facing page).

This suggests that the effect of attractiveness on the decision-making process varies depending on other factors, which makes firm conclusions difficult.

Application: Research has implications for real criminal trials.

Jurors are human beings subject to biases which may affect their neutrality, so should be reminded to remain impartial and not let extra-legal factors distort their judgement.

The Pfeifer and Ogloff study showed that the *racial bias effect* disappeared when jurors were reminded their guilty decision had to be beyond reasonable doubt.

This knowledge of jury bias may reduce miscarriages of justice in the future.

I&D extra: Mock trial research adds to credibility of psychology as a science.

Most experimental studies that look at characteristics of the defendant and pre-trial publicity use the mock trial method.

Extraneous variables are controlled more than in a real trial, so the effect of the studied variable (e.g. race) can be observed and measured (cause-and-effect relationships).

This means the internal validity of such studies is increased, as is their scientific value.

CA However, the external validity of mock trial experiments is low. Isolating one variable at a time is not representative of real trials, where race, attractiveness and accent of the defendant are likely to have a combined effect in the minds of jurors.

Revision booster

Read the specification carefully so you know what you can be examined on – in this case 'pre-trial publicity' and 'characteristics of the defendant' are in the specification. This means each could potentially be the basis of an extended response question (essay). If that is the case there is enough description on this spread but most especially focus on making sure your evaluation is effective and not just more description. Students often think they are evaluating when really they are simply describing more studies. For example, if all you do is say what Abwender and Hough found that's description. You then need to explain why this is a strength or weakness, and what we can conclude.

✓ Check it

1. Describe **two** ways in which characteristics of the defendant may influence jury decision-making. [4]

2. Describe the findings of research into pre-trial publicity. [4]

3. **Standard essay:** Evaluate research on factors that influence jury decision-making. [8] or [16]

4. **Methods essay:** Evaluate the credibility of research into factors affecting jury decision-making. [8] or [16]

Spec spotlight

6.3.1 Classic study: Loftus and Palmer (1974) Reconstruction of automobile destruction: An example of the interaction between language and memory.

Concepts

Dr Lee is testing the effect of leading questions on children's ability to recall an incident involving harm. He uses a picture of a crying boy with a round red mark on his thigh. Participants are asked to estimate how big the red mark was, on a scale of 1–10 (1 = small). The question they are asked says the boy was either pushed, smacked or walloped. A week later the participants were asked whether they saw 'the' or 'a' handprint on the child's thigh.

1. (a) Identify the independent variable in Dr Lee's study. (1)
   (b) Identify the dependent variable in Dr Lee's study. (1)

2. Explain which participants in the group that heard 'the handprint' would be most likely to say 'yes'. (2)

3. **Context essay:** Evaluate Dr Lee's experiment. (8)

Graph 1: Speed estimates for verbs used in Experiment 1.

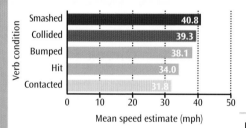

Graph 2: Presence of broken glass.

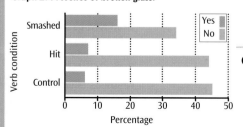

Aims	To investigate whether memory is influenced by information which occurs after an event (*post-event information*, including *leading questions*, see page 114).	
Experiment 1 – Procedure	Opportunity sample – 45 students (five equal groups) shown film clips of traffic accidents (from safety films, 5–30 seconds each).	

Aims — To investigate whether memory is influenced by information which occurs after an event (*post-event information*, including *leading questions*, see page 114).

Experiment 1 – Procedure — Opportunity sample – 45 students (five equal groups) shown film clips of traffic accidents (from safety films, 5–30 seconds each).

Afterwards, participants were asked a 'critical' question = '*About how fast were the cars going when they _____ (into) each other?*'

Independent variable = different verb in the gap: *smashed, collided, bumped, hit* or *contacted*.

Dependent variable = the participants' speed estimates.

Findings — The phrasing of the question produced differences in speed estimate, e.g. 'smashed' elicited a significantly higher estimate than 'contacted' (see Graph 1 on left).

Conclusion — The first study provided powerful evidence of the effect that post-event information can have on the recall of that event.

But does the information in the verb/leading question bias a person's response or does it alter their memory of the event?

Experiment 2 – Procedure — Sample – 150 participants shown a one-minute film including a short scene of a car accident.

Independent variable = the wording of the critical question:

- Group 1 – '*How fast were the cars going when they hit each other?*'
- Group 2 – '*How fast were the cars going when they smashed into each other?*'
- Control group – No question about speed.

A week later participants returned and were asked questions about the film, including, '*Did you see any broken glass?*' (at a random point for each participant in a longer interview).

Findings — Participants in the 'smashed' condition:

- Gave the highest estimate of speed.
- Significantly more likely to report seeing broken glass (even though there was none) – see Graph 2 on left.

Conclusions — Post-event information did not simply create a response bias.

It altered the initial memory of the event and generated expectations (i.e. the likelihood that there would be broken glass).

A strength of the study was its well-controlled procedure.

The lab setting allowed control of variables, the only change participants experienced was the wording of the critical question in each case.	The content of the interviews was standardised for each participant, as was the stimulus material (the video clips).	This suggests that the internal validity of the experiments was high.

CA Watching a crash on video is very different from witnessing one in real life. A film clip is unlikely to elicit the same level of emotional arousal as a real crash. There is also not the same emotional investment and there is no risk of someone going to prison should the estimate of speed be incorrect. For these reasons, it could be argued that the laboratory setting took away from the external validity of the research.

A weakness is that the study had sampling issues.

The participants were college students, so their level of education may have affected the findings (intelligent people may make better witnesses).	But students may have less experience of driving, affecting their judgement of speed. Either way, a student sample is not representative.	Therefore, the biased sample may reduce the external validity of Loftus and Palmer's findings.

Another weakness is that some studies provide contradicting evidence.

Yuille and Cutshall (1986) interviewed eye-witnesses to a real-life gun shooting in Canada.	Witnesses gave accurate reports of the crime four months after the event even though they had initially been given two misleading questions.	This suggests that in real situations (when the stakes may be higher), witnesses are less influenced by post-event information.

Application: Loftus' work on EWT has led to changes in the legal system.

The Devlin Report (1976) used EWT research, e.g. recommended that juries should not convict on a single eye-witness statement.	Loftus' work also contributed to changes in police interviewing (e.g. the cognitive interview was based on some of her evidence).	This shows that Loftus' research has implications that stretch beyond the laboratory.

I&D extra: The study illustrates how psychological understanding changes.

Loftus' research focus has changed over time – in the 1990s she looked at whether it is possible to implant false memories for events that did not take place.	She became involved in controversial and high profile legal cases about whether so-called 'recovered memories' of childhood abuse were in fact false memories suggested during therapy.	This led to stricter controls on the use of recovered memories in court.

So we're looking for a snappy dresser with an extensive gun collection who's very conscious about levels of air pollution?

Check it

1. Loftus and Palmer (1974) used an opportunity sample of 45 students in their classic study. Explain **one** strength and **one** weakness of using an opportunity sample in this study. (4)

2. Describe the findings of Loftus and Palmer's (1974) classic study. (4)

3. **Standard essay:** Evaluate the classic study by Loftus and Palmer (1974). (8) or (16)

4. **Prompt essay:** Research in criminological psychology has significantly improved the criminal justice system.

   Evaluate the practical applications of your classic and contemporary studies for criminological psychology. (8) or (16)

Contemporary study: Bradbury and Williams (2013)

Spec spotlight

6.3.2 One contemporary study, for example: Bradbury and Williams (2013) Diversity and citizen participation: The effects of race on juror decision-making.

A jovial bunch of jurors.

Examples of the control variables in this study:

- Strength of case for prosecution compared to the defence.
- Length of trial.
- How long the jury deliberated for.
- Case type, e.g. drug, violence.

 **Methods**

Dr May is collecting data from court cases where the majority of jurors were either the same racial group as the defendant, or a different racial group. She is rating the court decision on a points scale, adding a point for each conviction and doubling points for a serious conviction such as murder.

1. Explain why the aim of Dr May's study could justify the deception of participants. (2)

2. (a) Identify the independent variable in Dr May's study. (1)
   (b) Identify the dependent variable in Dr May's study. (1)

3. Context/Methods essay: Evaluate the use of objective measures of dependent variables in experiments. You must refer to the context in your answer. (8)

Aims

To investigate whether the racial composition of a jury (and the race of the defendant) affect the decision-making process.

To see if jury members show:

- *Ingroup bias* – jurors of same ethnicity as defendant are more likely to acquit, and/or
- *Outgroup bias* – jurors of different ethnicity are more likely to convict.

To see if a majority white or a majority Hispanic jury are more likely to convict a black defendant.

Procedure

Secondary data from a study of juries 12 years earlier (Hannaford-Agor *et al.* 2002) – analysed trials in US states Arizona, California, New York, Washington.

Only used trials with black defendants (60% of cases), because there were too few cases with white/Hispanic defendants.

Independent variable = racial make-up of jury (percentage of black, white, Hispanic).

Dependent variable = whether or not trial led to a conviction.

Seven 'control variables' taken into account (see left).

Data analysed using *logistic regression* (for nominal data, whether there was a conviction or not).

Findings

Juries with a higher percentage of white jurors (than black or Hispanic) were *more* likely to convict black defendants.

Juries with a higher percentage of Hispanic jurors (than black or white) were *more* likely to convict black defendants (but this relationship was less strong than that of majority white jurors).

Juries with a higher percentage of black jurors (than white or Hispanic) were *less* likely to convict black defendants.

Black defendants were *more* likely to be convicted of drug crime than violent crime or crime against property, regardless of jury composition.

No other control variable significantly influenced convictions.

Conclusions

Racial composition of a jury has a significant effect on the likelihood of conviction.

- Ingroup bias – black defendants are less likely to be convicted by majority black juries.
- Outgroup bias – black defendants are more likely to be convicted by a mostly white/Hispanic jury than by a black jury.

Balance of race is an important consideration in jury selection, as it may have a significant bearing on the outcome.

A strength of the study is that it collected data from real juries.

The researchers used secondary data from real trials.	This is an advantage over previous studies that set up mock trials using imaginary defendants to gather data.	This means possible demand characteristics were avoided, which increases the external validity of their findings.

CA The trials were conducted in real courtrooms, but the generalisability of the findings may still be low. All trials were based in US states so may reflect bias unique to the American system. Also, all defendants were black, so we cannot know if the findings represent the experience of defendants from other racial groups.

A weakness is that other characteristics of the defendant were not controlled.

Bradbury and Williams controlled other factors that risked confounding the findings, but other characteristics of the defendant may have influenced the jury.	Evidence shows that the defendant's gender, age, attractiveness and clothing can affect decision-making (see page 116).	This reduces the validity of the evidence because it is unlikely that jurors based their judgement on race alone.

The local police knew him as The Birdman, and he was about to swoop.

Another weakness of the study is its flawed measurement of conviction.

The dependent variable was whether a conviction occurred in a particular trial, recorded as 'yes' if there was a conviction, or 'no' if there was not.	But some defendants faced multiple charges in the same trial (they may have been found innocent of other charges, some of which may have been more serious).	This simple method of coding convictions could mean that important variations in the data were ignored.

Application: The study has implications for how real juries are selected.

The *peremptory challenge* (US practice) allows the defence or prosecution to object to a jury's composition on the grounds that it might prejudice the outcome.	However, the so-called *Batson rule* prohibits such an objection on the grounds of race.	The findings of this study suggest that the racial mix of a jury should be carefully considered to promote fairness, particularly when defendants are black.

I&D extra: The study is socially sensitive in its focus on race.

For all to have faith in the legal system, defendants must feel they are getting a fair trial, and believe that the judgement of guilt or innocence is based solely on the evidence.	Bradbury and Williams' research is controversial in this sense as it suggests that other extra-legal factors may prejudice the outcome.	This kind of research is vital if miscarriages of justice are to be avoided.

Check it

1. Describe the findings of **one** contemporary study from criminological psychology. [2]

2. Explain **one** practical application of the findings of **one** contemporary study from criminological psychology. [3]

3. **Standard essay:** Evaluate **one** contemporary study from criminological psychology. [8] or [16]

4. **Methods essay:** Evaluate the validity of **one** contemporary study from criminological psychology. [8] or [16]

Spec spotlight

6.3.3 One contemporary study, for example: Valentine and Mesout (2009) Eye-witness identification under stress in the London Dungeon.

'Oi! That's my parking space! I've got a scythe you know.'

Aims

To investigate eye-witness identification in an everyday situation in which anxiety would be high and participants would not realise their memory was being tested.

Procedure

Setting – the Labyrinth (London Dungeon), with 'scary person' ('wounded' man who suddenly steps out to block visitors). Pre-test of visitors showed the Labyrinth did lead to increased heart rate, suggesting elevated levels of arousal/fear (which were necessary for the independent variable of high anxiety).

Sample – 56 visitors agreed to complete questionnaires in exchange for a reduced ticket price (unaware they were part of a psychological study).

Each volunteer/participant walked around the Labyrinth. In the first 7 minutes they met the scary person.

Then spent 45 minutes on the rest of the exhibit. At the end informed consent was sought from participants (aims explained, right to withdraw).

Consenting participants completed three questionnaires:

- *Trait anxiety inventory* (TAI) – measured the participants' typical state of anxiety (how they generally feel).
- *State anxiety inventory* (SAI) – measured how participants felt when they were in the Labyrinth.
- *Memory questionnaire* tested participants' recall of the scary person – included free recall description, cued recall elements, scored for accuracy by an independent panel.

Participants identified the scary person from a group of nine photos (the 'line-up') – photos were matched to the scary person actor (sex, age, ethnic origin).

Findings

Mean SAI score in the Labyrinth (49.0) was significantly higher than the mean TAI score (36.8) – participants found the Labyrinth anxiety-inducing.

Witnesses with higher state anxiety recalled fewer correct descriptors of the scary person than less anxious witnesses.

Participants were divided into two groups:

- High state anxiety (higher than median score) – 17% correctly identified the scary person from the line-up.
- Low state anxiety – 75% correct identification.

Conclusions

Accurate eye-witness identification is impaired under conditions of high anxiety presumably because memory is negatively affected by increased physiological arousal.

Lab studies may underestimate the effect of stress on the reliability of eye-witness testimony because they do not replicate the experience of real-life anxiety – the higher the stress in a real crime scenario, the harder it is to correctly identify the perpetrator.

Apply it   Methods

Grant is testing the effect of anxiety on eye-witness testimony. He plans to block a pavement at dusk and divert walkers through a cemetery. A confederate, carrying a watering can, will suddenly confront the walkers. On rejoining the pavement, the walkers will be asked if they are willing to answer questions. These questions will assess the walkers' anxiety and their recall of the confederate. Grant expects low anxiety people to have better recall.

1. Explain how Grant could test recall. (2)

2. Grant's statistical test shows a significant difference between high- and low-anxiety participants but the high-anxiety group had better recall. Explain whether Grant should accept his alternate hypothesis. (1)

3. **Context/Methods essay:** Assess the validity of Grant's study. (8)

A strength of the study is the level of control.

Validity of anxiety questionnaire tested using other participants. The subjective anxiety score showed high correlation with their heart rate (objective) as they walked around the Labyrinth.

Also, in the real investigation, the time participants spent in the Labyrinth and their overall experience at the London Dungeon were carefully standardised.

This improved the internal validity of the investigation.

David Walliams wasn't looking well that day.

CA The sample may have been unusual in some respects. We can probably assume that those people visiting the London Dungeon would have a preference for scary activities, which may have influenced the anxiety they experienced during the visit. Generalising from such a select group is potentially problematic.

A weakness is that the findings are contradicted by other research.

Christianson and Hübinette (1993) interviewed 110 witnesses of 22 real-life bank robberies.

Witnesses who had been directly threatened or attacked (high anxiety) were more accurate in their recall of events than onlookers (low anxiety).

This suggests that high anxiety may enhance recall at least under some circumstances, contradicting the findings of Valentine and Mesout.

Revision booster

For each of the strengths and weaknesses you learn for a classic or contemporary study, focus first on the 'point' you are making. Test yourself by thinking about another study that you could apply the same point to and compare the way you would elaborate the point – the elaborations should be different. Your answers will sound more authentic if you are able to express the point objectively and link it effectively to the study.

Another strength of the study is the absence of demand characteristics.

During the tour, the dungeon visitors did not know they were participants in a study (the aim was only revealed after they experienced the Labyrinth).

Participants did not know they would be asked to remember the scary person, reducing demand characteristics (in a lab study the object of recall would be more obvious).

This further enhances the ecological validity of the study because, in real situations, eye-witnesses do not generally know they will be witnessing an important event.

Application: The study has important implications for real-life criminal trials.

The findings suggest eye-witness accounts should be treated with caution, particularly if the eye-witness has experienced trauma and stress during the incident.

Anxiety may improve recall of central details (e.g. sequence of events), but memory for peripheral details (face or clothing) is adversely affected (Burke and Mathews 1992).

This supports the view that eye-witness' memories, which are inevitably formed under stress, should be treated with caution.

I&D extra: The study was broadly ethically sound.

Participants went through a scary experience without coercion from the researchers (despite lack of consent at the start).

Participants gave consent retrospectively after the first phase, having already done the Labyrinth tour (given right to withdraw).

This procedure was ethically acceptable and justified because it preserved the validity of the witness experience.

✓ Check it

1. Describe **one** contemporary study from criminological psychology. (5)

2. Explain **two** weaknesses of **one** contemporary study from criminological psychology. (4)

3. **Standard essay:** Evaluate **one** contemporary study from criminological psychology. (8) or (16)

4. **Methods essay:** Evaluate **one** contemporary study from criminological psychology, with reference to objectivity and ethical issues. (16)

Spec spotlight

6.3.4 One contemporary study, for example: Howells et al. (2005) Brief anger management programs with offenders: Outcomes and predictors of change.

Rod wondered whether his new job as cage dancer at the local nightclub was right for him.

Methods

Prison Governor Fox is carrying out research on anger management. One group of participants attend ten sessions of anger management which each last two hours. Another group also attend ten sessions of two hours each but the sessions are in a library discussion group. Participants are interviewed each week about their anger level and sense of control.

1. Explain why Governor Fox should measure aggression before the study begins. (1)

2. (a) Suggest **one** reason why using a 'library' group is better than using a wait-list control. (2)

   (b) Suggest **one** problem with using the 'library' group as a control. (2)

3. **Context/Methods essay:** Evaluate the use of controls in experiments such as Governor Fox's. (8)

Aims

To test whether a prison-based anger management programme is more effective than having no treatment at all.

To test this hypothesis with serious offenders, explore why some offenders benefit from treatment more than others and identify pre-treatment characteristics that determine success.

Procedure

Sample – 418 male prisoners were recruited from Australian institutions (86% from prisons, 14% from a community-based correction centre) – only 21 completed a six-month follow-up assessment.

Control group was drawn from the same target population but members were on a waiting list for the anger programme.

- All participants completed behavioural measures of anger before and after the experimental group's intervention.

- Selected participants completed the measures two and six months later, after the control group had begun their own programme.

Programme = 10 two-hour sessions similar to programme on page 110 (e.g. cognitive preparation, relaxation skills).

Measures of success included:

- Questionnaires for anger intensity, expression, control, effectiveness in dealing with anger, motivation to change.

- Prison staff's observational measures to monitor progress.

Findings

Testing immediately after intervention showed only modest improvement (mostly not significantly better than controls).

Anger management group had significantly better knowledge of their anger than the control group at the end of the intervention (but difference was less marked after six months).

The biggest improvements were in prisoners who had the most intense anger and least control at the beginning (in some cases whether they went through the intervention or not).

Most improvement was in those most open to change at the beginning and highly committed to treatment ('readiness').

Conclusions

Overall impact of anger management programmes is small.

Gains for the experimental group on some measures were not significantly different from the control group (which also had positive outcomes, so just analysing one's anger with self-report assessments may be beneficial without treatment).

Anger management's best function may be educational.

There are important individual differences in who is likely to benefit from anger management intervention (readiness), which should be considered when deciding suitability for treatment.

A strength of the study is that its initial sample was very large.

Earlier studies of anger management were often restricted to one prison or young offenders' institute.

Such research inevitably produced samples that were small and unrepresentative.

Therefore, Howells *et al.*'s study is an improvement on previous research.

CA 418 participants were involved at the start of the study, but only 78 completed the two-month follow-up (just 21 at six-month follow-up) because of practical problems. This means Howells *et al.*'s final analysis of the long-term effects of the programme may be biased because individuals with particular kinds of problems may have dropped out (e.g. the most angry or least receptive criminals).

A weakness is lack of random allocation to experimental and control groups.

The control group came from a list of offenders waiting for anger management who had not been approved for a programme (unlike the experimental group).

The researchers judged this was a 'natural' comparison group, but individual differences between the groups were not controlled.

This may have affected the validity of the conclusions drawn.

Another weakness is that measures of anger were subjective self-reports.

To measure pre- and post-treatment anger, Howells *et al.* used an impressive range of assessment measures.

But using questionnaires to measure self-reported anger has been criticised. Anger is hard to quantify and differs from person to person.

This may reduce the scientific value of the data obtained.

Application: The findings may generalise to other forms of treatment.

The notion that offenders are more successful if they accept the need for change is a key part of other sorts of prison-based therapy, such as social skills training.

Motivational enhancement therapy (MET) is a behavioural therapy which aims to develop treatment readiness before embarking on treatment.

Therefore, Howells *et al.*'s study adds to the growing body of evidence that acceptance of the need for treatment is important for therapeutic progress.

I&D extra: There are gender and cultural issues in this study.

All the offenders in the study were male (because most people serving prison sentences are male).

We are still left with little insight into how female offenders respond to anger management. Also, there are cultural issues because the Australian sample had 86% violent criminals (UK is 23%).

This means that the conclusions Howells *et al.* drew about the effectiveness of anger management programmes may not be universal.

Miranda really hated spam emails. Not that you'd know...

✓ Check it

1. Describe the procedure of **one** contemporary study from criminological psychology. (5)

2. Explain **one** weakness of **one** contemporary study from criminological psychology. (2)

3. **Standard essay:** Evaluate **one** contemporary study from criminological psychology. (8) or (16)

4. **Methods essay:** Evaluate **one** contemporary study from criminological psychology in terms of the way that the data was collected and analysed. (8) or (16)

Attachment, deprivation and privation: Bowlby's work on attachment

A01
Description

You can never be too careful in the workplace.

John Bowlby worked as a psychiatrist in London in the 1930s, treating disturbed children. His early work focused on the negative effects of deprivation (see page 130). His later work focused on the positive effects of attachment, as covered on this page.

Apply it Concepts

Felix and Ana have a new baby, Lucy. They are struck by how helpless their baby is and also amazed at the strength of their immediate attachment to her. At first, they both spend a lot of time interacting with her and trying to sense what she is feeling, but then Felix returns to work and he has very little energy at the end of the day for interactions.

1. (a) How do psychologists explain why Lucy forms the primary attachment with Ana? (1)

   (b) Explain what might have happened if Ana was an insensitive mother. (2)

2. Explain how the attachment will benefit Lucy later in life if it is maintained in infancy. (2)

3. **Context essay:** Discuss the formation of Lucy's attachment. (8)

Why attachments form

The behaviour is naturally selected.

Attachment behaviour evolved because it benefited both babies and parents:

- Individuals are more likely to survive and pass on their genes if they are well-protected as babies – our distant baby ancestors would have been in danger if they did not stay close to a carer and attachment promotes proximity.

- Parents become attached to their babies – this parental attachment behaviour evolved because parents who were not good carers were less reproductively successful (so their genes were not passed on).

When and how attachments form

The critical period is about six months.

Bowlby claimed babies form attachments at about six months.

Any baby not forming an attachment around this age may never be able to form attachments.

Babies attach to carers who are most sensitive to their needs – more responsive, cooperative, accessible.

Social releasers

- Baby-like behaviours and features that elicit caregiving ('make' a carer want to look after the baby).

- These behaviours (and our response) have been naturally selected because they lead to survival and reproductive success.

Monotropy

Forming one primary attachment.

Babies form one (mono) special emotional bond to a *primary attachment figure* – often the biological mother but not always.

It is the person who responds most sensitively to the baby's needs, not the one who spends most time with them.

Babies form *secondary attachments* that provide an emotional safety net – many babies prefer their mother if upset but are equally well-comforted by their father, grandparent or sibling if the mother is absent.

Consequences of attachment

Forming an internal working model of relationships.

Monotropy is important because this special relationship forms the basis for a 'template' about what relationships are like – the *internal working model*, which has two consequences:

- Short-term – gives the child insight into the carer's behaviour and enables the child to influence it (so a true partnership can be formed).

- Long-term – a template for future relationships, creating expectations about what good relationships are like.

Continuity hypothesis – there is continuity from infancy to adulthood in terms of emotional type:

- Individuals who are strongly attached in infancy continue to be socially and emotionally competent.

- Babies who are not strongly attached have more social and emotional difficulties in childhood and adulthood.

A strength is research support for the importance of sensitivity.

Isabella (1993) observed mothers and babies at one, four and nine months, assessing quality of attachment at one year.

He found that the most strongly-attached babies had mothers who were more sensitively responsive.

This supports the importance of sensitivity in the formation of a close attachment.

A weakness is that the temperament hypothesis is an alternative explanation.

Kagan's (1984) *temperament hypothesis* says that a baby's innate temperament (personality) has an important influence on the attachment relationship.

Some babies are emotionally 'difficult' from birth and this affects the mother's ability to form a close relationship.

This means that how attachments form depends on more than just the sensitivity of the mother/caregiver (both nature and nurture matter).

Oh dear, someone's not happy... Some children are just born (not made) bad-tempered (according to Kagan).

Another strength is support for the idea of a critical period.

According to Bowlby it should not be possible to form attachments beyond the age of six months.

Rutter *et al.* (2011) agree that it is less likely attachments form after this period. But they believe it is not impossible (a *sensitive period* rather than a *critical period*).

This means that children are most receptive to forming certain behaviours at a particular time, but such developments can still occur outside this period.

Application: Bowlby's theory has had a major impact on working mothers.

Bowlby's theory has had a considerable impact on attitudes towards mothers going out to work.

It implies that mothers should stay at home to care for children because separation is harmful to emotional development.

Therefore, some feminists criticised Bowlby for discouraging women from being a mother and a career woman.

'CA' stands for 'competing argument'.

CA But this argument missed a key part of attachment theory – attachment is related to the quality of time spent with a baby, not the amount. Fox (1977) tested babies raised on an Israeli kibbutz (a metapelet looks after all the children during the day). The babies spent less time with their mothers, but the attachment bond was almost as strong to the mother as it was to the metapelet.

I&D extra: We can compare different ways of explaining attachment.

The behaviourist view is that attachment is about food (unconditioned stimulus) which creates pleasure (unconditioned response). The 'feeder' is associated with this pleasure and becomes a conditioned stimulus.

Harlow's (1959) research with monkeys showed that attachment was about contact comfort not food, and paved the way for alternative theories of attachment such as Bowlby's.

This view continues as a commonly held attitude – that feeding a baby establishes an important bond. However, Bowlby's theory challenges this.

✓ Check it

1. Describe Bowlby's work on attachment. [5]

2. Explain **one** concept from Bowlby's work that demonstrates the role of nature in attachment. [3]

3. **Standard essay:** Evaluate Bowlby's work on attachment. [8] or [16]

4. **I&D/Synoptic essay:** Assess the issues presented by socially sensitive research with reference to your chosen application (criminological, child or health) **and** clinical psychology. [20]

Attachment, deprivation and privation: Ainsworth's work on attachment

Spec spotlight

7.1.2 Ainsworth's work on attachment, including types of attachment and the Strange Situation procedure.

Episodes (about 3 minutes' duration)	Behaviour assessed
1. Parent and infant play.	–
2. Parent sits while infant plays.	Use of parent as secure base
3. Stranger enters and talks to parent.	Stranger anxiety
4. Parent leaves, infant plays, stranger offers comfort if needed.	Separation anxiety
5. Parent returns, greets infant, offers comfort if needed; stranger leaves.	Reunion behaviour
6. Parent leaves, infant alone.	Separation anxiety
7. Stranger enters and offers comfort.	Stranger anxiety
8. Parent returns, greets and comforts infant.	Reunion behaviour

The eight episodes of Ainsworth's SSP.

A dog playing a violin – now that's what I call a strange situation.

Apply it Concepts

Baby Duncan is playing at home while his mother Elle chats to her friend Lyn. Elle leaves the room to make tea while Lyn looks after Duncan. When Elle returns Lyn realises she has left something in the car and leaves the room, and then Elle realises she forgot the milk – so Duncan is briefly left alone.

1. (a) Explain how Duncan might react when Elle leaves. (2)
   (b) Explain how Duncan might react when Elle returns. (2)
2. Duncan has never met Lyn before. Explain how he might react when alone with her. (2)
3. Context essay: Discuss how Duncan might respond to Elle and Lyn at different times. (8)

Strange Situation procedure (SSP)

A method of assessing attachment type that is still the standard test used today.

Ainsworth developed the Strange Situation procedure:

- Structured observation in room that is new (i.e. 'strange').
- 9 × 9 foot square is marked off into 16 squares to help record the babies' movements.
- Eight 'episodes' (see table on the left), each designed to highlight certain behaviours.
- Key feature of the episodes is caregiver and stranger alternatively stay with the baby or leave.

This enables observation of the baby's response to:

- Separation from caregiver – babies show *separation anxiety* when left alone without caregiver (attachment figure, e.g. mother or father).
- Reunion with caregiver – babies have characteristic ways of greeting the caregiver on their return.
- A stranger – babies respond to an unfamiliar person in different ways (e.g. *stranger anxiety*).
- Novel environment aims to encourage exploration and thus tests the *secure base* concept.

Data collection methods

Using video recorder or two-way mirror.

Note what the baby is doing every 15 seconds (time sampling).

Use behavioural categories (e.g. contact-seeking behaviours or interaction-avoiding behaviours).

Each item is also scored for intensity on a scale of 1 to 7.

Types of attachment

Ainsworth *et al.* (1978) combined several studies, for a total of 106 middle-class babies observed in the SSP.

Three consistent clusters of behaviours formed qualitatively different attachment types (A, B and C, subtypes within each):

Insecure–avoidant (Type A) – 22% of babies:

- High willingness to explore, low stranger anxiety, indifferent separation anxiety, indifferent to departure or return of caregiver (i.e. 'avoidant').
- May develop due to caregiver insensitivity (so quiet baby).

Secure (Type B) – 66% of babies:

- Low separation anxiety and some stranger anxiety.
- Reunion behaviour was enthusiastic, used caregiver as a secure base from which to explore.

Insecure–resistant (Type C) – 12% of babies:

- High stranger anxiety, high separation anxiety and low willingness to explore.
- Reunion behaviour was angry resistance to being picked up, but also trying other means to maintain proximity.

A strength of the study is that the observations were highly reliable.

The study used a panel of experienced observers which meant that inter-observer reliability could be calculated.

Almost perfect agreement when rating exploratory behaviour (a correlation of +.94 between raters' scoring on the SSP).

This means that the observations can be trusted.

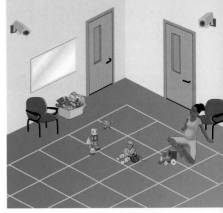

Layout of the Strange Situation procedure (SSP).

A weakness is that the study may have overlooked other types of attachment.

Main and Solomon (1990) analysed over 200 SSP videos and found Type D – *insecure–disorganised* (lack of consistent patterns of behaviour).

A fifth type has been identified – *disinhibited attachment*, characteristic of children who have experienced severe privation (see page 132).

This means that the initial research may have oversimplified a more complex situation and, as such, lacked validity.

Another weakness is low internal validity.

The SSP aims to measure the attachment type of a child, but it actually measures the quality of one specific relationship.

Main and Weston (1981) found that classification of attachment type depended on which parent a baby was with.

This suggests that attachment type may not be valid because what we are measuring is one relationship rather than a personal characteristic.

CA However, it could be argued that the relationship between child and primary caregiver is the key factor in determining attachment type. So if the relationship being measured is with the primary attachment figure then the outcome is valid.

Revision booster

The Strange Situation is a sequence. Some stages are more important to remember than others because the responses to these are used to identify attachment types. You need to learn both the whole sequence and which responses relate to which attachment type. You could use a flowchart to help you to remember.

You should also remember the general details, such as where the study was conducted.

Application: Processes of attachment can be applied to childcare situations.

In cases of disordered attachments, intervention strategies can be developed, e.g. *circle of security* teaches carers to understand babies' distress signals and increase understanding of how it feels to be anxious.

In a study of *circle of security* users, Cooper et al. (2005) found a decrease in the number of caregivers classified as disordered (from 60% to 15%) and an increase in securely attached babies (from 32% to 40%).

This supports the research on attachment types because such research can be used to improve children's lives and such strategies can only be trusted if they have a valid theoretical basis.

Check it

1. Describe Ainsworth's Strange Situation procedure. [4]

2. Explain **one** strength and **one** weakness of Ainsworth's work on attachment. [4]

3. **Standard essay:** Evaluate Ainsworth's work on attachment. [8] or [16]

4. **Methods essay:** Evaluate the validity and reliability of Ainsworth's Strange Situation procedure. [8] or [16]

I&D extra: Culture biases are a key issue for the use of the SSP.

The SSP is built on Western (individualist) assumptions about ideals for behaviour (valuing independence), whereas in collectivist societies interdependence is expected.

In the SSP a baby who appears to be dependent on their caregiver would not be categorised as securely attached.

This means that the SSP is not measuring universal behaviour.

Attachment, deprivation and privation: Research on deprivation

Spec spotlight

7.1.3 Research into deprivation (short-term and long-term effects) and how negative effects can be reduced.

Mother love: take once a day for two-and-a-half years.

Apply it Methods

Dr Mills is planning to change visiting hours on his children's ward. Previously parents were permitted to visit at any time between 9am and 6pm but now visiting will be allowed at any time of day or night. Dr Mills wants to measure any changes in the children's distress levels. He is developing a scoring system that will record three categories: protest, despair and detachment in children.

1. (a) Suggest **one** behaviour Dr Mills could record for each of the three categories. (3)
   (b) Suggest a scoring system for **one** of these categories. (1)

2. Dr Mills is planning a follow-up study with colleagues for 30 years' time. Explain what might be measured in this follow-up study. (2)

3. **Context/Methods essay:** Evaluate the contribution Dr Mills' study could make to the children. (8)

Short-term effects
PDD model

Based on Robertson and Bowlby's (1952) observations of young children experiencing brief separations.

In the 1950s parents could visit their children in hospital for about one hour each day. Also, if mothers were hospitalised, children were not allowed to visit, resulting in separations.

Protest–despair–detachment (PDD) model – child's responses to separation changed over time:

- *Protest* – child's initial response is acute distress. Behaviour directed at getting caregiver to return. Lasting a few hours or even weeks.

- *Despair* – child is less active, cries, rocks for self-comfort. Quietness sometimes misinterpreted as a sign that the distress is over, but actually it signals hopelessness.

- *Detachment* – child welcomes attentions of others, sociable. Apparent well-being is superficial as the child does not show normal greeting if a caregiver visits (remote and apathetic).

Long-term effects
Maternal deprivation hypothesis (MDH)

'Mother-love in infancy and childhood is as important for mental health as are vitamins and proteins for physical health' (Bowlby 1953).

Children need a 'warm, intimate and continuous relationship' with a mother (or permanent mother-substitute) for continuing normal mental health.

Critical (sensitive) period for the effects of deprivation:

- Inevitable negative effects before the age of about two-and-a-half years (and no mother-substitute available).

- A continuing risk up to five years.

The long-term consequence of deprivation is vulnerability to mental health problems such as depression.

> e.g. Bowlby's 44 thieves study – children who experienced prolonged separations at a young age developed mental health issues (affectionless psychopathy).

Reducing negative effects

Providing a substitute 'mother' can compensate for loss of emotional care.

Loss of maternal care is sometimes unavoidable, e.g. if a mother is depressed or needs to be hospitalised.

In childcare situations the aim is to provide secondary attachment figures (e.g. in day care, page 134).

Robertson and Robertson (1967–1973) demonstrated how substitute care is beneficial:

- Cared for young children in their own home while the children's mothers were in hospital.

- Showed there were fewer ill effects from separation if good quality substitute care was provided (e.g. one-to-one caregiving).

- Therefore, separation need not necessarily result in emotional deprivation if substitute emotional care is provided – it is emotional deprivation that can cause long-term harm.

A strength of the PDD model is that observations of Laura were meticulous.

James Robertson (1952) recorded Laura's (aged 2) behaviour in hospital. The research design was very careful to ensure no bias.

Laura was filmed during two 40-minute sessions at the same time each day to ensure filming was not only at the times she was distressed.

This provided high validity because the setting was natural and the very detailed recordings could be checked by others.

CA However, this detailed evidence is a study of just one individual, challenging the generalisability of the findings – though Laura was a fairly average child and the observations did fit with anecdotal data from medical staff. Also the same PDD cycle can be observed in the way people respond generally to situations of threat.

A weakness of Bowlby's research is that it was correlational.

In the 44 thieves study there were other factors which could explain why early separations were associated with later affectionless psychopathy.

There may have been an intervening variable (discord in the home) which caused both the separations and the psychopathy.

Thus, we cannot conclude separation or deprivation *causes* mental health problems. Most likely a vulnerability is created (life stresses increase the chances of later mental health problems).

Another weakness is a lack of distinction between deprivation and privation.

Rutter (1981) criticised Bowlby for not making it clear whether the child's attachment bond had formed but been broken, or had never formed in the first place.

Rutter felt that Bowlby's research mixed the two issues together when they are actually quite different (with different consequences).

This suggests that Bowlby's conclusions lack validity – it is not clear if subsequent effects are due to being deprived of emotional care or having never had it initially.

Application: This research has changed how children are cared for in hospital.

In the 1950s visits to a child in hospital were usually just an hour a day, or forbidden because children were often distressed by such visits.

Today it is unthinkable for children to be separated from their families, who often stay at the hospital in special rooms.

This was a major social change in the way children were cared for, which happened because of this research.

I&D extra: This research shows how psychology has developed over time.

The research on this spread is quite old because the findings changed the way children were cared for, so there was no need to continue this line of research.

Bowlby's research allowed people to make an important distinction between separation (with no emotional deprivation), emotional deprivation and privation.

This led to a changed focus of research which allows us to understand how related mental health issues can be prevented because we more clearly understand their roots.

The films taken by Robertson showed two-year-old Laura alternating between periods of calm and distress. Her parents occasionally visited, and her distress at their departure was heartbreaking. One doctor felt that he and his profession had been slandered in this film but reported that, the next time he walked down his children's ward, he saw things differently, 'I really heard the children crying for the first time'.

✓ Check it

1. Explain the term 'deprivation' with reference to research evidence. [3]

2. Explain **two** weaknesses of research into deprivation. [4]

3. **Standard essay:** Evaluate research into the short- and long-term effects of deprivation. [8] or [16]

4. **Prompt essay:** Many psychologists believe that the separation from our caregivers does not necessarily lead to long-lasting negatives outcomes.

   Assess **two** or more ways in which the negative effects of deprivation can be reduced. [20]

Attachment, deprivation and privation: Research on privation

Spec spotlight

7.1.4 *Research into privation and whether the negative effects can be reversed.*

7.2.4 *The ethics of researching with children, including children's rights and the UNCRC (1989), and issues around participation and protection.*

Read the UNCRC guidelines on page 176.

Institutionalised Romanian orphans. No joke.

Apply it Methods

Dr Kerr is conducting a meta-analysis on privation. She is worried about confounding variables in her chosen studies. She plans to separately analyse studies with long- and short-term follow-up periods. She is also interviewing adults over 70 who experienced privation.

1. Describe Dr Kerr's primary and secondary data. (2)

2. (a) Explain why Dr Kerr will separate the long- and short-term follow-up studies. (3)

   (b) Suggest **one** other reason why Dr Kerr may select or eliminate studies. (2)

3. **Context/Methods essay:** Discuss research into privation. You must refer to the context in your answer. (8)

Case studies of privation e.g. Czech twins.	A case study of 'isolated' children was the 'Czech twins': • Spent first seven years locked up by a stepmother. • When they were first 'discovered' they couldn't talk and were then fostered by two loving sisters. • The twins recovered and had good relationships with their foster family and their own children (Koluchová 1991).
Rutter's ERA study English and Romanian Adoptees (ERA) study (Rutter *et al.* 2011).	A study of 165 Romanian orphans since the early 1990s: • Spent early lives in Romanian institutions with almost no emotional care, then adopted in England. • Tested at adoption, and ages 4, 6, 11, 15 and early adulthood. Physical, cognitive and social development assessed (Kumsta *et al.* 2015). Control group of 52 English children who had not lived in institutions and were adopted before the age of six months. • Romanian adoptees were smaller than controls, weighed less and were classified as mentally retarded. • By age 4, almost all Romanian babies adopted before six months had caught up with the British adoptees. • Later follow-ups confirmed that significant deficits remained in some children adopted after six months.
Effects of privation Disinhibited attachment, physical under-development and poor parenting.	*Disinhibited attachment* (disorder listed in the DSM and ICD) • Form of insecure attachment – shown by many Romanian orphans adopted after six months. • Such children treat near-strangers with inappropriate familiarity (overfriendliness) and may be attention-seeking. Physical underdevelopment • Children in institutional care are usually physically small. • Lack of emotional care (not poor nourishment) is the cause of *deprivation dwarfism* (Gardner 1972). Poor parenting • Quinton *et al.* (1984) compared 50 women brought up in children's homes with 50 women brought up at home (control). • Ex-institutional women (by their 20s) experienced extreme difficulties acting as parents, e.g. children in care.
Can the negative effects be reversed? Yes.	Some Romanian adoptees recovered – so negative effects can be reversed if good emotional and physical care is provided. Applies mainly to those adopted *before* six months (Bowlby's critical age for formation of attachments, so age is important). Recovery for older adoptees (and Czech twins) is also possible if a child has an innate resilience or quality of care is good.

A strength of the ERA study is the careful methodology.

A large sample was used, a control group identified (UK adoptees) and the study has continued over a number of years to allow follow-up.	Also, a wide variety of dependent variables was measured and used to make comparisons (e.g. intellectual, language and emotional development).	This provides a wealth of information from which to draw valid conclusions.

CA In contrast, evidence from case studies (e.g. the Czech twins) should be treated with caution, but often isn't. People sometimes ignore the bits that don't fit the 'story' which means the evidence is misleading. In addition, the fact that we do not know the full details of what happened in the early lives of case studies means we cannot draw clear conclusions.

A weakness is that privation was not the only factor in the ERA study.

The Romanian orphans experienced more than emotional deprivation – physical conditions were appalling (health impact), lack of cognitive stimulus affected development too.	In many cases of privation, poor care in infancy is followed by poor subsequent care (living in poverty, parental disharmony, etc., Turner and Lloyd 1995).	These arguments mean that privation alone is unlikely to be the sole cause of later developmental problems (nor the most important factor).

Another weakness is that the long-term effects are not clear.

Children adopted later also spent longer in the institution, which may explain differences rather than age of adoption.	Late-adopted children may also just lag behind developmentally (and will catch up eventually) rather than have deficits which are permanent.	This means it is difficult to draw clear conclusions about the effects of age and privation at this time.

Application: The lives of children experiencing privation can be improved.

Research has shown the damage caused by large-scale institutional care – consequently such places have disappeared in most countries of the world.	The adoption process has also been refined by psychological research because we realise how important early adoptions are (before six months).	This impact is a tremendous strength of this body of research.

I&D extra: This research illustrates ethical and practical considerations.

Privation can't be ethically manipulated. You can't randomly allocate children to a group with or without emotional care, so research depends on the variable of interest occurring naturally.	However, children in such situations may feel it is an invasion of their privacy to be observed and tested, especially as they are vulnerable and had no chance to give consent.	This raises the question of whether the personal costs justify the benefits in terms of the knowledge we can gain from such a study.

They flipped a coin to see who would get to wear the matching T-shirt.

Revision booster

The Apply it question on the facing page is about research methods, which should remind you that exam questions may require you to relate the content of child psychology to research methods – in particular observation, questionnaires/interviews, cross-cultural research, meta-analysis, ethics and quantitative and qualitative data analysis.

✓ Check it

1. Describe evidence that suggests that privation is reversible. [4]

2. Explain **one** way privation researchers can ensure that UNCRC (1989) guidelines are upheld in their work. [4]

3. **Standard essay:** Evaluate research into privation. [8] or [16]

4. **Context essay:** Abdi was abandoned in a forest as a baby and was raised by monkeys. A team of dedicated professionals are now supporting him, following his discovery aged 14.

   Assess the likelihood that Abdi will overcome the negative effects of privation. [16]

Attachment, deprivation and privation: Research into day care

Spec spotlight

7.1.5 Research into day care, including advantages and disadvantages for the child, and what makes good- and poor-quality day care.

They'd been sat there for hours. Leaves on the line apparently.

Apply it Methods

Ode is studying the effects on children of attending the day care centre she runs. In her advertising she states that the centre helps children with their cognitive and social development, including becoming a more confident and independent child. Some prospective parents want reassurance about potential problems with day care.

1. **(a)** Suggest **one** way that Ode could measure each of the three benefits she states. (3)

   (b) Identify **one** problem Ode could investigate. (1)

2. If Ode wants to show that her day care centre is the best, why should she conduct her study over many years? (2)

3. **Context/Methods essay:** Ode has designed a longitudinal study to show the benefits of her day care centre. Evaluate the use of longitudinal designs in child psychology. You must refer to the context in your answer. (8)

Kinds of day care research studies

Meta-analysis and longitudinal studies.

Violato and Russell (2000) conducted a meta-analysis of 88 studies:

- Day care for over 20 hours per week had a negative effect on social development, attachment and aggression.
- But the studies were all short-term.

In the 1990s longitudinal studies were started to examine the effects of day care over the long-term:

- NICHD study in the US included 1,394 families studied over 16 years (see more on page 154).
- EPPE study in the UK followed 3000 children from different social backgrounds from age 3 to 7.
- Both compared children in day care with those receiving parental care.

Disadvantages for the child

Day care may create emotional deprivation with negative effects on attachment.

Disobedience and aggression – the longer a 5-year-old spent in day care (any quality), the more adults rated them as disobedient/aggressive (NICHD 2003).

Aggression – link remained between day care and aggression in same children at the end of primary schooling (Belsky *et al.* 2007).

Behaviour problems (e.g. lying, unpredictable conduct, hitting) three times more likely in children in full-time day care than those cared for by mothers at home (NICHD 2003).

Advantages for the child

Day care may help develop social and intellectual skills.

Independence and sociability – increased in children who had attended day care (EPPE study, Sylva *et al.* 2004).

Number of friends – positively correlated with time in full-time day care once children went to school (Field 1991).

Cognitive skills – boosted in US Head Start preschool care so disadvantaged children start school on an even footing:

- Head Start children had IQ gains of 10 points in the first year, which usually disappeared (Zigler and Styfco 1993).
- But long-term effects were observed (e.g. participants were more likely to obtain a high school certificate).

Good quality day care

Substitute emotional care may avoid ill effects but quality of care must be high.

The key factors of good quality day care are:

- Good staff-to-child ratio (about 1:3 for babies and 1:5 for older children).
- Staff should be given responsibility for individual children so they can become secondary attachment figures.
- Staff should be trained and encouraged to stay in their job to reduce staff turnover.

Li *et al.* (2013, page 154) found high quality of care included warmth and sensitivity, cognitive stimulation, encouraging greater exploration and being less emotionally detached.

A strength of this research area is good methodology.

Large-scale longitudinal studies (e.g. NICHD) produce a wealth of data about both children and their families.

Also, the NICHD sample was large and represented a wide range of different backgrounds.

This means we can feel more confident about making generalisations about the effects of day care.

CA However, the research is still correlational, so the data cannot show that day care caused the behavioural issues. Dingfelder (2004) argues that the findings are meaningless unless one knows the processes by which aggression is increased.

The MasterChef judges seem to get younger every year.

A weakness is that there may be more than one conclusion to be drawn.

Other NICHD findings did not receive quite as much media attention as the aggression/day-care link – Friedman pointed out that the findings relating to aggression can be stated differently (Lang 2006).

83% of children in day care for 10–30 hours a week didn't show higher aggression compared to children who had less or no day care. Age and hours in day care must be considered.

This is the danger of selective reporting by people who have a view to promote. Friedman's alternative emphasis suggests most children were not disadvantaged by day care.

Revision booster

When answering any extended response question (essay) it is always important to provide a balanced answer, citing at least one strength and one weakness and a competing argument for good measure. Remember that conclusions are not required when the command term is 'Discuss'.

Another weakness is that there are other factors that affect aggression.

NICHD data showed that a mother's sensitivity to her child was a better predictor of problem behaviours than time in day care (more sensitive mothering linked to fewer problem behaviours).

Higher maternal education and family income also predicted lower levels of children's problem behaviours (NICHD 2003).

Therefore, children's development appears to be more strongly affected by factors at home than in day care.

Application: Research can help improve day care for parents at work.

The recommendations on the facing page are research-based and suggest that the key issue is ensuring adequate substitute emotional care.

The advantages of day care should also be emphasised – research shows that the experience is good for social development.

Therefore, day care places should focus on maximising the benefits and minimising the factors associated with negative outcomes.

Check it

1. Explain **one** advantage of day care for the child, with reference to research evidence. [3]

2. Describe **two** features of good quality day care. [4]

3. **Standard essay:** Evaluate research into day care. [8] or [16]

4. **Standard plus essay:** Assess research into day care. You must make reference to ethical issues in your answer. [8]

I&D extra: One issue is the socially sensitive nature of this research.

If day care is harmful to children, then this has consequences for parents who both wish to work.

Some research suggests children may best be at home with one parent providing a strong emotional basis for development (at least in the very early years).

This has implications for career aspirations and for poorer members of society who may feel that it is economically necessary for both parents to work.

Attachment, deprivation and privation: Cross-cultural research

A01
Description

Spec spotlight

7.1.6 Cross-cultural research into attachment types and nature–nurture issues that arise about development.

7.2.3 The use of the cross-cultural research method, including the Strange Situation, in child psychology, including nature–nurture issues and issues of cross-sectional versus longitudinal designs.

'I just need to learn the study by van Iz...van Izen...van Oozen...van Izling...aw – I give up.'

Psychology student Neville wasn't known for his cultural sensitivity.

Apply it **Concepts**

Zreik *et al.* (2017) studied different attachment types in Arab-Israeli and Jewish-Israeli, Western and non-Western mothers. There were no differences between the samples in terms of secure versus insecure attachments but a few differences when more detailed comparisons were made between attachment types A, B, C and D.

1. **(a)** Explain why this could be described as a cross-cultural study. (1)
   (b) Describe **two** reasons why Zreik *et al.* may have found differences in attachment between the four cultural groups. (4)

2. Suggest why the ABCD comparison found differences. (1)

3. **Context essay:** Discuss the nature–nurture debate. You must refer to the context in your answer. (8)

Cultural similarities – Nature

Bowlby proposed that attachment behaviours are naturally selected.

Therefore, we would expect them to be genetically determined and universal. If they are, then this supports Bowlby's argument.

Cross-cultural research allows us to test this.

Research evidence

van IJzendoorn and Kroonenberg (1988, page 148) found much cross-cultural similarity in attachment types around the world (secure attachment was invariably most common).

Meta-analysis by Cassibba *et al.* (2013, page 150) also found similarities in a comparison of Italian and US samples.

Tronick *et al.* (1992) support this:

- Efé babies were looked after and breastfed by different women but usually slept with their own mother at night.
- Different from child-rearing in the UK and yet at six months babies still showed one primary attachment (like in UK).
- So forming a primary attachment is a universal behaviour even when children have multiple carers.

Cultural differences – Nurture

Different cultures often have different child-rearing practices (as in the Efé above).

Cultural differences in attachment behaviours (nurture) might lead to differences in adult behaviour.

Research evidence

Takahashi (1990) studied 60 middle-class Japanese babies/mothers:

- Secure attachment rates similar to Ainsworth *et al.* but Japanese babies showed more insecure–resistant attachment (32%), may be related to culture.
- Japanese babies particularly distressed being left alone.
- Japanese babies are rarely separated from their mothers, physical closeness develops a sense of oneness (*amae*).
- Western parents encourage babies to be more separated, e.g. by putting babies in their own bedroom.

Grossmann and Grossmann (1990) studied infants and families in Germany:

- Northern German babies had a greater tendency to be classed as insecure–avoidant in the Strange Situation procedure (SSP).
- German culture encourages distance between parents and children (to get independent, non-clingy babies, who do not make demands on parents, but obey their commands).
- Attachments in southern Germany more similar to US samples (less emotionally distant subculture in the south).

A strength is that many studies were carried out by indigenous researchers.

For example, the Grossmanns are German and Takahashi is Japanese.	This avoids many issues in cross-cultural research (e.g. misunderstanding participants' language or difficulty communicating instructions).	This enhances the validity of the data collected.

CA But this was not true of all the research, e.g. Tronick *et al.* were outsiders from America. Their observations may have been biased by expectations about Africans.

A weakness is that even 'indigenous' studies applied an imposed etic.

The Grossmanns and Takahashi used the SSP to assess attachment type – but various assumptions underlie this technique which may make it invalid in other cultures.	For example, a child who happily plays at a distance from an attachment figure is judged as securely attached. But clinginess is the norm in Japanese children.	This means that both the German and Japanese children may appear to be insecurely attached but weren't. They were responding in a culturally-appropriate way.

Gross(ed out)man.

Revision booster

Cross-cultural research, evolutionary explanations and the nature–nurture debate are all covered on this spread and go hand-in-hand. Remember that you may be able to use these ideas in a question on issues and debates in Paper 3.

Another weakness is that most studies include countries rather than cultures.

These are not the same – within any country there are different cultures, e.g. van IJzendoorn and Sagi (2001) found attachment rates similar to Western studies in an urban Japanese sample but not in a rural sample.	Furthermore the classic study for this topic (van IJzendoorn and Kroonenberg, page 148) found more variation in attachment rates within cultures than between cultures.	This suggests that data about countries may be fairly meaningless and research should focus on relating cultural ideals to attachment outcomes.

Application: Attachment research should change focus.

Rothbaum *et al.* (2000) argued the solution is to produce theories rooted in individual cultures and related to unique childcare practices linked to emotionally healthy outcomes.	Nevertheless they agree about some universal principles related to attachment (e.g. providing a form of protection for a defenceless baby).	This suggests that both nature and nurture are involved in attachment behaviours.

I&D extra: This topic illustrates the nature–nurture debate.

Cross-cultural research on attachment often shows that nurture is a stronger influence than nature.	However, there is also evidence to support cross-cultural similarities in attachment, which are the product of nature.	This supports the widely accepted position that our innate predispositions (nature) are modified by life experiences (nurture).

✓ Check it

1. Explain how cross-cultural research on attachment supports the view that nature is more important than nurture. (4)

2. Explain **one** weakness of cross-cultural studies which use the Strange Situation. (2)

3. **Standard essay:** Evaluate cross-cultural research into attachment. (8) or (16)

4. **I&D/Synoptic essay:** Assess the role of nature in understanding human behaviour. You must use examples from your chosen application (criminological, child or health) **and** social psychology. (20)

Autism: The features of autism

Spec spotlight

7.1.7 The features of autism.

Reach out and celebrate difference.

Apply it Concepts

Hiran has been diagnosed with autism. A typical behaviour he shows is watching his marbles roll down a ramp over and over again but he doesn't play marbles with other children. They find him strange as he rarely talks, often sniffs at things and won't join new games. He loves sweets, which are kept in a jar at the top of a kitchen cupboard. When he points at the jar his mum reaches up and gives him a sweet. One day she sees him standing pointing at the cupboard all alone.

1. Explain Hiran's behaviours:
   (a) With the marbles. (4)
   (b) With other children. (2)

2. Explain why Hiran would point at the cupboard even if there was nobody there to see him. (3)

3. **Context essay:** Discuss Hiran's symptoms of autism. (8)

Autism

Autism spectrum disorder (ASD).

Two broad categories of symptoms are considered for a diagnosis of ASD:

- Social communication difficulties.
- Repetitive behaviours.

Social communication difficulties

Social-emotional reciprocity deficits

- May not use communication to share interests or emotions, initiate interactions or respond to others.
- Lack back-and-forth of everyday communication.

Nonverbal communication deficits

- Use nonverbal signals (e.g. eye contact and social smiling) inappropriately.
- Facial expressions can be limited or exaggerated, gestures may be used in the wrong contexts.
- Mismatch between facial expression and tone of voice.

Problems developing and maintaining relationships

- Lack understanding that other people have minds, so have trouble seeing the world from another's viewpoint.
- Unaware of social norms, which makes it hard to change behaviour to suit the context (e.g. laughing at the wrong time).
- Lack of understanding means difficulty making friends (e.g. children with ASD do not play cooperatively).

Restricted and repetitive behaviours

Repetitive behaviours

- Use language unusually, e.g. repeating what has just been heard (*echolalia*).
- Physical movements can be repetitive (e.g. rocking).
- Use objects over and over again in the same restricted ways (e.g. lining them up).

Routines and rituals

- Stick inflexibly to routines (e.g. step-by-step sequence).
- Use verbal rituals, insisting other people use words in a 'set' pattern (e.g. when answering questions).
- Can be resistant to change and variations in routines.

Unusual reactions to sensory input

- Find touch aversive so try to avoid it (e.g. hair brushing).
- May be obsessively interested in movements of objects, (opening, closing) looking at them for long periods.
- First response to an object (or in some cases a person) may be to lick or sniff it.
- Can be easily distressed by stimuli they're not used to yet and may appear indifferent to pain (both their own and other people's).

A strength is that diagnosis of ASD is valid.

Frazier et al. (2012) support the division of ASD symptoms into two broad categories (communication difficulties and restricted/ repetitive behaviours).

They found that this dyadic (two-category) model of ASD was confirmed by a statistical technique called factor analysis. This means that the DSM-5's classification is valid because it reflects the reality of the disorder's symptoms.

This is important as valid classification is the first step in planning an effective treatment programme – it improves the accuracy of diagnosis so symptoms can be more effectively targeted.

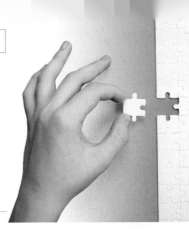

CA The validity of the DSM-5 classification may be valid but the reliability of the DSM-5 classification is questionable. In an Australian study by Taylor et al. (2017), 27 clinicians used the DSM-5 criteria to classify symptoms observed in nine video clips. The findings were mixed – reliability was 100% for three of the clips, but 'poor' for the other six. This suggests that the reliability of a diagnosis of ASD under the DSM-5 has not yet been fully established.

Autism may include a preoccupation with detail.

A weakness is that diagnosis of ASD focuses on deficits.

Frith (2003) rejects the focus on what people with ASD cannot do in favour of a focus on superior abilities.

For example, people with ASD do have problems with global processing (seeing the 'bigger picture'). But they are more skilled in local processing (i.e. they can identify and understand details such as specific information in a conversation).

The issue is that the traditional focus on deficits overlooks the strengths of people with ASD and maintains the stigma associated with it.

Case studies of autism spectrum disorder

Nina is six years old and shows no signs of wanting to make friends with other children. She is completely perplexed when children try to involve her in 'pretend' games, for example by riding an imaginary horse. She gets angry and upset whenever her class is taught by a supply teacher. Nina seems to enjoy attention from adults. She is obsessed with bikes, so speaks to adults about them at great length and very formally. She uses technical language about bikes that not even most adults understand. She hates the sound Velcro® makes when it is being unfastened.

Guy is 32 and lives with his parents. He is socially withdrawn and has no friends. He takes what other people say very seriously and literally. Guy eats the same meals every day at the same times. He is fascinated by time, and collects clocks and books about clocks. He will talk about clocks endlessly but doesn't notice when others become bored. Guy frequently smiles to himself but never to other people. He rocks back and forth in his room switching his desk light on and off for hours on end.

Adapted from genuine cases studies.

Check it

1. Leo displays various features of autism.

   Describe **two** behaviours which would suggest Leo has autism. [4]

2. State **two** questions a child psychologist might ask Leo's mother to help work out whether he has autism. [4]

3. **Standard essay:** Evaluate the features of autism. [8] or [16]

4. **Methods essay:** Evaluate **two** ways child psychologists can ensure they meet UNCRC standards when working with children with autism. [8]

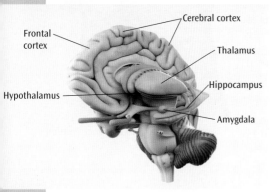

Frontal cortex
Cerebral cortex
Thalamus
Hypothalamus
Hippocampus
Amygdala

A slice through the middle of the brain showing some of the areas and structures that may be involved in ASD, including the amygdala.

ASD = autism spectrum disorder.

Methods

Dr Cox conducted a longitudinal study of amygdala size and function in boys diagnosed with autism. He also used a questionnaire which measured levels of fear. He measured amygdala and total brain volume using MRI scans and amygdala activity using fMRI.

1. Dr Cox intends to have a control group. Suggest **two** characteristics that should be used to select members of the control group. (2)

2. (a) Explain why the MRI scans are likely to be more objective than Dr Cox's score of fear. (2)
   (b) Explain why amygdala **and** total brain size were measured. (1)

3. **Context/Methods essay:** To what extent should studies in child psychology collect many types of data? You must refer to the context in your answer. (20)

Amygdala dysfunction explanation for autism (ASD)

Structure and functions of the amygdala.

The *amygdala* consists of 13 densely-packed collections of neuron cell bodies (*nuclei*) in each of the brain's medial temporal cortex.

There are two amygdala, one in each hemisphere.

A highly networked structure, densely interconnected with other structures and regions (e.g. *hypothalamus, prefrontal cortex*).

The amygdala has a powerful influence through these connections on behaviours associated with motivation, emotion and social interaction.

Amygdala development and ASD

Amygdala development differs between children with and without ASD, according to Nordahl *et al.* (2012):

- Amygdala of children with ASD is 6–9% larger from two years of age than in children without a diagnosis of ASD.
- As children with ASD get older, volume growth stalls.
- But it continues in children without ASD, so by late adolescence there is no difference in volume.

This early development in ASD may be partly responsible for any abnormal neural organisation and impaired functioning of the amygdala.

Link between frontal cortex and amygdala

The amygdala has a central role in influencing social behaviour, so is part of the human 'social brain'.

Baron-Cohen *et al.* (2000) applied this idea to ASD:

- Amygdala has neural connections with the *frontal/ prefrontal cortex* (major role in processing social information).
- Abnormal amygdala development in childhood affects the operation of these parts of the brain.
- This is a key cause of social and behavioural deficits in ASD (e.g. impairments of social-emotional reciprocity).

Role of the amygdala in impaired social processing

People with ASD often do not fully understand the emotional expressions of others.

Baron-Cohen *et al.* (1999) showed that this is due to amygdala dysfunction impairing social processing:

- Gave participants (with and without ASD) the 'eyes test' (photos of people making various facial expressions, showing just the eye areas – see top of facing page).
- People with ASD found it hard to choose the correct description of each expression from a choice of two (e.g. concerned/unconcerned).
- fMRI scans showed that, relative to controls, people with ASD had underactive left amygdala.

A strength of amygdala dysfunction theory is support from clinical studies.

Kennedy et al. (2009) studied 'SM' who did not have ASD, but a rare genetic disorder impaired her amygdala function.

Her preferred personal space distance for social interaction was about half of that for matched control participants.

This finding shows that amygdala dysfunction is associated with social deficits that are similar to those found in ASD.

CA However, findings about the role of the amygdala are inconsistent. Herbert et al. (2003) reported smaller amygdala volumes in children with ASD compared with controls. But other research findings from various age groups differ. This casts doubt on the validity of the theory and means the role of the amygdala is still unclear.

A weakness is that the ASD-amygdala dysfunction link may be indirect.

People with amygdala damage cannot process anxiety-related information normally, so social functioning is impaired (anxiety is co-morbid with ASD, i.e. they often occur together).

White et al. (2009) suggest there may be a link between amygdala dysfunction and social behaviour deficits that are due to abnormal processing of anxiety.

This shows that the role of the amygdala in ASD is more complex than the conventional dysfunction explanation suggests.

Another weakness is that neural factors in ASD are oversimplified.

Several other brain structures are just as dysfunctional in ASD as the amygdala.

Paul et al. (2010) studied two women who only had amygdala damage. Their social behaviour was not impaired to the extent found in ASD.

Therefore, amygdala dysfunction on its own is probably not enough to fully account for symptoms of ASD.

Application: The dysfunction explanation offers a potential target for treatment.

More research remains to be done to identify the biochemical abnormalities associated with amygdala dysfunction that may explain ASD symptoms.

A drug treatment that corrects amygdala functioning is possible. Also, if amygdala dysfunction is reliably linked to ASD, it could lead to earlier diagnosis.

This could help shorten the 'diagnostic journey', the drawn-out and highly stressful process many families go through to get a diagnosis.

I&D extra: Research into ASD is socially sensitive.

Some people with ASD do not believe they have a 'disorder' that needs to be 'treated'. Language about ASD is often negative, with an emphasis on deficits and impairments.

It is unusual for theories to highlight the strengths of people with ASD – they are seen as 'all deficits', unable to function in everyday life with nothing to contribute to society.

Therefore, psychologists have a responsibility to be active in dispelling the myths and misunderstandings surrounding ASD.

One of these facial expressions is fear, and the other is anger. But which is which? Most people find it straightforward to identify the two emotions. But some people with ASD find it difficult because they have trouble processing emotional expressions.

 Check it

1. Explain **two** features of **one** biological explanation for autism. [4]

2. Describe **one** practical application of **one** biological explanation for autism. [2]

3. **Standard essay:** Evaluate **one** biological explanation for autism. [8] or [16]

4. **I&D/Synoptic essay:** Assess the view that biological explanations of behaviour are reductionist. You must refer to **two** applications in psychology (clinical, criminological, child or health). [20]

Autism: One other explanation

Spec spotlight

7.1.7 One other explanation for autism.

Apply it Concepts

The Sally–Anne test does not work well with adults with autism. Another test uses 'strange stories'. One story is about penguins huddling together in the cold and moving between the middle and edge of the group. A person with autism finds it hard to explain why the penguins behave like this.

1. **(a)** Suggest why the Sally–Anne test does not work with adults. (1)

2. **(a)** State how an adult not diagnosed with autism would respond to the 'strange stories' question. (1)

   (b) Explain why an adult diagnosed with autism could not answer the 'strange stories' question about penguins. (4)

3. **Context essay:** One approach to explaining autism is biological. Discuss the 'strange stories' method using **one** other explanation for autism. (8)

Sally–Anne test

A child is told the following story.

Sally puts her marble in her basket and leaves the room.

Anne moves the marble to her box.

Sally returns. Where will she look for the marble?

Theory of mind

We are aware that other people are able to represent the world in their minds.

Understanding other people's internal mental states means we can interpret and predict their behaviour – when we develop this understanding, we possess a *theory of mind* (ToM):

- The recognition that other people have thoughts, emotions and intentions of their own.
- We infer people's mental states from their behaviour.

This ability is impaired in ASD (Baron-Cohen 1995):

- People with ASD have 'mindblindness', a reduced ability to understand the internal mental states of other people.
- Dysfunctional ToM is a central deficit of ASD, accounting for social and communication impairments.

Foundations of a ToM

Two abilities:

Distinguish between physical and mental things.

Distinguish between appearance and reality.

Physical versus mental

- A child listens to a story about two characters.
- One holds a glass of pop (a physical experience), the other thinks about a glass of pop (a mental experience).
- The child answers questions about what each character can do (e.g. 'Which child can drink the pop?').
- Neurotypical four-year-olds find this easy because they can distinguish between physical and mental – but it is very difficult for a child with ASD.

Appearance versus reality

- Neurotypical four-year-olds usually know that an object that looks like one thing can really be something else (e.g. a football-shaped birthday cake is still a cake).
- Children with ASD may not always grasp that an object's appearance and its real nature are not always the same.

Testing ToM deficits

The Sally–Anne test (see left).

Children listen to the Sally–Anne story and are asked questions, including one that tests ToM, 'Where will Sally look for her marble?'.

The correct answer ('in the basket') reflects the understanding that another person can hold a different view of the world (i.e. Sally's 'belief' about the marble's location is different from the child's).

Baron-Cohen *et al.* (1985) tested three groups of children:

- Neurotypical four-year-olds – 85% correct.
- Children with Down syndrome (low intelligence, acting as a control group) – 86% correct.
- Children with ASD – 20% correct.

Conclusion – processing tasks that require a ToM are hard for people with ASD, these skills are independent of intelligence.

A strength is experimental support for the ToM explanation.

Baron-Cohen et al. (2001) tested ToM using the 'eyes test' (see previous spread), where participants identify emotions by selecting a response from four options (e.g. serious, ashamed).

Adults with ASD performed worse than controls, suggesting an impaired ability to infer emotional states from facial expressions.

This finding supports the validity of a ToM deficit as a feature of ASD, especially given that the task did not depend on language abilities (participants were given glossaries to define words).

A weakness is ToM dysfunction is an incomplete explanation.

ToM deficits do not account for the non-social features of ASD, including the repetitive behaviours and interests that are part of the diagnosis under the DSM-5 (Tager-Flusberg 2007).

Also, as Frith and Happé (1994) point out, some people with ASD pass both the Sally–Anne and the eyes tests.

This means that the ToM explanation lacks validity because it is not a comprehensive theory of ASD.

Another weakness is that ToM lacks explanatory power.

ToM dysfunction may be a symptom of ASD and not a cause. A neurological impairment could be the underlying cause of the ToM deficit and thus the cause of ASD.

Or, looking back through the chain of cause and effect, the ultimate cause could be genetic (e.g. the genes responsible for development of brain organisation).

Therefore, ToM may not explain a great deal about ASD, at least not without involving other (biological) mechanisms.

Application: The ToM explanation offers a target for intervention.

Kasari et al. (2012) studied children with ASD in a programme to improve their joint attention skills.

Compared with controls, the language skills of these children were significantly improved and this improvement was apparent even after five years.

This shows that treating ASD as a ToM deficit produces beneficial outcomes, especially when children can start school with better language skills.

CA However, other studies are not so positive. Fletcher-Watson et al. (2014) reviewed interventions based on ToM. They found that ToM can be developed in children with ASD. But the improvements are short-lived and do not generalise beyond the situations in which the skills were learned. Predictions based on ToM deficits may have only limited application.

I&D extra: ToM shows how psychological understanding has developed over time.

ToM was a starting point for development of theories that could explain more findings, e.g. once it was found that ToM deficits could not explain repetitive behaviours, Frith (1989) developed a theory that could.

Weak central coherence theory suggests that people with ASD are less likely to pay attention to the broader context of a situation and tend to focus on isolated details instead.

This shows how psychological understanding progresses through testing and revising theories, extending or even abandoning them when they are no longer able to explain the bulk of research findings.

ALWAYS UNIQUE TOTALLY INTELLIGENT SOMETIMES MYSTERIOUS

Says it all.

Revision booster

You have studied two explanations for autism – one biological and one other. Sometimes, when you have studied two explanations you may be able to use one of the explanations as evidence against the other – but take care because this might not always be the case. It may be possible for the two explanations to exist side-by-side, so neither one is wrong.

Also, don't forget that, if you are using an explanation as evaluation then description of the explanation is not creditworthy – you must focus on comparative strengths or weaknesses.

Check it

1. You have studied **two** explanations of autism.

   Describe how a child psychologist might explain the causes of autism to a parent. [3]

2. Explain **one** strength of **one** explanation for autism, with reference to research evidence. [3]

3. **Standard essay:** Evaluate **one** explanation for autism. [8] or [16]

4. **Standard plus essay:** Evaluate **one** explanation for autism with reference to practical applications. You must include at least **one** comparison with an alternative explanation for autism in your answer. [8] or [16]

Autism: Therapies for helping children with autism (1)

A01
Description

Spec spotlight

7.1.7 Therapies for helping children with autism.

ball

pens

toy kitchen

trampoline

In PECS children have cards with pictures of objects or activities they are interested in, such as those above. When a child wants one of these things they are encouraged to select the card and a picture exchange takes place where a facilitator helps the child hand the card to the teacher.

Apply it Methods

Jan thinks there are practical and ethical challenges in testing therapies for children with autism. These include small sample sizes, delay in the development of speech, problems with participants maintaining behaviours over time, and withholding basic rights (such as playthings).

1. (a) Describe **one** practical problem with testing a therapy for children with autism. (2)
   (b) Describe **one** ethical problem with testing a therapy for children with autism. (2)

2. Design a practical, ethical test of any **one** therapy for children with autism. (6)

3. **Context/Methods essay:** Evaluate **one** therapy for helping children with autism using the practical and ethical problems that Jan has raised. (8)

Picture Exchange Communication System (PECS)
Bondy and Frost (1985)

A therapy used with people with limited or no vocal speech, to develop functional communication.

Based on *applied behavioural analysis* (APA), a general approach using behaviourist principles (e.g. reinforcement) to improve social behaviour (including communication).

Children with ASD usually do not initiate conversation, so have few opportunities for communication behaviour to be reinforced (e.g. rewarded with praise). PECS therefore aims to provide opportunities for reinforcement.

PECS is designed to help the child make the first move in communication rather than simply responding to others.

The PECS protocol
A preparation phase plus six stages (Frost and Bondy 2002).

Pre-programme preparation
- Discover which objects (toys, food, etc.) and activities the child is interested in and finds motivating.
- Picture cards created for each object/activity (see left).

Stage 1 Physical exchange
- Teacher (communication partner) shows object, e.g. ball.
- Another adult behind the child (facilitator) prompts child to pick up picture of the object.
- 'Picture exchange', facilitator helps child hand card over.
- Teacher responds by saying 'ball' or 'I want the ball' and gives the object to the child – positively reinforcing.
- Process repeated with different objects, leads to generalisation.

Stage 2 Increasing independence, distance and persistence
- PECS less structured – pictures arranged in a binder.

Stage 3 Learning to discriminate
- Range of pictures in the book becomes wider.

Stage 4 Sentence structure
- Child builds sentences by placing pictures on a 'sentence strip' (e.g. add 'I want' picture to a ball picture).

Stage 5 Answering direct questions
- Child learns to construct and exchange a sentence strip in response to questions such as 'What do you want?'.

Stage 6 Commenting
- Questions expanded to include social ones (e.g. 'What do you have?') – child can comment on experiences.

A strength is research evidence to support the effectiveness of PECS.

Charlop-Christy et al. (2002) found that three boys with ASD made more spontaneous speech utterances after PECS training (one boy went from 28% to 100%).

Eye contact and joint attention (shared gaze on same object) also improved significantly, and there was a marked reduction in problem behaviours such as tantrums.

These suggest that PECS can help children with ASD acquire spontaneous speech, as well as bringing additional benefits.

CA This study has methodological weaknesses. There were only three participants, so the study has no power to draw conclusions. There was no statistical analysis of the data, so it is unclear if improvements were *statistically* significant. These limitations partly undermine the positive conclusions about success of PECS.

A weakness is that there is only limited support from meta-analyses.

Flippin et al. (2010) analysed three group studies and eight experiments, concluding that PECS is 'fairly effective' in improving communication in children with ASD.

But there was no evidence that improvements were maintained over time or generalised across situations (gains in spontaneous speech were at best small).

This suggests PECS has limited application. But, although the quality of evidence is poor, PECS should not be abandoned but subjected to more rigorous testing with more participants.

Another weakness is that PECS has potential negative effects.

PECS focuses on just one form of functional communication – requests ('comments' in Stage 6 are responses to prompts and not self-generated).

Flippin et al. argue that training in *initiating* communication is missing from the standard PECS programme.

This is a weakness because focusing on a very limited type of communication may delay spontaneous speech development.

Application: There is some evidence that PECS is a cost-effective therapy.

PECS can be expensive. However, this needs to be balanced against the costs of other therapies that are less effective.

Successful PECS may contribute to greater independence, so that people with ASD are able to work and make a living.

This means that investment in PECS would lower costs to wider society of social care and welfare benefits.

I&D extra: PECS illustrates ethical issues in psychology.

Baron-Cohen (2009) criticises therapies that rely on withholding external rewards.

In PECS stage 1, the teacher withholds a ball until the child has exchanged a picture. The ball is a reward to be earned, but the child should be able to play with it freely.

Therefore, Baron-Cohen suggests that therapies should focus on the child's interests that are intrinsically rewarding, so there is no need to withhold external rewards.

A different kind of pecs training!

Check it

1. Describe how **one** therapy for autism can help improve a child's functioning. [4]

2. Explain **one** practical issue that might affect the delivery of **one** therapy for autism. [2]

3. **Standard essay:** Evaluate **one** therapy for autism. [8] or [16]

4. **I&D essay:** Psychological research is powerful as it can greatly improve the quality of people's lives.

   Evaluate **two** or more uses of psychological knowledge in society, using examples from criminological, child or health psychology. [20]

Autism: Therapies for helping children with autism (2)

Spec spotlight

7.1.7 Therapies for helping children with autism.

Behaviourist methods are those based on learning theory – learning through classical and operant conditioning, and also extended to the principles of social learning theory (modelling).

Model behaviour.

Concepts

Max has been diagnosed with autism and his parents are considering a possible therapy to help him. He is five years old so he could attend school but cannot because he lacks basic skills. For example, he cannot put his socks on or pull a jumper over his head. He eats with his fingers and rarely speaks. Max can understand speech as he follows instructions occasionally, but often has tantrums when asked to do a simple task.

1. (a) Name **one** therapy for autism and suggest how this could reduce Max's tantrums. (1)

   (b) Explain how the therapy identified in part (a) could improve either Max's language or his socialisation. (4)

2. **Context essay:** Discuss how **one** therapy for autism could help Max. (8)

Early intensive behavioural intervention (EIBI)

Early + intensive + focused on behaviour.

EIBI is evidence-based, i.e. based on research into what is most effective (e.g. parental involvement, behaviourist methods):

- Early – therapy for children under five years of age, with greatest success achieved with children under two years.
- Intensive – highly structured, between 20 and 50 hours/week, one-to-one therapy (in a home or school setting over a period of one to four years).
- Focused on behaviour – based on *applied behaviour analysis* (ABA), a therapy that uses behaviourist techniques (e.g. modelling) to replace unwanted behaviours (tantrums) with desirable behaviours (eye contact, spontaneous communication).

Elements of EIBI

Various 'flavours' of EIBI all have several features in common.

Personnel

- Sessions delivered by a trained behaviour therapist and programme supervised by a qualified professional (measures and monitors the child's progress).
- Parents and other family members become closely involved with day-to-day application of EIBI methods.

The target behaviours/goals are communication/language development, social interaction, self-care.

Enables generalisation – uses strategies to let the child practise learned skills in new environments outside the home and classroom.

Stages of EIBI

Lovaas (2002) proposed an EIBI programme involving four main stages.

Stage 1 Establish cooperation and reduce tantrums

- Therapist makes simple requests and reinforces the child's cooperative behaviour.

Stage 2 Foundational skills

- Several skills are developed, from simple to more complex, e.g. the child sorts 2D/3D objects into categories.
- Therapist models behaviours for the child to imitate including gross movements (e.g. folding arms) and fine movements (e.g. making a 'peace' sign).
- Child imitates facial expressions and develops play skills.

Stage 3 Early communicative language

- Receptive language is reinforced, beginning with ability to follow instructions ('sit there') and eventually to identify objects, people and behaviours (e.g. selecting a cup).

Stage 4 Grammatical language/early socialisation

- Focus switches to expressive language, reinforcing those behaviours that turn thoughts into grammatically-correct sentences (e.g. verbal imitation, utterances, writing).
- Self-care skills are also developed (e.g. eating with a spoon, dressing and undressing).

A strength is support for EIBI from meta-analyses.

Reichow *et al.* (2012) included five studies of EIBI effectiveness in their meta-analysis. All of the studies had a control group (treatment-as-usual) to compare outcomes.

Children who received EIBI showed significantly greater improvements than controls in IQ, receptive and expressive language, communication skills, socialisation and self-care skills.

This shows that EIBI is an effective therapy for some children with ASD.

CA However, there were methodological issues with some of the included studies. Only one was a randomised controlled trial (RCT) in which children were randomly allocated to groups. The researchers rated the overall quality of the studies as 'low'. Therefore, the evidence-base supporting EIBI is promising but not conclusive.

Could therapy remodel the autistic brain?

A weakness of EIBI is a lack of treatment fidelity.

EIBI therapists carry out the therapy in varied ways, e.g. behaviourist techniques used by therapists adhering to one 'brand' of EIBI are not used by others.

Healy and Lydon (2013) claim some of these techniques are outdated and unsupported by evidence, so it is hard to know what the 'core' techniques of EIBI are.

This makes it hard to conduct meaningful research and highlights the need for standardised, high-quality training to enhance effectiveness.

Another weakness is that success may be due to non-specific factors.

Boucher (2009) identified four such factors – the intensity of the therapy, its early implementation, its highly-structured nature and family involvement.

These are independent of the specific behaviourist techniques used in EIBI. They are factors found in any successful therapy.

This suggests that there is nothing 'special' or unique about EIBI that explains its effectiveness.

Application: EIBI/ABA has the potential to prevent ASD.

Dawson (2008) claims early intervention can change the course of brain development before 'full' autism occurs.

This optimistic outlook is based on brain plasticity in childhood and progress in other fields (e.g. neuroscience, genetics).

The prevention of ASD could result in huge cost savings and improve the quality of life of affected individuals and families.

I&D extra: EIBI illustrates the influence of reductionism in psychology.

EIBI is firmly based on a behaviourist view of therapy, using the behaviourist principles of applied behaviour analysis (e.g. modelling, reinforcement, imitation).

But there are other interacting psychological and biological factors involved in ASD, which if addressed in treatment, could lead to symptom improvement.

This suggests that reductionist explanations are limited because they rarely reflect the true complexity of the causes of ASD.

Check it

1. Describe **one** therapy for children with autism. [4]

2. Explain **one** weakness of **one** therapy for autism. [2]

3. **Standard essay:** Evaluate **one** therapy for autism. [8] or [16]

4. **Prompt essay:** Some therapies for autism appear more successful than others.

   Evaluate **one** therapy for autism. You must include a comparison with another therapy for autism in your answer. [8] or [16]

Classic study: van IJzendoorn and Kroonenberg (1988)

Spec spotlight

7.3.1 van IJzendoorn and Kroonenberg (1988) Cross-cultural patterns of attachment: A meta-analysis of the Strange Situation.

7.2.3 The use of meta-analysis using cross-cultural research to draw conclusions about the universality of attachment types.

Aims

To see if patterns of attachment are better understood if a large data set is examined, not just individual smaller samples.

To look at attachment differences between cultures (intercultural) and within cultures (intracultural).

Procedure

Meta-analysis of 32 studies that used the Strange Situation procedure (SSP) to classify mother–infant attachment.

Eight different countries, 1,990 SSP classifications.

Exclusions – studies with overlapping samples, special groups (e.g. twins), children older than 24 months.

Findings

Type B (secure) was the modal classification in all samples except one German sample.

Samples were examined to see if there were significant deviations in frequency of a particular classification:

- Fewer Type Cs (insecure–resistant) and more Type As (insecure–avoidant) in the four European countries (Britain, Sweden, Netherlands, Germany) than in the 'average' of all the samples.
- The opposite was true for Israel and Japan.

Intercultural (between) and intracultural (within) differences

- Significant intercultural differences ($p < 0.0001$).
- Significant intracultural differences, e.g. between the two German samples ($p < 0.01$), same for Japan ($p < 0.01$) and US ($p < 0.0001$) samples.
- Most significant feature was that the intracultural variation was 1.5 times the intercultural variation.

Similarities and differences

- Overall US sample was near the global centre but US sample U7 was more like the Japanese sample J1.
- Israel and Japanese samples had similar profiles and were different from Great Britain and Sweden.

Apply it Methods

Dr Ely conducted a meta-analysis of intra- and intercultural differences in attachment. All the chosen studies used the Strange Situation procedure (SSP). For each study in the sample, there was at least one other study from the same country that used a different kind of population, such as from rural or urban areas. Dr Ely did not know the exact steps of the SSP in each study.

1. (a) Explain why Dr Ely wanted **two** samples from each country. (3)

   (b) Suggest **one** problem with not knowing the exact way the SSP was conducted. (2)

2. Explain how Dr Ely is testing for both intra- and intercultural differences. (2)

3. **Context/Methods essay:** Evaluate Dr Ely's study. (8)

Conclusions

Intracultural differences were quite considerable.

The same researchers often obtained data within each country, so differences were not due to procedural variations.

The universal high levels of Type B might suggest attachment is an innate and biological process.

However, this similarity may be explained by global mass media – TV and books that advocate particular parenting styles.

Graph showing proportions of the three different attachment types across the eight countries studied.

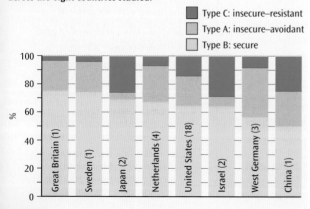

- Type C: insecure–resistant
- Type A: insecure–avoidant
- Type B: secure

A strength of this study was the very large sample of participants.

Using a larger sample across many different countries/cultures should increase the representativeness of the data.

Large samples also reduce the impact of anomalous findings caused by poor methodology or unusual participants.

Therefore, this study provides a useful benchmark of a global average for all attachment research.

CA However, some countries were barely represented. In three of the eight countries there was just one sample (and just two samples in two other countries). This makes intercultural comparisons meaningless because each sample may be atypical and/or affected by poor methodology.

Van Eejen...Van Ooja...Van Uzi...no, me neither.

A weakness of the study lies in the method of meta-analysis.

In this meta-analysis the method (SSP) was the same in all studies – but the *meaning* of this procedure varies from one country/culture to another.

The SSP is an *imposed etic* (see right), which is an issue, and also there is some doubt that the procedure is used the same way in different countries (Sagi and Lewkowicz 1987).

This makes it difficult to draw conclusions about the universality of attachment types.

An *imposed etic* is a technique used in (i.e. imposed upon) one culture even though it was designed for use in another culture.

Another weakness is the issue of country versus culture.

This meta-analysis drew conclusions about cultural differences yet it was actually comparing countries.

We have no information about the cultural background of each sample (e.g. urban or rural, university town or industrial centre etc.).

This means that other comparisons could be made (e.g. between all rural communities) which might be more interesting/revealing.

Application: Knowledge of cultural differences is important for day care.

If there are cultural differences then staff working in day-care facilities should shape their behaviours to the child's expectations of how a parent (or parent-substitute) should behave.

An example is encouraging dependence or independence, depending on culture.

The 'wrong' kind of behaviour could confuse a young child because they are used to other kinds of attachment behaviours at home.

I&D extra: This research goes to the heart of culture bias in psychology.

The method used to study attachment (SSP) was an imposed etic so some cultures end up appearing deficient – their babies are classified as more insecurely attached than US children.

Furthermore this research highlights the fact that attachment theory as a whole is culture-biased in its assumptions that independence and self-reliance are the traits that should be fostered.

This is an individualist assumption whereas collectivist cultures wish to develop cooperation and dependence in their children.

Spec spotlight

7.3.2 One contemporary study: Cassibba et al. (2013) Attachment the Italian way.

Methods

Riya is planning a cross-cultural study of attachment in European countries, to compare infants in the UK, France and Italy. She hopes to observe infants at home.

1. Riya will use the Strange Situation procedure. Explain whether the observation will be:
   (a) Participant or non-participant. (2)
   (b) Covert or overt. (2)

2. Operationalise **two** behaviours that Riya could record in the infants' homes. (2)

3. **Context/Methods essay:** To what extent should child psychology use observational methods? You must refer to the context in your answer. (20)

Tables showing percentage of individuals in each classification.

Studies used 3 categories (grey rows) or 4 categories (white rows).

Child samples: Types A (insecure–avoidant), B (secure), C (insecure–resistant) and D (disorganised).

Attachment type	A	B	C	D
US normative samples	21	67	12	
	23	55	7	15
Nonclinical samples	33	53	14	
	28	44	6	22
Clinical samples	40	32	28	
	28	27	10	35

Adult samples: AAI classifications were D (dismissing), F (secure), E (preoccupied), U (unresolved).

Attachment type	D	F	E	U
N. American normative samples	23	58	19	
	16	56	19	18
Nonclinical samples	22	59	19	
	19	60	11	10
Adolescent samples	27	61	12	
	24	62	10	4
Clinical samples	35	38	27	
	27	25	15	33

Aims

To test the universality of attachment theory in a meta-analysis comparing Italian samples to standard samples.

To investigate attachment types in clinical samples (i.e. individuals with psychological problems).

Procedure

Database search of studies (PsychINFO) and books from 1990–2009 using key words *attachment, Italian, Strange Situation procedure (SSP)* and *AAI (Adult Attachment interview)*.

Sample – 17 SSP studies (23 samples, 627 participants) and 50 AAI studies (72 samples, 2258 participants).

Child SSP samples compared with normative data from 21 US samples (van IJzendoorn *et al.* 1992).

Adult AAI samples compared with nonclinical sample of North American mothers (Bakermans-Kranenburg and van IJzendoorn 2009).

Findings

Child attachment (see first table on left)

- In the nonclinical Italian samples the majority of infants were classified as Type B (53% or 44%).
- Clinical Italian samples showed more insecure attachments (A or D) than nonclinical samples.
- Significant difference between nonclinical and normative sample ($p < 0.01$) when three types were measured.
- Clinical Italian samples showed a significant deviation from Italian nonclinical samples ($p < 0.001$), more Types A and D in the clinical sample.

Adult attachment (see second table on left)

- In the nonclinical Italian sample of mothers the modal category was Type F.
- Significant deviation of the nonclinical sample from the normative sample found only in the four-way samples, with fewer Type U ($p < 0.01$).
- Adolescent Italian samples diverged significantly from the norm with fewer Type E and U ($p < 0.01$).
- Clinical Italian samples differed significantly from Italian nonclinical sample with fewer Type F ($p < 0.0001$).

Conclusions

Cross-cultural similarities – secure attachment was the modal group, which is evidence for the innate basis of attachment.

Also cultural differences, e.g. nonclinical Italian infants showed overrepresentation of avoidant attachments (Type A) compared to norm.

Italian nonclinical adults showed fewer cases of unresolved loss than the norm – the cultural difference may be because Italy is almost completely Catholic (support from belief in an afterlife).

A strength of the study is the large representative sample.

There were almost 3000 participants, offering a good cross-section of Italians (and representing both individualist and collectivist groups).	The sample also included unpublished papers (e.g. doctoral theses), avoiding the *file-drawer effect*.	This allows us to feel confident about the validity of the conclusions drawn.

CA As the researchers note, the sample was large but it was also 'heterogenous' (the people studied were all quite different). So they suggest that conclusions about cultural differences between the sample and global populations are tentative.

A weakness is that the comparison sample was only from the US.

Making comparisons between two sets of data is desirable but it is not reasonable to assume that one is a universal norm whereas the other is a deviation.	The 'norm' was formed by van IJzendoorn et al.'s (1992) US samples, which produced a distribution almost identical to the first data produced by Ainsworth et al. (1978).	This means that we know there were differences between the two groups, but we do not know the significance of the difference or which is deviant (the Italian sample is implied as the deviant).

'File drawer effect' refers to academic journals not publishing research that lacks conclusive findings (i.e. filing it away).

A weakness was the use of methods designed in other cultures (imposed etic).

The assumptions underlying the SSP and the AAI are related to individualist cultures where independence is valued.	Cassibba et al. acknowledge that Italian culture is in part individualist but this is not true of all family groups.	Thus some of the sample may have been 'unfairly' tested using methods based on individualist assumptions, making the findings meaningless.

Application: Data on clinical samples may be useful in terms of treatments.

There appears to be an association between attachment type and psychological problems as Types A and D were more common in the clinical sample.	But we do not know if the infant's attachment experiences caused the psychological problems or vice versa (having a psychological problem may make secure attachment difficult).	This suggests that approaches such as 'attachment parenting' may help with psychological problems (a parent focuses on sensitivity to their infant's 'signals' and emotional needs).

I&D extra: There are practical issues in the design of a meta-analysis.

To make the analysis in this study valid the methods used in the studies must be comparable (i.e. very similar).	This may not be true for SSP studies, but the AAI procedure is more firmly standardised and coders are very carefully trained to categorise the data.	This meant that the selection criteria for the adult part of the study were very clear – only studies using trained coders were included.

✓ Check it

1. Describe **one** contemporary study from child psychology. (5)

2. Explain **one** ethical issue relating to **one** contemporary study from child psychology. (2)

3. **Standard essay:** Evaluate **one** contemporary study from child psychology. (8) or (16)

4. **Methods essay:** Evaluate **one** contemporary study from child psychology in terms of the way that the data was collected and analysed. (16)

Contemporary study:
Gagnon-Oosterwaal *et al.* (2012)

Spec spotlight

7.3.3 One contemporary study: Gagnon-Oosterwaal et al. (2012) Pre-adoption adversity and self-reported behaviour problems in 7-year-old international adoptees.

Internalising problems are self-focused (e.g. separation anxiety), externalising problems are directed towards others (e.g. conduct disorder).

Examples from the DI. Children express their feelings by answering yes/no questions about Dominic who is presented as male/female/different ethnicities.

Apply it Concepts

Dr Day hopes to test internationally adopted children who join culture-matched (CM) families (e.g. Chinese adoptees being adopted by Chinese families in other countries) and culture-unmatched ones (CU).

1. Explain why Dr Day uses culture-matched and culture-unmatched adoptions. (2)

2. Explain why Dr Day should consider the wealth of the adoptive families. (2)

3. **Context/Methods essay:** Assess the use of controls in Dr Day's study. (8)

Aims

To build on previous research into the effects of early deprivation on later behaviour problems in internationally adopted (IA) children.

To test the accuracy of child self-report to measure internalising and externalising problems.

Procedure

Sample – 95 adopted children (69 girls, 26 boys) from e.g. China and other East Asian countries, Russia. 92% of children adopted from orphanages, 8% from foster care.

Children's mean age at assessment was 7 years 4 months (SD = 4 months, range = 6.5–8.6 years).

95 mothers of the children, mean age 44.4 years, average 15 years' schooling, 93.6% had family income of over 40K Canadian dollars.

Comparison sample – 91 French-speaking children from regular Montreal schools. Mean age at assessment was 7 years 8 months (SD = 10 months, range = 6.5–8.8). Families had average/high income, mothers had a college degree.

Measures

• Health and developmental status at arrival – medical data and anthropometric measures (e.g. height). *Bayley Scales* assessed mental and psychomotor development.

• *Dominic Interactive* (DI) – computerised pictorial self-report to assess most frequent internalising/externalising symptoms in children aged 6–11 years.

• *Child Behaviour Checklist* (CBCL) – 118-item survey on internalising/externalising problems. Parent responds on 3-point scale (not true, sometimes, often).

Findings

IA children reported more internalising problems than non-adopted peers ($p = 0.07$). There were no group differences for externalising.

IA children reported more symptoms of specific phobia than non-adopted peers ($p = 0.0001$).

Positive correlation between mothers' and children's reports but only significant for externalising problems ($p = 0.001$).

Significant correlations between developmental status at adoption and characteristics at age 7.

e.g. negative correlation between weight/height ratio and depression ($p < 0.05$), specific phobias ($p < 0.05$) and conduct disorder ($p < 0.01$).

Conclusions

IA children are well-adjusted when adopted to well-off families.

Use of child self-report is important for studying internalising problems as mothers' reports only accurate for externalising.

Height and weight may be significant risk factors because they are associated with malnutrition (also affects brain growth, especially areas of the brain in regulation of emotion).

A strength of the study is the design which controlled many key variables.

For example, samples were matched on several variables including affluence (to exclude sociodemographic factors).

If circumstances are poor after adoption we don't know whether later mental health problems are due to pre-adoption or post-adoption adversity.

This control enhanced the validity of the findings.

CA One key variable was not controlled – potential cultural influences. The UNCRC (page 176) says IA should only happen if there are no alternative placements in the home country (Article 21). This acknowledges the stress created for IA children living in a foreign culture. Such stress might have acted as a confounding variable.

A weakness is the differences in the age of the samples.

The two samples only differed in terms of one disorder – specific phobias, which appears early in development.

Therefore, differences were apparent whereas other internalising and externalising disorders have a later onset, so they were not detected.

This means that, in order to fully investigate the effect of pre-adoption adversity on later development, the sample needs to be older.

The Simons brothers were well aware of the difference in their anthropometric measures.

Another weakness is the ability of Dominic interactive (DI) to assess disorders.

The DI does not measure all the DSM criteria for the seven disorders and so is not a fully valid measure of the different conditions.

Also, the reliability and validity of children's self-report may vary depending on the type of symptoms assessed.

This means that the main dependent variable in this study may lack reliability and validity.

Application: The findings can help to guide adoption processes.

A key finding is that early experiences of deprivation and also international adoption are not necessarily harmful.

Previous research found these factors are linked to later behaviour problems – the lack of problems in this study may be due to high quality carers.

This suggests adoption agencies should focus on the adoption home and do what they can to improve the sociodemographic quality of that home.

I&D extra: Social sensitivity is an issue related to this research.

Studying the effects of adoption is challenging but necessary – the world will always have children whose parents cannot care for them and psychologists want to investigate ways to avoid subsequent mental health problems.

However, findings may indicate solutions which are not feasible. The suggestion that children should be adopted into affluent homes implies that those not adopted to such homes are being harmed.

This does not mean that such research should not be done, just that researchers must be aware of the implications of their findings.

✓ Check it

1. Describe **one** or more practical issue(s) that might have affected the researchers whilst conducting **one** contemporary study from child psychology. [3]

2. Explain **one** strength and **one** weakness of **one** contemporary study from child psychology. [4]

3. **Standard essay:** Evaluate **one** contemporary study from child psychology. [8] or [16]

4. **Methods essay:** Evaluate **one** contemporary study from child psychology in terms of credibility. [8]

Spec spotlight

7.3.4 One contemporary study: Li et al.
(2013) Timing of High-Quality Child Care
and Cognitive, Language and Preacademic
Development.

*Janine was having one of her 'low quality
childcare' moments...*

Apply it — Methods

Dr Coll is researching the effects of
childcare. She was planning to use
observations and rating scales to assess the
quality of childcare provision as well as
testing children's cognitive skills. However, in
the end she has decided instead to interview
parents about their satisfaction with carer
sensitivity and their child's development.

1. (a) Suggest **one** closed question Dr Coll
   could use to assess beliefs about carer
   sensitivity. (1)

   (b) Suggest **one** open question Dr Coll
   could use to assess language skills. (1)

2. Explain **one** strength and **one** weakness
   of Dr Coll's choice to use an interview
   rather than to observe. (4)

3. **Context/Methods essay:** Discuss
   Dr Coll's choice of method for testing
   childcare quality. (8)

Aims

To study low quality (LQ) and high quality (HQ) care in infant–
toddlers (Period 1, P1 → 24 months) and preschool children
(Period 2, P2 → 54 months).

Three specific hypotheses tested in the study:

1. HQ in P1 → positive outcomes after P2 if HQ care in P2.
2. HQ + HQ in P1 and P2 better than HQ + LQ in P1 and P2.
3. HQ + HQ in P1 and P2 → best outcome.

Procedure

Sample – from NICHD study of 1,364 US families (see page
134).

Care quality assessed at 6, 15, 24, 26 and 54 months using
ORCE (*Observational Record of Caregiving Environment*). Each
assessment was four × 44-minute observations.

Quality rated on four-point scales, average > 3.0 = HQ.

HQ care = caregivers more sensitive to child, greater
cognitive stimulation, fostered greater exploration, less
emotionally detached (Vandell *et al*. 2010).

General mental development was measured at 24 months of
age using the *Bayley Mental Developmental Index*.

Specific competencies (memory, language, and preacademic
skills) measured at 54 months using a range of *Woodcock–
Johnson* tests and the *PLS Expressive and Receptive* tests.

Findings

Cognitive, language and preacademic skills for language
(letter–word identification) and maths (applied problem-
solving) highest among children who had HQ care in both P1
and P2.

Skills lower in children with HQ during only one of these
periods.

Skills lowest in children with LQ care during both periods.

HQ in P2 (irrespective of P1) linked to better outcomes.

HQ in P1 (irrespective of P2) linked to better memory skills at
the end of P2.

Conclusions

No 'clear winners' – some functions (language) were better
with later HQ care, others (memory) benefited more from
early HQ.

Patterns in memory skills vs. language/pre-academic
outcomes were consistent with Huttenlocher's (1979) theory
of brain development:

• Development of cognitive functions (early language, joint
  attention) is related to formation of synapses.

• Synapses develop most rapidly in first three years of life
  (importance of early HQ care). Growth continues into
  adolescence (secondary role of later HQ care).

Findings suggest early and later HQ care are both important,
but early HQ care doesn't 'inoculate' children against later
poor quality care.

A strength is that the study used a broad and large data set.

It used secondary data from the NICHD study – over 1000 families, variety of cognitive measures and assessments of childcare.

Such large data sets even out anomalies that inevitably occur and may bias smaller data sets.

This suggests that the study's findings were high in generalisability.

CA On the other hand the original NICHD sample as a whole excluded, for example, teenage mothers and low birth-weight babies. Also, the sample used at P1 (24 months) tended to be relatively economically advantaged with more white families than the original NICHD sample. Factors such as this (also the study is American) restrict generalisability because there are cultural differences in attachment.

A weakness is the analysis did not account for different kinds of childcare.

The only factors examined in relation to the quality of care all focused on the emotional support offered to children.

Other variables may moderate the effects of day care on development, e.g. the form of day care (childminding or nursery) and the hours per week a child is in day care.

This suggests that factors such as these may have acted as confounding variables, lowering the internal validity of the study.

Another weakness is that measurement was only short-term (54 months).

It might be more revealing to look at how the sample did during their school years in terms of both cognitive and social development.

We might find that any early differences had disappeared later or that early high quality care ultimately had a more lasting effect.

This means that the conclusions drawn are rather limited because they focus on very short-term differences.

Application: The study aimed to consider ways to best invest in day care.

The question is whether it is better to focus on providing quality care early or later in order to boost subsequent school performance.

The findings suggest high quality care at either point has benefits. But in terms of brain development (Huttenlocher's theory) it may be better to focus on earlier high quality care.

This is important because it provides empirically-based advice for government initiatives in terms of where money is best spent.

I&D extra: One issue is the reductionist nature of this research.

The aims of the NICHD research are far from reductionist but the focus in this study is on high versus low quality care.

This overlooks other possible issues such as whether low quality childcare is better than home care for some children, studying a variety of outcome measures rather than just cognitive development.

This seems to reduce the debate and childcare experience to only a small set of variables, making conclusions rather trivial. For some children any childcare may be better than what they are currently getting.

Nick Head NIC HD – get it?

Check it

1. Describe the procedure of **one** contemporary study from child psychology. (5)

2. Explain how ethical issues relating to participation and protection of children would have affected **one** contemporary study from child psychology. (2)

3. **Standard essay:** Evaluate **one** contemporary study from child psychology. (8) or (16)

4. **Methods essay:** Evaluate ethical issues relating to **one** contemporary study from child psychology. You must refer to BPS ethical guidelines and UNCRC standards in your answer. (16)

Go on, you know you want one…
Saying no to a cigarette (or three) is
not easy when you are addicted.

Apply it Concepts

Hua has smoked since she was 16. Now she is in her 30s she wants to stop. However quitting is hard as she has such a craving for cigarettes, especially during work breaks. As for the long train journey home from work, she feels physically unwell until she has a cigarette. The problem now is that she smokes so many a day – it was only one or two a day for fun at 16, but it's now become a real habit.

1. Explain **one** example from the context of:
   (a) Physical dependency. (1)
   (b) Psychological dependency. (1)

2. Describe how tolerance has affected Hua. (2)

3. **Context essay:** Discuss issues around Hua's drug use. (8)

Dependency

Can be psychological and/or physiological.

Psychological dependency – compulsion to experience the effects of a drug ('craving') because drug is reinforcing:

- Increased pleasure = positive reinforcement.
- Decreased discomfort = negative reinforcement.
- Result = addict more likely to take drug again.

Physical dependency – only established when a person stops taking a drug and experiences a withdrawal syndrome.

Withdrawal

Abstaining or reducing intake after a period of drug use produces symptoms typical of withdrawal.

Withdrawal syndrome = set of symptoms that reliably occur together.

The specific collection of symptoms is unique to each category of drug (e.g. opioids, sedatives, etc.) and is predictable.

Symptoms are usually the 'opposite' of the drug's effects (e.g. alcohol relaxes an alcoholic, but withdrawal produces anxiety).

Withdrawal indicates that physical dependency has developed:

- The addict experiences some symptoms of withdrawal whenever they cannot get the drug.
- This happens often so they become familiar with the symptoms (unpleasant and cause discomfort).
- So people continue to take a drug not only to experience pleasurable positive effects but to avoid negative ones.

Withdrawal typically has two phases:

- Acute withdrawal phase begins within hours of abstaining, and the symptoms gradually diminish over days.
- Prolonged withdrawal phase includes symptoms that continue past acute withdrawal (i.e. weeks and months).

The withdrawing addict becomes even more sensitive to the cues they associate with the drug (e.g. rituals, locations), so relapse into drug-seeking and drug-taking is common.

Tolerance

Develops when the response to a given amount of a drug decreases.

A larger dose is needed for the same effects (e.g. pleasure).

Tolerance is the outcome of repeated exposure to the effects of a drug – three common types:

- Functional tolerance – postsynaptic receptors become less sensitive to a drug.
- Behavioural tolerance – people learn through experience to adjust behaviour to compensate for a drug's effects (e.g. alcoholics learn to walk more slowly).
- Cross-tolerance – tolerance to one drug generalises to another (e.g. alcohol addicts develop tolerance to sedative effects, so need higher dose of anaesthetic in surgery).

Addiction

Specific meaning in psychology and medicine – a complex and multifaceted behaviour, outcome of dependency and tolerance.

A strength is that addiction can be explained in terms of neural mechanisms.

Repeated exposure to the effects of a drug can cause changes to brain structure and function, for example *downregulation*.	Chronic drug-taking means a reduction in number of postsynaptic receptors available for binding with a neurotransmitter, altering synaptic transmission.	This understanding of the neural mechanisms involved helps to make the causes of addiction clearer.

CA Some brain mechanisms in addiction are not well understood. The *mesocorticolimbic circuit* (see next spread) and *dopamine* are key elements of addiction because of their roles in reward. But a focus on these is limited because there are other neurochemical mechanisms involved (e.g. *GABA* and *serotonin*). Although dopamine is central, it interacts with other brain processes.

A weakness is that research on rats is hard to generalise to humans.

The neural mechanisms underlying tolerance, dependency, withdrawal and addiction are similar in human and rat brains, but they are not identical.	In the rat park, Alexander *et al*. (1978) showed that the social environment affects addiction in rats. Psychological and sociocultural factors are even more critical in humans.	This means we must be cautious about interpreting findings from animal studies and applying them uncritically to human addiction.

Another strength is that there are controlled animal studies on tolerance.

Siegel *et al*. (1982) injected rats with heroin every other day for 30 days, and then finally with a very large dose. 32% died, but the rest developed tolerance.	Siegel (1984) also found tolerance in humans – the most frequent victims of fatal heroin intake were 'weekend' users who did not use the drug enough to develop tolerance.	This is strong support for the key role of tolerance, in studies that cannot ethically be conducted on humans.

Application: As knowledge increases, more treatments become available.

Understanding physical dependency in nicotine addiction has led to effective treatments (e.g. *nicotine replacement therapy* to manage withdrawal).	Psychological dependency is addressed by helping smokers avoid the cues they associate with the rewarding effects of nicotine.	This means the research has led to ways in which the personal and social costs linked to drug-taking can be significantly reduced.

I&D extra: These concepts illustrate different ways of explaining addiction.

One biological explanation for heroin addiction focuses on neural mechanisms in the CNS involving reward pathways and neurotransmitters.	But these interact with psychological processes (e.g. learning) and social factors that increase the risk of addiction (e.g. peer/family relationships, sources of stress).	This shows how explanations in psychology can combine to provide a fuller explanation for a behaviour.

NicoDerm. CQ.
Nicotine Transdermal System 21 mg Delivered over 24 Hours
STOP SMOKING AID
CLEAR PATCH EXTENDED RELEASE in HOURS
STEP 1 · 21 mg
14 clear patches (2-week kit)

One a day to keep the craving at bay.

'CA' stands for 'competing argument'.

Revision booster

The terms in the specification relating to issues around drug taking are interlinked – addiction, tolerance, dependency and withdrawal – but it is important to be able to distinguish between them clearly as they will be used in exam questions and you need to provide specific answers.

Check it

1. Explain **two** issues associated with drug-taking. [4]

2. Frieda is addicted to heroin. She has not had any heroin for nine days.

   Explain how this might affect Frieda. [3]

3. **Standard essay:** Evaluate issues around drug-taking. [8] or [16]

4. **I&D essay:** Assess the use of psychological knowledge in society using examples from your chosen application (criminological, child or health). [16]

On this spread (and the next three spreads) you can be asked questions on all three addictions and must have explanations specific to each addiction.

Mesocorticolimbic circuit

Blue arrow = mesolimbic from VTA to NA.

Red arrow = mesocortical from VTA to prefrontal cortex.

The outcome is increased dopamine in the NA and prefrontal cortex.

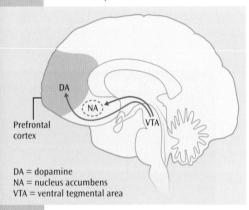

DA = dopamine
NA = nucleus accumbens
VTA = ventral tegmental area

Apply it Concepts

Dr Kay is investigating the mechanism of action of a new designer drug that people are becoming addicted to. His studies with rats have shown that it has a similar biological action to alcohol. He is hoping to develop a treatment for the addicts.

1. **(a)** Identify a neurotransmitter that the new drug may affect and explain how it might work. (3)
   (b) Explain whether a treatment for addiction to the new drug would need to be an opioid agonist or antagonist. (2)
2. Explain why doctors may lack confidence in Dr Kay's conclusions. (2)
3. **Context essay:** Discuss the neurotransmitters and brain areas that Dr Kay would study to understand the action of the new drug. (8)

Alcohol addiction

Alcohol operates on GABA (gamma-aminobutyric acid), the brain's main inhibitory neurotransmitter.

Alcohol
- Increases *GABA*'s effects, leads to relaxation etc.
- Decreases *glutamate* (main excitatory neurotransmitter).

Mesocorticolimbic circuit (see left) is activated by alcohol, *dopamine* is transmitted from the VTA along the:

(1) *Mesolimbic pathway* to the *nucleus accumbens* (NA).

(2) *Mesocortical pathway* to the *prefrontal cortex*.

The activation of the mesocorticolimbic circuit reinforces alcohol-seeking and intake (see next spread).

Heroin addiction

Heroin has profound effects on a class of neurotransmitters called endogenous opioids (endorphins and enkephalins).

Endorphins and *enkephalins* naturally reduce pain and provide intense euphoria (e.g. the 'runner's high').

Heroin is a direct agonist of endogenous opioids (it binds with the same receptors, stimulating and activating them).

This produces an initial euphoric 'high' (more intense than naturally-occurring), followed by relaxation and anxiety reduction.

Three endogenous opioid receptors (*mu*, *delta*, *kappa*), heroin binds especially readily with the mu receptor:

- Reduces GABA in the VGA by binding with mu-opioid receptors on GABA-producing neurons (Tomkins and Sellers 2001).
- Prevents GABA, an inhibitory neurotransmitter, from restricting dopamine production.
- Therefore, heroin causes more dopamine transmission in the mesocorticolimbic circuit.

Nicotine addiction

Dani and Heinemann's (1996) desensitisation hypothesis explains nicotine addiction in terms of dopamine.

The surfaces of dopamine-producing neurons are covered in receptors that bind with *acetylcholine* (ACh).

When enough ACh molecules bind with receptors, the electrical impulse continues from presynaptic to postsynaptic neuron.

One ACh receptor subtype (the *nicotinic acetylcholine receptor*, nAChR) binds with both ACh and nicotine.

When nAChRs bind with nicotine, the neuron is stimulated and transmits dopamine through the mesocorticolimbic circuit.

nAChRs are concentrated in the VTA – when stimulated by nicotine, dopamine increases in the NA, along the mesolimbic and mesocortical pathways and in the prefrontal cortex.

Immediately after stimulation nAChRs shut down and cannot respond to neurotransmitters – they are 'desensitised', which leads to downregulation (fewer receptors available).

Continuous exposure of nAChRs to nicotine causes a permanent reduction in the number of active neurons.

A strength is research support for the central role of dopamine in addiction.

Berrendero et al. (2010) point out that all neurotransmitter systems interact with dopamine to produce their effects.

Martinez et al. (2012) showed that heroin addiction is linked with changes to the D2 and D3 dopamine receptors, which also occur in other chemical addictions.

Therefore, taken together, findings such as this increase the validity of neurotransmission as an explanation for addiction.

CA However, drugs differ in their effects on dopamine. For instance, alcohol's effects are indirect – it changes GABA activity first. But heroin is more direct – it changes neurotransmitters directly responsible for the natural opiate response. The reality is that several neurotransmitter systems interact in complex ways to cause addiction.

Biochemical explanations might account for how people become addicted to cigarettes but not why. Perhaps the 'why' is more to do with social factors.

A weakness of biochemical theories is that they only explain proximate causes.

The desensitisation hypothesis explains biochemical events in the brain that lead to nicotine addiction – this is a proximate explanation (the immediate cause).

But this can't explain how the biochemical events themselves are ultimately caused. Studies show that genes (the ultimate cause) determine how neurons respond to drugs.

This shows that biochemical theories are not sufficient, and need to be combined with genetics for a fuller picture of the causes of addiction.

Revision booster

The brain structures, pathways and neurotransmitters involved in the action of the three drugs (alcohol, heroin and nicotine) overlap. To help you to separate the processes when revising, try drawing the sequence for each drug as a flowchart.

Another weakness is that most knowledge comes from animal studies.

There are important differences between human and rat responses to drugs.

For instance, rats are not as influenced by complex psychological and social factors in the same ways that humans are.

Therefore, we should be cautious in applying the findings of animal studies to humans uncritically.

Application: Knowledge of how neurotransmitters work has led to treatments.

Methadone is used to treat heroin addiction because it is an opioid agonist (occupies opioid receptors, prevents heroin binding, provides intense but controllable high).

In contrast *naltrexone* (used with alcoholics) is an opioid antagonist, blocking opioid receptors and so reducing the pleasurable effects of drinking alcohol.

This means that the treatments stemming from knowledge of neurotransmitters improve quality of life and also have economic benefits.

I&D extra: Biochemical explanations are reductionist accounts of addiction.

Biochemical accounts explain addiction at the fundamental level of neurotransmitter molecules, rather than at 'higher' levels (which may be more valid).

Choi et al. (2003) found that psychosocial factors (e.g. having friends who smoke) best explained the adolescents most likely to become dependent on nicotine.

Therefore, biochemical theories can explain *how* addiction occurs but not *why*, oversimplifying a complex behaviour.

Check it

1. Explain **one** biological explanation for alcohol addiction. [4]

2. Compare the mode of action for addiction to alcohol and for addiction to heroin. [4]

3. **Standard essay:** Evaluate **one** biological explanation for alcohol addiction. [8] or [16]

   [Same question is possible for heroin or nicotine.]

4. **Methods/Prompt essay:** Research into the biology of addiction requires samples of willing addicts to act as participants.

   Evaluate practical and ethical issues relating to the use of humans in research into the biology of addiction. [8] or [16]

Spec spotlight

8.1.3 One learning explanation each for alcohol, heroin and nicotine addiction. Explanations may apply to more than one drug.

Would they still be friends if they stopped drinking?

Apply it Concepts

When Sia first started taking heroin she experienced a great sense of euphoria. However, now she regrets ever trying it, as all she does is suffer when she can't get any heroin and she only begins to feel normal when she has her faithful syringe in her hand.

1. (a) Explain how learning was involved in the initial stages of Sia's addiction. (2)
   (b) Explain how learning is involved in Sia's continued addiction. (2)

2. Suggest why Sia begins to feel normal before injecting. (2)

3. **Context essay:** Discuss learning explanations for Sia's addiction. (8)

Operant conditioning – Positive reinforcement

Explains how people become addicted to a drug in the first place.

Rewarding consequences of a behaviour (e.g. pleasure) make that behaviour more likely to occur again (e.g. taking a drug).

All three drugs are powerful reinforcers because of their physiological effects on the *dopamine* reward system of the *mesocorticolimbic circuit* (see previous spread).

Each drug ultimately stimulates release of dopamine into the *prefrontal cortex* – this produces feelings of mild euphoria (or extreme for heroin) which are rewarding, so positively reinforce the addictive behaviour.

Operant conditioning – Negative reinforcement

Continuing dependence is better explained by negative reinforcement.

Abstaining after long-term use leads to an acute withdrawal syndrome.

All three forms of addiction share symptoms – behavioural effects (e.g. disturbed sleep), cognitive effects (e.g. poor concentration) and mood disturbances (e.g. depression).

Addicts relapse because wide-ranging withdrawal symptoms make it hard to abstain for long – so taking the drug again is negatively reinforcing because it stops an unpleasant event.

Negative reinforcement may be more powerful than positive reinforcement in predicting future drug abuse (Blume 2001).

People also use these drugs to escape stressful reality, to self-medicate (e.g. reduce pain) and to avoid losing friends (all examples of negative reinforcement).

Classical conditioning

Another learning explanation for how an addiction forms.

- The drug (e.g. nicotine) = unconditioned stimulus (UCS).
- Produces feeling of well-being (due to dopamine release) = unconditioned response (UCR).
- This is an intrinsic response to the drug and is not learned.

In a drug-taking situation, there are several stimuli that are initially neutral stimuli (NS), e.g. lighter, syringe, glass.

- The lighter (or syringe, glass, etc.) becomes a conditioned stimulus (CS) through repeated association with the UCS.
- When the now CS occurs on its own, it produces a conditioned response (CR, feeling of well-being).

Cue reactivity theory

Conditioned stimuli also act as cues.

Conditioned stimuli (CS) produce a similar physiological and psychological response as there is to the drug itself. There are two key elements:

- Subjective desire (craving) for the drug.
- Physiological signs of reactivity (e.g. autonomic responses such as increased heart rate and skin temperature).

Learning explanations

A strength is considerable research support for the learning explanation.

Carter and Tiffany's (1999) meta-analysis into cue reactivity included 41 studies of alcohol, heroin and nicotine (and other) addictions.

Addicts showed cravings and increased physiological arousal to drug-related cues (e.g. lighters) compared with neutral cues.

These findings are consistent with predictions derived from cue reactivity theory.

CA However, the studies in this meta-analysis (and other recent ones) may lack ecological validity. Shiffman et al. (2015) compared addicted smokers' responses to cues presented in lab conditions and in real-life situations. They found no agreement between the two sets of responses.

Cravings might be triggered by drug-related cues.

A weakness is that addiction is a multifaceted behaviour.

Brain biochemistry is an important cause of addiction, genes also play a crucial role, as do psychological factors such as cognitive biases.

So learning processes must be seen in the context of a wider collection of causes and risk factors, all of which contribute to addiction.

Therefore, any theory seeking to explain addiction in terms of a limited set of factors is going to lack validity.

Another weakness is that the explanation is based on research with animals.

In lab studies of rats, the link between behaviour and reinforcement is predictable, immediate and studied in a controlled environment.

But addiction in humans is about seeking drugs as well as taking them. In real-life it is a 'messier' business (e.g. delayed reinforcement).

This means the learning explanation has limited application to real-world addictive behaviour in humans.

Application: There are several treatments based on conditioning principles.

Aversion therapy uses classical conditioning to reduce addiction by associating pleasurable effects of the drug with an unpleasant stimulus (e.g. a painful electric shock).

Some research studies (e.g. Smith et al. 1988 in relation to nicotine addiction) have found this to be an effective treatment.

This shows that applications of learning theory can have significant practical benefits in terms of reducing NHS spending and improving health.

I&D extra: The learning explanation for addiction illustrates gender issues.

Women do less well at giving up smoking than men. More men are addicted to heroin and alcohol, but women progress from casual use to addiction more quickly (Kennedy et al. 2013).

These differences reflect biochemical influences but are at least partly due to psychological factors such as cue sensitivity (greater in women, Carpenter et al. 2014).

Therefore, understanding gender differences helps to direct treatment more effectively, as men and women respond differently to drug-related cues.

Revision booster

There is more to evaluating an explanation than just writing down a strength or weakness of it. So try practising the following:

- Explore what a strength or weakness *means*.
- Consider whether it is *justified*.
- Use research *evidence* to support or contradict your criticism.
- Think of a *contrasting* point to balance your argument.

✓ Check it

1. Describe **one** learning explanation for alcohol addiction. [3]
2. Compare **one** biological and **one** learning explanation for addiction. [4]
3. **Standard essay:** Evaluate **one** learning explanation for alcohol addiction. [8] or [16]
   [Same question is possible for heroin or nicotine.]
4. **Prompt essay:** Many people say that taking drugs allows them to escape the pressures of everyday life and have fun.
   Evaluate **one** learning explanation for drug addiction. [8] or [16]

Treatments for drug addiction: Aversion therapy

Spec spotlight

8.1.4 Treatments for drug addiction: Two treatments each for alcohol, heroin and nicotine addiction, including aversion therapy. Treatments may apply to more than one drug.

Aversion therapy could include imagining unpleasant images while smoking.

Aversive stimuli

Addictions can be treated using an emetic drug (causes vomiting) or mild electric shocks.

An emetic quickly causes severe nausea (sick feeling).

At the same time, the client prepares to consume the drug (e.g. pouring a drink, lighting a cigarette, preparing heroin). Vomiting (emesis) begins almost immediately.

Several repetitions using higher doses over a week or two, plus 'booster' treatments (single-day sessions over a few weeks).

Classical conditioning means the client associates taking the drug with unpleasant effects (fear of the effects may be enough to prevent the client taking the drug).

Electric shocks have also been used as the aversive stimulus (e.g. for nicotine addiction). Useful for people with medical conditions worsened by vomiting (e.g. high blood pressure).

Alcohol addiction treated with *disulfiram* (e.g. Antabuse):

- Interferes with normal bodily process of metabolising alcohol into harmless chemicals.
- Drinking alcohol while taking the drug causes severe nausea and vomiting (instant hangover).

Heroin addiction treated using a drug that causes vomiting:

- Addict is injected with a drug (*apomorphine*) just before they inject heroin, so heroin is associated with vomiting.

Nicotine addiction treated using *rapid smoking*:

- Smokers sit in a closed room and puff on a cigarette every six seconds until they feel sick.
- UCS (intensive smoking) creates the UCR (nausea).

Covert sensitisation

A type of aversion therapy that occurs *in vitro* (outside normal biological context).

The client does not actually experience the aversive stimulus but *imagines* how it would feel.

- The client is encouraged to relax as the therapist reads a script instructing the client to imagine an aversive situation.
- The script is based on information given by the client about how they prepare to take a drug (for realism).
- The client imagines themselves preparing and smoking (or injecting or drinking), followed by unpleasant (aversive) consequences (e.g. nausea, vomiting).
- The more vivid the imagined scene the better. The therapist goes into graphic and disgusting detail, e.g. imagine handling drug-related materials covered in faeces.
- Towards the end of a session, the client imagines 'turning their back' on the drug and experiencing relief.

Apply it Methods

Dr Pitt is planning a study of a new aversion therapy for smoking. She has considered many ways to measure effectiveness, including reduction in number of cigarettes smoked a day, a self-report scale of urge to smoke, dropout rate from the treatment and percentage relapse after one year.

1. Explain why either the self-report or the dropout rate:
   (a) Would be more reliable as a measure of the effectiveness of the new therapy. (2)
   (b) Would be more valid as a measure of the effectiveness of the new therapy. (2)

2. Explain why both number of cigarettes smoked per day **and** relapse rates are useful for understanding the effectiveness of the new therapy. (4)

3. **Context/Methods essay:** Evaluate the use of **two** of Dr Pitt's measures of aversion therapy effectiveness. (8)

A strength is research support for the effectiveness of covert sensitisation.

Tongas (1979) found that one year after completing covert sensitisation, 56% of nicotine addicts were still abstaining.

Elkins (1991) found similarly positive outcomes for emetic aversion therapy for alcohol addiction.

This shows that therapies based on learning theory are effective interventions for addictions.

CA However, Hajek and Stead (2011) found they could not judge the effectiveness of aversion therapy programmes because all but one of the studies suffered from 'glaring' methodological problems. For example, the researchers who evaluated the outcomes of the studies knew which participants received the therapy or a placebo.

Probably best not to watch the next bit.

A weakness is that aversion therapy suffers from treatment adherence issues.

Because aversion therapy uses stimuli that are unpleasant, many people drop out of treatment before it is completed.

There may be a systematic pattern to which people drop out (those less likely to respond to treatment tend to leave early).

This makes it hard to assess aversion therapy and means the available research probably overestimates its effectiveness.

Another weakness is that traditional aversion therapy lacks effectiveness.

This is especially true of therapy using shock as the aversive stimulus, e.g. Cannon et al. (1981) gave alcoholics treatment plus shock aversion or just treatment (control).

Control participants had more days of abstinence after 12 months. The addition of shock aversion was ineffective in treating alcoholism.

This suggests that the pain and discomfort caused by the therapy is not justified by the findings.

Revision booster

Students often start their essays with an introduction. For example, it's tempting to 'set the scene' by defining addiction, but unless the question asks for it, that won't earn you marks. On the other hand you do need an 'ending' (a conclusion) or mini-conclusions for all essays except 'discuss' questions.
Make sure your 'ending' is a real conclusion, not just a repetition or summary of what has been said.

Application: The therapy can improve an addict's quality of life.

Although the benefits of aversion therapy seem to be mostly short-term, this can be overcome by providing booster sessions (or 'recaps').

Wiens and Menustik (1983) found 24% of alcohol addicts treated with aversion were abstaining after one year. But with six recap sessions, 99% abstained.

This shows that aversion therapy can be used in a way that brings long-term changes and benefits in real-life situations.

I&D extra: Aversion therapy illustrates ethical issues in psychology.

Psychologists abide by a code of conduct and ethical principles that determine how research participants and clients in therapy are treated.

It is unlikely that aversion therapy can be carried out in a way that meets these criteria but covert sensitisation is less traumatic and more ethically acceptable.

The pressure to seek ethical solutions helps psychologists investigate preferable means of treatment.

Check it

1. Explain **one** treatment for nicotine addiction. [4]

2. Compare **two** treatments for any **one** addiction. [6]

3. **Standard essay:** Evaluate aversion therapy as a treatment for alcohol addiction. [8] or [16]

   [Same question is possible for heroin or nicotine.]

4. **Standard plus essay:** Evaluate ethical issues related to the use of aversion therapy. [16]

Treatments for drug addiction:
One other treatment (drug therapy)

Spec spotlight

8.1.4 Treatments for drug addiction: Two treatments each for alcohol, heroin and nicotine addiction, including aversion therapy. Treatments may apply to more than one drug.

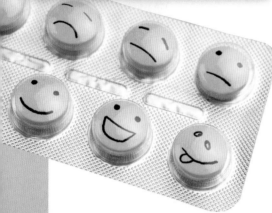

Drug therapy. For the addict's ever-changing moods.

Revision booster

In an essay question with a scenario, take time to identify what you can use in your answer. Underline key parts of the text and make notes around it to help you. In the example below you might underline 'UK' and 'Finland' and the three drugs, which could give you ideas for ways to collect data. Finally there is the point about attitudes to seeking therapy.

Apply it Methods

Cath works at a UK drug rehabilitation centre and also works at a similar one in Finland, where heroin is very hard to obtain, drinking is increasing and smoking is decreasing. She wants to know whether Fins have different attitudes to seeking therapy compared to people in the UK.

1. Explain why this is a cross-cultural study. (1)

2. (a) Suggest **two** ways for Cath to collect data for her study. (4)
   (b) Explain **one** advantage of using **one** of these methods in Cath's cross-cultural study. (2)

3. **Context/Methods essay:** Discuss the use of cross-cultural studies to learn about drug misuse. You must refer to the context in your answer. (8)

Agonists
Activate receptors, with a similar effect to the addictive drug.

Agonists 'stabilise' an addict in two ways.
- They control the withdrawal syndrome, allowing a gradual reduction in dose and symptoms.
- By replacing one source of the drug with another, some of the cues that reinforced the addiction are removed – this reduces cue-related cravings, so relapse is less likely.

Heroin treatment

Methadone is an opioid agonist that binds to the same receptors as heroin (especially *mu*-opioid):
- Treatment aims to satisfy the addict's craving for euphoria with fewer harmful side effects.
- Methadone is 'cleaner' than heroin, and safer (given under medical supervision in treatment centres).

Nicotine treatment

Nicotine replacement therapy (NRT) is another agonist:
- Nicotine is the major addictive chemical in tobacco, but is not the most harmful ingredient of smoking.
- NRT gives a clean, controlled dose of nicotine. It operates neurochemically by binding to nAChRs in the *mesolimbic pathway* of the brain.
- This stimulates *dopamine* release in the *nucleus accumbens*, as it does in cigarette smoking (page 158).
- The amount of nicotine is reduced over time by using smaller and smaller patches (or less gum, etc.).

Antagonists
Bind to same receptors as an addictive drug.

This means the drug of dependence cannot have its usual effects, especially the feeling of euphoria.

Alcohol treatment

Naltrexone is a selective alcohol antagonist ('selective' because it prevents only one of alcohol's effects, the other effects are still experienced).
- Its 'blocking' action means someone who drinks alcohol will not experience the usual pleasurable sensations.
- This gives them 'breathing space' to think again about their behaviour and avoid a full relapse.

Heroin treatment

Opioid antagonists have an indirect effect on the dopamine reward system (normally activated by alcohol):
- They reduce the release of dopamine in the nucleus accumbens by enhancing the release of *GABA* in other parts of the mesolimbic pathway.
- The outcome of this neurochemical activity is a dampening down of the cravings associated with the addiction.

One other treatment (drug therapy)

A strength is that research supports drug therapy for all three addictions.

Anton *et al.* (2006) showed that naltrexone helped alcoholics to drink less and go longer before bingeing than control participants.

Veilleux *et al.* (2010) showed that methadone produced better results than abstinence/placebo. Stead *et al.* (2008) found NRT was more effective than no treatment/ placebo.

This shows that drugs are effective treatments for addiction, and that the biochemical explanation may yet lead to further life-saving drug therapies.

CA But even effective drugs treat the *symptoms* of addiction rather than the causes. There are psychosocial reasons why people become addicted (e.g. stress). Drug therapy does not remove these psychosocial cues and therefore there is a greater chance of relapse than is the case with psychological treatments.

A weakness is that all drug therapies have side effects.

These depend on the size of the dose required to have beneficial effects, which can be quite high in some cases.

Common side effects for all addictions include sleep problems, dizziness, stomach cramps, depression and weight loss or gain.

This means that clients could discontinue therapy, especially when they get no benefits from the drug of dependence (i.e. 'all pain, no gain').

Patch essential. Big sign optional.

Another strength is the ethical benefits associated with drug therapy.

Research has supported the biological basis of addiction, eroding the view that addiction is a form of psychological weakness.

Addiction therefore becomes less shameful as more people accept that a neurochemical imbalance is hardly the addict's 'fault'.

This means that as the stigma associated with addiction diminishes, more people come forward for treatment.

Application: There are limits to drug therapies in real-life situations.

Drug therapy is meant to be convenient because the client just takes a tablet rather than having to change their thought processes or lifestyle.

But many addicts are addicted to the cues associated with their drug of addiction, which maintain their chaotic and disorganised lifestyle.

This means those addicts simply can't cope with the demand of taking a daily medication, and this leads to non-compliance.

I&D extra: Drug therapy illustrates psychology as a science.

The most valid study is the randomised controlled trial (RCT). Participants are allocated randomly to either a treatment or control condition (evens out pre-existing participant differences).

Other procedures are also used to remove bias (e.g. 'blinding', so the researcher does not know who has taken the active drug). Findings then guide practical use of the treatment.

This means the most effective drug treatments are the ones that are used – some are abandoned, others are refined and new ones are developed.

 Check it

1. Describe **one** way of treating nicotine addiction other than aversion therapy. [3]

2. Explain **one** strength and **one** weakness of a treatment for heroin addiction. [4]

3. **Standard essay:** Evaluate the use of **one** therapy for alcohol addiction other than aversion therapy. [8] or [16]

   [Same question is possible for heroin or nicotine.]

4. **Context essay:** Dan was addicted to heroin. He was given aversion therapy a few years ago but quickly relapsed. His doctor wants him to try another form of treatment.

   Discuss **two** arguments the doctor might use to persuade Dan to try out **one** treatment other than aversion therapy. [8]

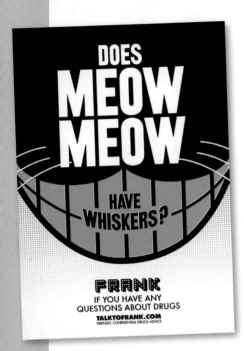

Talk to Frank campaign

The longest-running anti-drug campaign in the UK.

Frank is not a physical character but a label for anti-drug communications (e.g. TV ads, poster campaigns, website).

The campaign is aimed mainly at young people aged 11 to 18 and partly at parents (to increase knowledge of drugs and confidence in starting conversations with their children).

Talk to Frank employs several psychological strategies.

Psychological strategy 1 – Identification

Based on social learning theory (SLT).

Some behaviours are learned indirectly through modelling.

• Observing behaviour of another person (model) and imitating it.

• More likely to happen if observer identifies with model (e.g. the model has desirable characteristics).

Frank is also a kind of virtual 'older brother'.

• 'He' is friendly, straight-talking, trustworthy and credible.

• Young people take notice of Frank because he is the expert on drugs and is worth listening to.

• Frank is an alternative 'model' to drug-using peers.

Psychological strategy 2 – Emotional appeal

Campaigns that appeal to our emotions are more likely to be effective.

Hafstad *et al*. (1996) found a positive emotional response to an anti-smoking campaign was the best predictor of change.

A defining feature of the *Frank* campaign is its unconventional use of humour – bizarre, surreal and surprising.

Frank's anti-drug message becomes associated with positive feelings that stem from laughter (classical conditioning).

This contrasts with earlier campaigns (*Heroin Screws You Up*) which used fear to associate drug use with negative feelings.

Apply it Concepts

Syd has some ideas for an anti-drug campaign. He plans to use strategies based on social learning theory, the Hovland-Yale model and appealing to emotions. He can't decide whether he wants a serious expert figurehead or someone friendly – or both! He also wonders if 'funny' or 'scary' is better.

1. Explain whether Syd's campaign should be 'scary' or 'funny' in order to be effective. (3)

2. (a) Explain why Syd may choose a 'serious expert'. (2)
   (b) Explain why Syd may choose a 'friendly' figurehead. (2)

3. **Context essay:** Discuss Syd's choices of strategies for his anti-drug campaign. (8)

Psychological strategy 3 – Hovland-Yale model

An advertising strategy to persuade people.

Hovland-Yale model identifies three factors that may change an individual's attitudes (Hovland *et al*. 1953):

1. Source – a credible source is more likely to be believed:

• A source's credibility comes from their expertise and attractiveness (so Frank is not a physical character as he would inevitably appear 'uncool').

2. Message – give both sides of an argument:

• Presenting just one side is less likely to change attitudes.

• Frank appears impartial and balanced, and even presents drug-taking as a rational choice (it has benefits).

3. Audience – allow audience to draw own conclusions:

• More persuasive, but depends on levels of intelligence and education (people with less education prefer one-sided arguments).

• Campaign must appeal to as many of the target group as possible (message has to adapt to the audience).

A strength is evidence that *Talk to Frank* is an effective campaign.

ONS (2014) report that the number of 16–24-year-olds claiming to take illegal drugs dropped from 28.3% (in 2003/2004 when *Frank* began) to 18.9% (in 2013/2014).

Also, nearly 40 million people visited the campaign website, and 3.5 million called the helpline.

These figures imply that the anti-drug message of *Talk to Frank* has worked, in that a proportion of young people stopped taking drugs.

CA But the link is misleading. Most of the decline was due to reduced cannabis use. The use of some drugs (e.g. cocaine, MDMA, LSD) *increased* overall (Crime Survey for England and Wales, ONS 2015). There is little to no evidence that young people have given up drugs or reduced their usage as a direct result of *Talk to Frank*.

A weakness is that there are issues with the underlying Hovland-Yale model.

The model shows steps involved in persuasion, but not an explanation for how persuasion occurs (i.e. how people go from accepting the message to actually giving up drugs).

Hafstad and Aarø (1997) argue the message must have emotional appeal – people who had an emotional response to an anti-smoking campaign were more likely to stop.

This suggests that *Talk to Frank* is based on an invalid and outdated psychological model of persuasion.

Another weakness is evidence that shows *Talk to Frank* is actually ineffective.

Gohel (2016) found that participants who watched *Frank* ads scored mean of 65.42 on 'perceived drug risk'. Control group (saw no ads) scored 66.75.

On 'intent to use drugs', *Frank* participants scored a mean of 29 and controls scored 33 (also not significantly different).

These findings suggest that *Talk to Frank* adverts have little or no effect on people's perceived risk of drug use or their intention to use drugs.

Application: Issues with *Talk to Frank* can be used to inform new strategies.

This campaign was itself based on lessons learned from previous campaigns (e.g. minimising fear-related messages, establishing credibility).

So the real value of *Talk to Frank* may be what we can learn for the next campaign (e.g. emotional involvement to go from accepting the message to changing behaviour).

The implication is that any future campaign will need to take into account the true complexity of real-life drug-taking.

I&D extra: Research into anti-drug campaigns involves social control.

Drug addiction can cause unemployment, crime, physical and mental illness, so is expensive and causes great misery.

Governments tackle addiction by controlling the behaviour of individual drug addicts, and anti-drug campaigns are one way of achieving this.

So psychological research that develops anti-drug campaigns supports government policies of social control (to benefit the community).

Talk to Frank, ask your Mum or Dad.

Check it

1. Describe **two** features of **one** anti-drug campaign. [4]

2. Explain **one** practical issue relevant to your chosen anti-drug campaign. [2]

3. **Standard essay:** Evaluate the effectiveness of **one** anti-drug campaign. [8] or [16]

4. **I&D/Synoptic essay:** Assess issues relating to the use of psychology as a means of social control. You must use examples from your chosen application (criminological, child or health) and the learning theories topic. [20]

Spec spotlight

8.3.1 Olds and Milner (1954) Positive reinforcement produced by electrical stimulation of septal area and other regions of rat brain.

Apply it — Methods

Dr Jha is exploring a new brain area believed to be involved in addiction. He is using rats and injects them daily with a new drug, or a harmless salt solution for the placebo group. The rats' ability to learn a new maze each day is scored. When the drug-group animals show signs of physical dependence the rats are all killed so their brains can be examined.

1. (a) Explain why Dr Jha needs a non-drug group. (1)
   (b) Explain how the pain of the injection for the placebo group can be justified. (2)

2. **Context/Methods essay:** To what extent is the use of animals in drug studies ethically justified? You must refer to the context in your answer. (20)

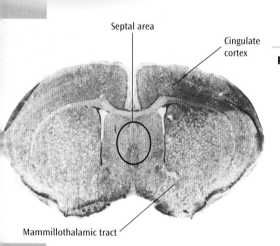

Septal area

Cingulate cortex

Mammillothalamic tract

A stained section through a rat brain, showing the main areas stimulated in Olds and Milner's study. This view is from the front of the brain, about halfway along (called a coronal section).

The first rats to be tested had 12 hours of acquisition testing but this was reduced to six hours for rats tested later. Therefore, the researchers used only the first six hours of data for all the rats.

Aims

To see if electrical self-stimulation of the brain (ESSB) acts as a reward, a punishment or a neutral stimulus.

To discover if stimulation has a reinforcing effect on behaviour and find brain structures involved in this reinforcing function.

Procedure

Animal laboratory experiment (brains of 15 male hooded rats):

- Independent variable = brain location of electrode.
- Dependent variable = number of lever presses when stimulation switched on (acquisition) and off (extinction).

Tested in Skinner box (stimulation only when rat pressed lever). Each rat had a one-hour pre-testing session on Day 4 after implantation (to find minimum voltage to produce an effect).

On two subsequent days, each rat was tested in two ways:

- Acquisition (three hours/day) – rats self-stimulated.
- Extinction (half hour/day) – no stimulation when pressing lever.

Scoring – acquisition score (proportion of time spent pressing lever when stimulation present) and extinction score (baseline score when no stimulation).

Acquisition score above extinction score = stimulation rewarding. Acquisition score below = stimulation punishing.

After testing, rats were killed and brains frozen, cut into sections, stained, examined (to see which areas had been stimulated).

Findings

Brain structures – stimulation rewarding in 7/15 rats:

- *Septal area* – four rats stimulated here spent 75–92% pressing lever in acquisition time, only 8–21% during extinction.
- *Mammillothalamic tract* – one rat stimulated here spent 71% lever-pressing in acquisition, 9% during extinction.
- *Cingulate cortex* – two rats stimulated here spent 36 and 37% lever-pressing in acquisition, 10 and 9% in extinction.

Behaviour of individual rats:

- Rat 34 (septal area) lever-pressed 7500 times in 12 hours, average 742 responses/hour (almost zero in extinction).
- Rat A-5 (mammillothalamic tract) gave 1250 responses on average per hour one day, a response every two seconds.

Conclusions

The septal area (and mammillothalamic tract and cingulate cortex to lesser extent) are part of a system associated with rewarding effects when stimulated – reward centres.

Stimulation of all other brain structures tested had either neutral or punishing effects – brain has 'punishment centres'.

A strength is that the findings were supported and extended by later research.

Olds (1958) reported that male rats deprived of food for 24 hours crossed an electrified floor to receive self-stimulation but not to get food.

This finding implies that self-stimulation is more rewarding than 'natural' sources of pleasure.

This confirms that there are reward centres in the brain that have powerful effects on behaviour when electrically stimulated.

CA However, later research showed that some conclusions were not valid, e.g. the *medial forebrain bundle* was identified as the brain's main pleasure centre. But researchers now believe this part of the brain is not a 'centre' but a pathway linking the *ventral tegmental area* to the *nucleus accumbens* (see diagram on page 158). Research has now focused on these structures rather than on those found by Olds and Milner.

A weakness is the artificial nature of the brain stimulation in the study.

The rewarding effects in the study are not the same as the effects of naturally-occurring rewards. The extreme responses in the study only occur in artificial lab conditions.

Also, the response is not satiated (satisfied) as the rat continues to lever-press to exhaustion. The animal does not reach a point where it has had enough stimulation (unlike with food or sex).

This means the findings have very limited application to pleasure-seeking behaviour in the real world.

Another weakness is that generalising from rats to humans is obviously risky.

We need a balanced approach – we cannot say for sure that the human and rat brain are similar enough to justify making generalisations.

On the other hand it is clear that there are reward centres in the human brain that parallel those in the rat brain.

Therefore, the differences are quantitative not qualitative. The human brain is more complex than the rat's but the two are not basically different, so research with rats is useful (with caution).

Application: The research has been used to explain addiction in humans.

Olds and Milner stimulated brain areas known to be involved in producing *catecholamine* neurotransmitters (e.g. Crow 1972).

One of these (*dopamine*) is central to how the brain's reward system responds to drugs such as nicotine, alcohol and heroin.

This is important because explaining addiction is a crucial step towards developing effective treatments and saving lives.

I&D extra: The study illustrates how understanding has developed over time.

Isaacson (1982) argues this study was a turning point because it directed focus away from observable behaviours to experiences (pleasure).

For behaviourists (learning theorists) at the time, even using words like 'pleasure' was considered unscientific and unmeasurable.

This study challenged the narrow limitations of behaviourism, freeing psychologists to measure less observable concepts such as 'pleasure'.

A hooded rat. Should findings from animal studies be applied to humans? Roland's not sure.

Revision booster

You can see that the findings of this study are relevant to your general understanding of the biological processes involved in addiction. But you need to know more than this study for the subtopic 'one biological explanation for addiction', covered on the spread starting page 158. On that spread you learned about other, more important, brain areas such as the ventral tegmental area (VTA) and the nucleus accumbens (NA).

This is a good example of the 'development of psychology over time' as Olds and Milner is a *classic* study, i.e. it is old. Think mnemonics: **Old**(s) and Milner.

✓ Check it

1. Describe the procedure of the classic study by Olds and Milner (1954). (5)

2. Explain **two** strengths of Old and Milner's (1954) classic study. (4)

3. **Standard essay:** Evaluate the classic study by Olds and Milner (1954). (8) or (16)

4. **Methods essay:** Evaluate the ethics of using animals to study drug addiction in studies such as Olds and Milner (1954). (8) or (16)

Spec spotlight

8.3.2 One contemporary study: Mundt et al. (2012) Peer selection and influence effects on adolescent alcohol use: a stochastic actor-based model.

It was time for the Mason family to start thinking about moving to a bigger house.

Apply it Concepts

Sam is pretty neutral about drinking alcohol. He has a group of friends, some of whom disapprove of it and others who will sometimes drink but who are also happy not to be drinking alcohol. Pete and his friends all go out regularly together for a drink, often consuming too much alcohol.

1. (a) Use evidence to explain whether Pete's friends' behaviour is likely to have affected his alcohol use. (4)

   (b) Suggest **two** other characteristics Pete's friends are likely to share with him. (2)

2. Explain **one** possible difference between Sam and Pete's families that could explain their drinking behaviours. (2)

3. **Context essay:** Discuss Sam and Pete's alcohol use. (8)

Aims

To assess the relationship between friendship networks and alcohol use in adolescence.

To see if adolescents select friends with similar alcohol use (selection) or match the alcohol consumption of their friends (influence).

Procedure

Longitudinal stage of the study divided into two 'waves'.

Data from US *National Longitudinal Study of Adolescent Health*.

Stratified sample – 90,118 students (aged 12–18) from 132 schools.

Wave 1 procedure

- Random sample – 20,745 students surveyed on e.g. parental education, risk behaviours, health.
- Selected five best male and five best female schoolfriends.
- Parents indicated how often they drank alcohol in the past year.
- Also all students from 13 schools (saturation sampling) provided data on peer networks within those schools.

Wave 2 procedure, a year later

- Sample – 14,738 from Wave 1 asked about alcohol use in past year.
- Again selected five best male/female schoolfriends.

Analysis – data from 2,563 students in Wave 1 saturation subsample (49.2% girls, 50.8% boys, mean age 15.8).

Measures e.g. alcohol use, friendship networks, family bonding.

Stochastic actor-based modelling (extent to which alcohol use and friendship ties developed from Wave 1 to Wave 2).

Findings

Evolution of friendship networks

- Friendship selection linked to similar alcohol consumption ($p < 0.001$) and also similar age, gender and ethnicity.
- Number of outgoing friendship nominations (each person names their friends) not significantly correlated to alcohol consumption but number of incoming friendship nominations (i.e. where each person is named) did.

Evolution of alcohol-use behaviours

- More frequent drinking by immediate friends not linked to increased alcohol consumption (friends did not influence each other's alcohol intake).
- Family bonding was protective against alcohol use.
- Parental alcohol use not associated with adolescent use.

Conclusions

The findings support *homophily* (forming friendships with similar people) to explain adolescent alcohol use (i.e. selection).

Other factors influence friendship formation – similar age, gender and ethnicity among them.

A strength of the study is that it used rigorous statistical analysis.

The researchers controlled for a problem with multiple statistical tests – obtaining a significant result where none exists (Type I error).	They avoided this by halving the significance level from the traditional $p = 0.05$ to $p = 0.025$.	This gives us confidence that the findings of the study are statistically significant and valid.

CA However, the analysis was partly weakened because friendship networks were limited to schools. This excluded other friendships outside school (common for adolescents). This was supported by the finding that the average number of reported friends was just two, lower than found in other studies. This suggests that friendships were under-reported in this study, which limits the validity of the conclusions.

Might people under-report their alcohol consumption?

A weakness is that the data was derived from self-reports.

At least some students and parents probably did not give accurate responses. There is evidence from the study that this was an issue.	There was an increase from Wave 1 to 2 in the number of participants not drinking. Also, only 44% of parents reported that they drank alcohol (60–70% in other studies).	This under-reporting of alcohol consumption undermined the validity of the findings and suggests they may not be generalisable.

Another weakness of the study is its narrow focus solely on alcohol use.

The researchers ignored the use of other drugs such as nicotine, which they acknowledge is a limitation of the study.	Peer influence (not found to be significant in relation to alcohol use) may have had more of an effect on the use of other drugs.	This means we cannot choose between the peer selection and peer influence explanations for wider drug use based on this study.

Application: The study provides valuable data to help guide interventions.

Knowing that adolescents select their friends based on similarity of alcohol use has implications for how it can be tackled.	Encouraging young people to pay attention to other characteristics of friends may be more effective than highlighting the dangers of alcohol.	This opens up a new direction for attempts to reduce drug use, ultimately improving the quality of life of many people.

I&D extra: The study illustrates issues related to socially-sensitive research.

The study may reinforce the perception of adolescents as risk-taking, indiscriminate in choice of friends and influenced into taking drugs by friendships.	This kind of thinking prevents the vote being extended to young people aged between 16 and 18 years, for example.	This is a weakness because careless generalisations can ultimately lead to a form of social discrimination against adolescents.

Revision booster

In an exam everyone feels some measure of anxiety. When you are anxious you may forget those things that are not well-learned or well-practised. So, practise, practise, practise.

You could try saying your answers out loud. Write some notes for an essay and put these on a PowerPoint, and then deliver the essay out loud. This has a surprising effect on improving memory.

✓ **Check it**

1. Describe **one** contemporary study from health psychology. (5)

2. Explain **one** ethical issue relating to **one** contemporary study from health psychology. (2)

3. **Standard essay:** Evaluate **one** contemporary study from health psychology. (8) or (16)

4. **Methods essay:** Evaluate **one** contemporary study from health psychology in terms of reliability and validity. (16)

Spec spotlight

8.3.3 One contemporary study: Dixit et al. (2012) Biosocial determinants of alcohol risk behaviour: An epidemiological study in urban and rural communities of Aligarh, Uttar Pradesh.

How prevalent is alcohol use in India?

Aims	To discover the prevalence of alcohol use in urban and rural areas of Uttar Pradesh, a northern state of India.
	To identify some of the factors associated with alcohol use, including age, religion, education, gender and occupation.
Procedure	Cross-sectional door-to-door survey of households.
	Sample – 848 participants (424 from urban, UHTC, and 424 from rural, RHTC, a systematic method was used (every tenth household).
	In consenting households, one or two people were randomly selected aged 15 or older – findings from 114 participants were not used.
	The researchers obtained 'informed verbal consent' from participants (and parents if they were aged 15–18 years).
	Structured interview schedule – demographic variables (e.g. occupation), alcohol type and reasons for use (e.g. stress).
Findings	Prevalence and patterns of alcohol use
	• 13.4% had used alcohol, of which 5.07% were current users.
	• Users significantly more likely to be:
	• 26–40 years.
	• Low socioeconomic status.
	• Members of Hindu religion.
	• Male (34.55% vs 0% for females).
	• People whose parents also used alcohol.
	• Rural (20.45%) rather than urban (10.99%).
	• Lowest caste in Indian society ('untouchables').
	Reasons for use
	• 55.5% of rural users and 85.7% of urban users started using alcohol between the ages of 15 and 25 years.
	• Peer pressure (86.1% of users), curiosity (68%), social acceptance (25%), unemployment (2.8%), health benefits (2.8%), anxiety/stress (1.4%).
Conclusions	Prevalence of alcohol use varies in different regions of India.
	5.07% was low compared with national figures (e.g. 13.4% in 15–49-year-olds in the *National Family Health Survey-3*).
	Difference may be due to the large proportion of Muslims in the study (57%), which reduced the overall prevalence figure.
	Alcohol risk behaviour is prevalent in the community and action should be taken to target vulnerable individuals (e.g. de-addiction centres, law enforcement, education programmes).

Apply it

Methods

Dr Kay studied reasons for smoking using a semi-structured interview. She used opportunity sampling to collect data by going to different houses in the streets near where she lived. In each household she selected one or two volunteers. Consent was obtained from households and also from individual participants. Where two individuals were tested, each was interviewed in isolation. They were told that they could answer any question with 'I would rather not say'.

1. (a) Suggest **one** reason why Dr Kay chose a semi-structured interview to obtain information about reasons for smoking. (2)

  (b) Suggest **one** weakness of using a semi-structured interview in Dr Kay's study. (2)

2. Explain **two** problems that Dr Kay may have with her sample of participants. (4)

3. **Context/Methods essay:** Discuss the ethics of Dr Kay's study. (8)

A strength is there is some support for the findings of this study.

As the researchers point out, their findings about religion, social status, occupation and gender have been confirmed in earlier research.

For example, Reddy and Chandrashekar (1998) found greater prevalence of alcohol use amongst rural participants than urban-dwellers.

These mutually supportive findings give this study (and the others) some degree of validity and reliability.

CA However, the reliability of the study is questionable. For example, there is little evidence from the research report of standardised procedures (e.g. questions that were used). Therefore, the extent to which all the participants experienced the procedure in a similar way is unclear. Replication of the study would be difficult. This means it is hard to know whether the findings were 'one-off flukes' or not.

A weakness is that the conclusions drawn are not justified.

The researchers claim that prevalence of alcohol use varies in different regions of the country, based on a survey of two areas of a single district in one state of India.

They also state that 'alcohol risk behaviour' is prevalent in the community studied, but their figure is less than half the national figure found in other studies.

This suggests the findings need to be supported by other studies before far-reaching conclusions can be drawn.

Another weakness is that some important variables were not measured.

The researchers did not measure the amount of alcohol participants drank.

Therefore, they could not distinguish between someone who had only ever had one drink and someone who drank every day.

This means there is no evidence of alcohol addiction in this study and the conclusions drawn were unjustified. Yet recommendations were made with potentially wide-ranging consequences.

Application: The researchers suggest several applications of their findings.

For instance they refer to setting up de-addiction centres, devising educational campaigns, enlisting the media and strictly enforcing laws.

These are all potentially useful ways of tackling risky alcohol-related behaviours.

These applications could help relieve the problems associated with alcohol addiction.

I&D extra: The study illustrates the (mis)use of psychological knowledge.

For example, the researchers call for government action to implement wide-ranging and potentially punitive actions (e.g. strictly enforce laws).

They made such recommendations even though there is no evidence in their study of alcohol addiction.

This counts as misuse when the data is methodologically flawed.

The study failed to measure the amount that individual participants drank.

Revision booster

Evidence is key in psychology. But whether it's description (AO1) or evaluation (AO3) depends on how you use it. Are you outlining what the evidence is or describing the procedure? That's AO1. Are you explaining what the evidence tells us about a theory or treatment or linking the findings of the study to the theory? That's AO3. Make sure you use your material in the right way for the question and make the difference clear to the examiner.

✓ Check it

1. Describe the procedure of **one** contemporary study from health psychology. (5)

2. Explain **one** strength and **one** weakness of **one** contemporary study from health psychology. (4)

3. **Standard essay:** Evaluate **one** contemporary study from health psychology. (8) or (16)

4. **Methods essay:** Evaluate **one** contemporary study from health psychology with regard to practical and ethical issues. (16)

Spec spotlight

8.3.4 One contemporary study: Pengpid et al. (2012) Screening and brief intervention for hazardous and harmful alcohol use among hospital outpatients in South Africa: results from a randomised controlled trial.

South Africa. It's not actually that colour.

Methods

Dr Bow is studying alcohol abuse in rural populations worldwide. A test he used in the UK to assess alcohol misuse has been translated into appropriate languages. In each community he has asked local health workers to check that the questions are meaningful.

1. (a) Dr Bow's test can be used as a questionnaire or interview. Justify why Dr Bow should choose **one** of these. (2)

   (b) Explain **one** disadvantage of your choice of method. (2)

2. Explain why Dr Bow's test should be used at several different stages of therapy. (2)

3. **Context/Methods essay:** Evaluate cross-cultural research. You must refer to the context in your answer (8)

Table showing mean AUDIT scores over time.

	Baseline	6 months	12 months
Intervention	12.0	7.0	7.2
Control	11.3	6.3	7.3

Aims To assess effectiveness of screening and brief intervention to reduce alcohol use in hospital outpatients in South Africa.

Procedure Sample – 1419 male and female hospital outpatients interviewed using the *Alcohol Use Disorder Identification Test* (AUDIT, Babor *et al.* 2001), in English or Tswana.

392 outpatients selected as 'hazardous or harmful' drinkers – men who scored 8–19 (out of 40) and women who scored 7–19.

Randomised controlled trial – computer-generated random numbers used to allocate participants.

Independent variable
- Intervention (one 20-minute counselling session on reducing alcohol use, included AUDIT feedback, a leaflet and advice).
- Control – health education leaflet on responsible drinking.

Dependent variables
- AUDIT scores at baseline, six months and 12 months.
- Data also collected on participants' age, gender, education, marital status, income and residential status.

Trained assistant nurse counsellors (ANCs) – interviewed outpatients using the AUDIT, another ANC scored the AUDIT (blind to allocation), delivered intervention (five-day workshop).

Findings Reliability of intervention implementation
- Intervention was fully delivered in 15 steps.
- External staff observed 10% of intervention sessions and found the ANCs implemented at least 13 steps in 85% of sessions (highly consistent delivery).

Alcohol use outcomes
- Both groups showed significant reductions in AUDIT scores over time (see table below left).
- No effect of intervention type – reduction in scores was not significantly greater for one group or another.

Conclusions Levels of harmful alcohol use can be reduced over one year in non-dependent outpatients by providing some further support.

The intervention was no more effective than the leaflet.

Just asking control participants questions about their drinking may have been enough to change their behaviour – questioning is a 'mini intervention' (McCambridge and Kypri 2011).

The effectiveness of the intervention may be underestimated, perhaps because the two groups were not comparable.

A strength of the study is that its procedures were reliable.

The procedures were standardised, e.g. a protocol for conducting the intervention was used, including the 15 steps the ANCs worked through.	Also, standardisation was maintained by training and quality assurance processes (e.g. observers).	This means outcomes for the two groups could be accurately compared as the participants' experiences of the study were similar.

CA However, other factors mean the two groups may not have been directly comparable after all. There were differences even though the researchers tried to control these by random allocation. The intervention participants had higher AUDIT scores on average, suggesting they were more harmful drinkers than the controls. This may be why the study probably underestimated the intervention's effectiveness.

A weakness is the conclusions were based on self-reports.

Some participants may not have been accurate or honest, some may have underestimated their use, others may have wanted to give a false impression.	This is especially likely given the personally sensitive nature of the questions concerning alcohol consumption.	This under-reporting of alcohol use may have undermined the validity of the researchers' conclusions about effectiveness.

Another weakness is the dropout rate at each follow-up point.

There was dropout in the intervention group (29%) and control group (27%). This is an issue if there is a pattern (a certain 'type' drops out and from one group more than another).	The researchers did an *attrition analysis* and found no differential dropout between the two groups. However, dropout could have been linked to a variable not measured.	This would result in treatment effectiveness being over- or underestimated, weakening the validity of the conclusions.

Application: The study provides valuable data to help guide interventions.

The researchers could not demonstrate the effectiveness of the intervention they used in this study.	But the findings provide support for the AUDIT as a screening instrument and for health education (i.e. leaflet and advice).	This gives a practical direction to reduce alcohol use in harmful drinkers, ultimately improving their quality of life.

I&D extra: This study illustrates issues concerning culture in research.

How the AUDIT was used is an example of an *imposed etic*, i.e. the assumption that a test developed in one culture can be used in another culture without changes.	Just translating the questionnaire is not enough – it should be validated within that culture (e.g. giving it to a representative sample of the population to establish its reliability and validity).	This shows how culture bias and ethnocentricity can creep into research, using a questionnaire developed in one culture as a standard against which to assess drinking behaviour.

The dropout rate in the study was high.

Revision booster

Learning the material you will need for the exam and knowing how to structure an essay is half the battle won. But you also need to be able to get it onto paper in the available time. Write a *very brief* essay plan for all our standard essays – the plans should just consist of key trigger words. Then practise writing essays in full using your plans and time yourself doing this. Allow yourself no more than 12 minutes for an 8-mark essay.

 Check it

1. Describe **one** or more practical issues relevant to **one** contemporary study from health psychology. [3]

2. Explain **one** ethical issue relating to **one** contemporary study from health psychology. [2]

3. **Standard essay:** Evaluate **one** contemporary study from health psychology. [8] or [16]

4. **Methods essay:** Evaluate **one** contemporary study from health psychology with reference to the way that the data was collected and analysed. [16]

Spec spotlight

The specification says...

Clinical psychology

5.2.1 Awareness of Health and Care Professions Council (HCPC) guidelines for clinical practitioners.

Criminological psychology

6.2.5 Ethical guidelines: British Psychological Society (BPS) Code of Ethics and Conduct (2009), including risk management when carrying out research in psychology and Health and Care Professions Council (HCPC) principles for undertaking psychological, formulation and intervention.

Child psychology

7.2.4 The ethics of researching with children, including children's rights and the UNCRC (1989), and issues around participation and protection.

Revision booster

When answering exam questions on the issues described on this page, remember to illustrate your answer with examples of studies or therapies.

You can also use these issues when answering exam questions on applications of psychology as ways to evaluate your application.

✓ Check it

1. The Health and Care Professions Council (HCPC) develops and maintains standards of conduct, performance and ethics among those who work in health-related professions.

   Describe **one** example of a standard related to conduct. [3]

2. Explain the role of the United Nations Convention on the Rights of the Child (UNCRC 1989). Refer to at least **one** of the rights in your answer. [4]

3. The British Psychological Society (BPS) code of ethics and conduct (2009) sets an expected standard for psychological research.

   Evaluate how well research in clinical psychology has met the requirements of this code. [12]

Health and Care Professions Council (HCPC)

The HCPC was set up by the government to develop and maintain standards amongst people who work in the 16 health-related professions, e.g. dieticians, paramedics, physiotherapists, practitioner psychologists (clinical, forensic and health).

In order to practise a person must be registered with the HCPC.

The HCPC produces *standards of conduct, performance and ethics* (SCPE 2016) that outline expectations about behaviour and conduct. This includes:

- Protecting the interests of service users and carers.
- Respecting confidentiality.
- Managing risk by taking all reasonable steps to reduce the risk of harm to service users, carers and colleagues.
- Being open when things go wrong.
- Being honest and trustworthy, making sure that therapists' conduct justifies the public's trust and confidence in them.
- Keeping records of their work.

British Psychological Society (BPS) Code of Ethics and Conduct (2009)

The BPS code is organised around four core principles, linked to the ethical issues:

1. Respect – includes informed consent, confidentiality, privacy and right to withdraw.
2. Competence – includes awareness of professional ethics and making ethical decisions.
3. Responsibility – includes protection from harm and debriefing.
4. Integrity – includes honesty (avoiding deception) and addressing misconduct.

United Nations Convention on the Rights of the Child (UNCRC 1989)

UNCRC has 54 'articles' setting out civil, political, economic, social and cultural rights that all children are entitled to.

The Convention aims to explain how adults and governments must work together to ensure all children can enjoy their rights.

Examples of these rights

Ethical issues, e.g. Article 12 (respect for the views of the child) – Every child has the right to express their views, feelings and wishes in all matters affecting them, and to have their views considered and taken seriously. This right applies at all times, for example during immigration proceedings, housing decisions or the child's day-to-day home life.

Deprivation and privation, e.g. Article 9 (separation from parents) – Children must not be separated from their parents against their will unless it is in their best interests (for example, if a parent is hurting or neglecting a child). Children whose parents have separated have the right to stay in contact.

Autism and mental health, e.g. Article 23 (children with a disability) – A child with a disability has the right to live a full and decent life with dignity and, as far as possible, independence and to play an active part in the community. Governments must do all they can to support disabled children and their families.